On This Journey

On This Journey

Daily Devotional for Young People

On This Journey

On This Journey

Daily Devotional for Young People

By

Rev. Onedia N. Gage, Ph. D.

Library of Congress

On This Journey
Daily Devotional for Young People

All Rights Reserved © 2004. 2015. 2020.
by Onedia N. Gage, Ph. D.

No part of this book may be reproduced or transmitted in any part of form or by any means, graphic, electronic or mechanical, including photocopying, recording, taping, or by any information storage of retrieval system, without the permission in writing from the publisher.

For information, please contact:
Purple Ink, Inc.
P O Box 300113
Houston, TX 77230
www.purpleink.net
onediagage@purpleink.net

Onedia Gage Ministries
www.onediagage.com
onediagage@onediagage.com

ISBN 97809801002-0-4

Printed in the United States

Books by

Onedia N. Gage, Ph. D.

Are You Ready for 9th Grade . . . Again? A Family's Guide to Success
As We Grow Together Daily Devotional for Expectant Couples
As We Grow Together Prayer Journal for Expectant Couples
As We Grow Together Bible Study: Her Workbook
As We Grow Together Bible Study: His Workbook
The Best 40 Days of My Life: A Journey of Spiritual Renewal
The Blue Print: Poetry for the Soul
From Fat to Fit in 90 Days: A Fitness Journal
From Two to One: The Notebook for the Christian Couple
Hannah's Voice: Powerful Lessons in Prayer
Her Story The Legacy of Her Fight: The Bible Study
Her Story The Legacy of Her Fight: The Devotional
Her Story The Legacy of Her Fight: The Legacy Journal
Her Story The Legacy of Her Fight: Prayers and Journal
I Am.: 90 Days of Powerful Words: Affirmation and Advice for Girls
ILY! A Mother Daughter Relationship Workbook
In Her Own Words: Notebook for the Christian Woman
In 90 Days: What Will You Do?
In Purple Ink: Poetry for the Spirit
In Your Hands: A Dad's Impact on Your Daughter's Self-Esteem
Intensive Couples Retreat: Her Workbook
Intensive Couples Retreat: His Workbook
Living A Whole Life: Sermons Which Prompt, Provoke and Provide Life
Love Letters to God from a Teenage Girl
The Measure of a Woman: The Details of Her Soul
The Notebook: For Me, About Me, By Me
The Notebook for the Christian Teen
On This Journey Daily Devotional for Young People
On This Journey Prayer Journal for Young People
On This Journey Prayer Journal for Young People, Vol. 2
One Day More Than We Deserve Prayer Journal for the Growing Christian
Promises, Promises: A Novel
Queen in the Making: 30 Week Bible Study for Teen Girls
Queen in the Making: 30 Week Bible Study for Teen Girls Leader's Guide
There's a Queen Within: Her Journey to Self—Worth
She Spoke Volumes . . . And Then Some
Six Months of Solitude: The Sanctity of Singleness Notebook
Six Months of Solitude: The Sanctity of Singleness Prayers and Journal
Tools for These Times: Timely Sermons for Uncertain Times
With An Anointed Voice: The Power of Prayer
A Woman Like Me: A Bible Study
A Woman Like Me: A Daily Devotional
A Woman Like Me: A Sermonic Study
Yielded and Submitted: A Woman's Journey for a Life Dedicated to God
Yielded and Submitted: A Woman's Journey for a Life Dedicated to God An Intimate Study
Yielded and Submitted: A Woman's Journey for a Life Dedicated to God Prayers and Journal

The Nehemiah Character Series

Nehemiah and His Basketball
Nehemiah and His Big Sister
Nehemiah and His Bike
Nehemiah and His Flag Football Team
Nehemiah and His Football
Nehemiah and His Golf Clubs
Nehemiah and Math
Nehemiah and the Bully
Nehemiah and the Busy Day
Nehemiah and the Class Field Trip
Nehemiah and the Substitute for the Substitute
Nehemiah Can Swim
Nehemiah Found the Mud
Nehemiah Reads to Mommy
Nehemiah Writes Just Like Mommy
Nehemiah, the Hot Dog, and the Broccoli
Nehemiah's Family Vacation
Nehemiah's Favorite Teacher Returns to School
Nehemiah's First Day of School
Nehemiah's Sister Moved
Nehemiah's Visit to the Hospital

What God Said

I can do all things through Christ who strengthens me.
Philippians 4:13 NIV

And He has said to me, "My grace is sufficient for you, for power is perfected in weakness." Most gladly, therefore, I will rather boast about my weaknesses, that the power of Christ may dwell in me.
2 Corinthians 12:9 NAS

"Come to Me, all who are weary and heavy-laden, and I will give you rest."
Matthew 11:28 NAS

On This Journey

Dedication

Hillary Nicole, may these words guide and motivate you to be faithful to God and the path He has planned for you. Lean on Him and depend on Him for all of your needs. When I started this project, I didn't know you would be born before I was finished. I love you and will always be here for you.

Nehemiah Christian, may these words inspire you to honor God through who you are. God has great plans for you. I look forward to the great works He has planned for you and through you. You were born before we printed this, so I am excited to have you here. I love you and will always be here for you.

To our children—our gifts from God—If I pray for you, then you will remain strong.

To my prayer warriors, may all of our prayers be answered.

To the youth whose lives this will touch: may these words inspire you to respond to God's calling. Keep your relationship with God healthy. May these words inspire you to desire to achieve the level God has planned for you. My prayers are for you daily.

On This Journey

Dear Hillary Nicole:

When I started writing this devotional in 1999, I had only dreamed of you—my little girl. I wrote this for you and now that you are here, I am so excited. I read and talk to you about God all the time. I pray over you everyday. I love you and your healthy spiritual wellness is extremely important to me.

When you are old enough to read this, I urge you to ask as many questions as you need. I am right here for you as your example of Christianity and your biggest supporter.

You will encounter things—all of which I may not mention specifically—for which I have prepared you. At that time, it may not seem as if I have but you are prepared and most importantly you are covered with my prayers and God's protection.

May the Lord bless you and keep you. May the light of His countenance shine on you and give you His peace. May He bless you as you go out and come in; rise early and settle late; in your labor and your leisure; in your laughter and in your tears.

I love you always!

Love,
Mommy
Onedia N. Gage

On This Journey

Dear Nehemiah Christian:

When I finished this project and was ready to print, you were due. I was excited for you to finally be here. I read and talk to you about God all the time. I pray over you everyday. I love you and your healthy spiritual wellness is extremely important to me.

When you are old enough to read this, I urge you to ask as many questions as you need. I am right here for you as your example of Christianity and your biggest supporter.

You will encounter things –all of which I may not mention specifically—for which I have prepared you. At that time, it may not seem as if I have but you are prepared and most importantly you are covered with my prayers and God's protection.

May the Lord bless you and keep you. May the light of His countenance shine on you and give you His peace. May He bless you as you go out and come in; rise early and settle late; in your labor and your leisure; in your laughter and in your tears.

I love you always!

Love,

Mommy

Onedia N. Gage

On This Journey

Dear Teen Christian:

It is awesome you've selected On This Journey Daily Devotional for Youth for use as your personal devotional. Your study of God's word is extremely important. OTJ will help you remain consistent. I started on a journey with Christ at a very early age. I accepted Jesus as my Lord and Savior at age 5. My journey has been one full of excitement and discovery. I have excited and disappointed God in my life. I have learned a lot, too.

Each devotional is dated such that you may start as soon as you receive your devotional. Each devotional starts with a scripture and ends with a prayer. The commentary documents some of my testimony, advice for a successful journey, and biblical resources. I have included some anecdotes describing my journey with Christ, which will prove beneficial to you as you journey.

I wrote OTJ because devotional resources for youth are limited and young people need resources to succeed. As a young person, I struggled to find resources to help me with my walk with God. I didn't want my child or others to have the same trouble. OTJ motivates, inspires and empowers you to remain faithful to God. OTJ shares how to witness to others, overcome peer pressure, avoid costly mistakes related to sex, drugs, alcohol and other related issues, and influences you to stand for God in all situations.

You should expect to spend 30 minutes daily: 10 minutes to read and 20 minutes writing in your journal. You also need to make time to pray, which may last two minutes or ten minutes. You and God will determine that time. You also should expect to address your issues in a new and honest way. For example, you may not have known how to talk to God before but now you'll know better about your conversations with God. Your growth and maturity will demand a new attitude about God, His word, your commitment, inclusive of your study time, prayer life and lifestyle. Our daily living is based on Luke 9:23-25. We are called to live for Christ daily. We are not called to be part-time Christians.

If you should need to reach me for questions, prayer or additional resources, please email me at onediagage@purpleink.net or onediagage@onediagage.com.

In Christ,

Onedia Gage
Onedia N. Gage

On This Journey

Daily Devotional for Young People

Dear Parent:

I just implore you as a parent to be attentive to your child, especially when they are highly inquisitive and precocious. Embrace their ideas and listen to them, even when you don't want to. They need your validation of who they are and whose they are. This validation stretches you in ways you may be unprepared to explore but without fear, I encourage your obedience as you approach the challenges your child presents. Your validity of them changes their life and strongly impacts their choices, leading them to what's right and away from what's wrong.

Life outside the parental box is far from easy. My short parenting journey thus far has proved interesting but doesn't make me an expert. Not even close. However, it does allow me to reflect on the type of child I was. Further, my childhood forces me to pray and ask my mother for forgiveness. Getting out of the box is required. First, abandoning the box means you are free to parent according to God's words. This means parenting with discipline and love and prayer, among other Christ-centered qualities and behaviors.

Secondly, the box is not good for either parent or child. Consider parenting to please the society and your child rather than using God's word as your source for instruction. The Bible clearly defines the parental role. The child's role is defined too. So the child cannot be in their role if you are not properly functioning within yours. Without the correct roles, friction, disobedience and discord results.

Lastly, the box presents a false sense of security and self-esteem. It also gives the illusion you have done the right thing. We compare our parenting to other parents rather than the Bible. This comparison gives a skewed snapshot of someone else's parental report card, if you will. The problem is that the next parents are presented with similar challenges as we ask them how they handled it then we decide what to do. This approach is disorderly. We are to ask God, refer to His Instructions and wait on His answer.

By the way, just because we made a better decision than another parent is not grounds for celebration. We need to pray for each other so that we are able to present a strong, united, Christ-centered front. It is safe to discard the "box." God does not operate in that box. He does not want us in the box but will allow us in our time to discard the "box." Just a tip I learned from the wise woman who mothered me: 'so if she jumps off the bridge, are you going to jump, too?' I stopped using others to persuade my mother for things I wanted. Stop listening to what others do.

If you have any questions, are in need of prayer, or need more resources, please email me at onediagage@onediagage.com.

In Christ,

Onedia N. Gage

On This Journey

TABLE OF CONTENTS

Dedication	11
Letters	13
"Goal Setting"	22
January	23
February	54
"True Love Waits"	83
March	85
April	116
"Your Personal Testimony"	146
May	147
June	178
"My View On Things" by Shannon Carroll	209
July	210
August	241
September	272
"How To Share Your Faith"	302
October	303
November	334
December	364
"With Your Whole Heart, Walk with God"	396
Resources for the Journey	397

On This Journey

GOAL SETTING

Goal setting has nothing to do with how old you are. Goal setting has everything to do with starting with the "end" in mind. Life's rule: God is in charge. The "end" will change—several times I might add.

If your "end" is attorney, you need to know the steps required to accomplish that "end." Requirements for attorney: complete all twelve grades of school, complete bachelor's degree in an accredited undergraduate college or university, passing the LSAT exam, complete law school and passing the bar exam. And just for the sake of conversation, at the average price of $40,000.

How will you pay for this? How will you achieve this? Both answers require planning, thus goal setting.

Establishing goals merely outlines the framework for the path and pace you desire. If you know that $16,000 is required for your undergraduate degree, then you start in ninth grade looking for scholarships and earning grades worthy of scholarships looking for you. Really focused goal setting includes knowing the entrance minimums for each level. For example, if the college of your choice has a freshman average grade point average (GPA) of 3.75 on a 4.0 scale, then you need to insure you earn the average or better. If the LSAT minimum at your law school of choice is 160 of 200 then you need to target the 175 mark. If you know that the best firms only offer jobs to the top 25% of your class, then you study with those facts in mind.

Goal setting includes now, then and later. If at age 20, you decide you want to retire at 50, then you have some decisions to make. You need to start saving that same day to accumulate the funds you need to save to retire in 30 years.

If you want to own your own business (entrepreneurship), then you need to save and do the applicable research for the business you desire.

Planning means tailoring everything to your goals. Prayer means more. Ask God to reveal to you what He has in store for you. He will reveal each item at its appointed time. Be prayerful and plan-minded when you make decisions and take action.

Lastly, goal setting is responsible, and respectable, but most of all, it deserves your time. Goal setting can start at any time of year, not like New Year's resolution.

Goals are written, measurable, attainable and achievable. Goals also require a date for completion. Your goals effect who you are and Whose you are.

JANUARY 1

³And God said, "Let there be light," and there was light.

Genesis 1:3

God, You have given me this Earth such that I may experience Your creation and it's miracles. Often we forget that You are responsible for all that we have and enjoy. We forget that without You, we would not be able to exploit the natural resources that were once so plentiful.

Lord, I am learning to appreciate Your wonders and Your works. The mountains and valleys, that are so perfectly shaped, are designed for us to acknowledge Your perfection.

Master, Your love is evident by what we have around us. You have commanded many things to come to pass. We experience this daily.

For Your power, Lord we thank You. Thank You for seeing into the void and creating something magnificent: the world and everything therein.

Lord, thank You for seeing in me what I can't see in myself. When You decide that You have plans for me, I am amazed that You love me so.

Thank You, God for Your creation.

On This Journey

JANUARY 2

⁴You shall not make for yourself an idol in the form of anything in heaven above or the earth beneath or in the waters below.

Exodus 20:4 - 6

God's second commandment is that we have no idols. Idols become idols because of our attention to an object or person. Idols become idols because of our worship of that object or person. An idol is anything you give priority to above God.

How does this happen? How do we have idols? How did we start worshipping things above God? We have shown those things our attention and affection and our money and our time. Consider your favorite thing(s). Is the TV show that comes on Thursday at 7 PM your favorite show? The difference between things you like and things you idolize is the amount of time you spend, the sacrifice you make, and the amount of time spent persuading others to like your object, too. Consider what you do when your show is on: (1) you don't answer the phone during your show; (2) you make sure that you are home on time so as not to miss any part of the show; (3) you don't want to be disturbed; (4) you know every detail about every character on the show; and, (5) you discuss the details of the show at every opportunity until the next show. Compare your attitude about the show to your relationship with Christ:

1) How much time do you spend with God each day?
2) Do you have a regular time you spend with God each day/week?
3) Do you let anything or anyone interrupt your time with God?
4) Do you know all the details about God and all of the details of Him, His Son, and the Holy Spirit?
5) Can you call an equal number of characters in the Bible as your TV show?
6) Do you recap the details of your intimate exchange with God and growth with God at every opportunity until the next time?

Is there something or someone with whom you spend more time than God? Can we change that? What would it take for you to worship God the way He deserves? Start today by designating time for God. Keep your appointed time with Him. It'll be the best thing that happens to you.

Lord, I only want to worship You.

Daily Devotional for Young People

JANUARY 3

⁷You shall not misuse the name of the Lord your God, for the Lord will not hold anyone guiltless who misuses His name.

Exodus 20:7

The misuse of God's name is at the least disrespectful of Him. At worst, it is degrading and reduces Him to a level where we would mistakenly think we were the same. He is not our equal.

God deserves our utmost respect, which includes His name. It is to be used with honor and reverence. He is holy. Throwing His name around will give the impression that we don't support who He is. Be cautious of your overall behavior. You never know when a non-believer or/and a new convert is watching you as an example of what Christianity is supposed to be.

Often non-believers meet Christians who happen to be having a non-Christ-like moment and are confused about the difference between Christians and non-Christians. This confusion then leads to a decision against Christianity and consequently turning away from God.

Do not misuse the Lord's name. It is a privilege to call His name. Don't misuse or abuse your privilege because of something ludicrous like the misuse of His name.

When you misuse His name, consider what happens when someone calls you something other than your name. Do you answer them? Does it offend you? Do you correct them? Do you consider their request seriously? Do you feel disrespected? Why would God react differently?

Lord, thank You for the privilege to call Your name.

On This Journey

JANUARY 4

[8]Remember the Sabbath day by keeping it holy.

Exodus 20:8-11

This comes down to the definition of holiness and non-holiness. Ask your parents or family what is acceptable to do on a Sunday and what is not. My grandmother would prefer I not work on Sunday. She also doesn't condone washing clothes on Sunday. She feels that chores should be done on other days of the week.

My mom agrees but mostly she was concerned about our spiritual wellness. They spoke in unison that church attendance was required if I had been out the night before. My grandmother was adamant about being on time to church, being alert in church, bringing your Bible and a notepad and pen to church, not talking or chewing gum in church, and not walking in church. It seems like lots of rules but ones I keep for myself even now and will pass this along to my children and their children.

Holy is about reverence and respect. God defines holiness because He is the creator of holiness and the Sabbath. Originally, it was a day of rest because He had created the world in six days. There is a debate between faiths, if you will, about whether the Sabbath is Saturday or Sunday. I observe the Sabbath on Sunday and won't debate the difference. I will, however, question or challenge how the day is spent. The only thing I want to argue is what you do on that day. There are things I won't do on that day at all, i.e. car washing and certain other chores. There are some things I only do if I have to, i.e. work, golf (or other sports), and shop. There are things that I feel are designed for that day, i.e. church, family time, and my favorite things, writing, reading, and quiet time.

You have to make a choice for yourself about your activity on the Sabbath. One last consideration: if you won't do it on the Sabbath, why not? If not on the Sabbath, when? If not acceptable on the Sabbath, is it ever acceptable? If not, then should you do it at all, whether Sabbath or not?

God, keep me Holy whether the Sabbath or not.

Daily Devotional for Young People

JANUARY 5

¹²Honor your father and your mother, so that you may live long in the land the Lord your God is giving you.

Exodus 20:12

Let's make a list:

Honorable	**Dishonorable**
Clean your room	Talking back/Arguing
Listen	Disobedient
Get good grades	Dishonesty
Talk to them	Disrespectful
Truthful/Honesty	Harming Yourself
Do not steal	Drugs
Respect	Sex
Obedience	Alcohol
Achievement	Suicide/Cutting
Appreciation	Skipping Classes/Missing School
Mannarable	Quitting on yourself

Parents are a gift as well as children are gifts. Some children don't have parents. Some of us with a parent(s) don't appreciate our parent(s). Consider what it costs them when you are disobedient. Not money, but hurt and pain. The items on the dishonorable list may keep them awake at night. Consider the worst thing: today you have a parent and tomorrow you don't. What would you do? How would you feel? Have you done anything that you'll regret later? This is not meant to scare you but to give you a reference point.

Parents are a blessing and the most certain way to lose a blessing is to take the blessing for granted. Thank the Lord for the gift of your parent(s). Hug them back when they hug you. Love them back. There will be times when you may not believe they do but remember how early they wake to prepare for work, how late they stay awake to prepare for your future, and the sacrifices they make for your comfort and your needs and your wants.

I appreciate my mother for paying our bills. I wanted a hug more often but I realized that she hugged me with every check she wrote, envelope she sealed, stamp she licked, for the lights, phone, cars, gas, insurance, cable, mortgage, and anything else that goes into making a house comfortable for me. Our lights always came on when I flipped a switch. That was her hug and her kiss at each one. Honoring them is a blessing.

Thank You Lord, for my parents, biological and spiritual.

On This Journey

JANUARY 6

[13] You shall not murder.

Exodus 20:13

Not to kill needs no explanation. Murder is wrong and it's invasive of another person's being. Death is very serious and taking another's life is also serious.

Two other types of murder need to be discussed though: murder of the spirit and suicide. Your soul and spirit need nurture and love. They thrive on support and nourishment. Your spirit will die without the proper care. They need love and care and the word of God. Your soul and spirit thrive based on what they are fed. Take care of what your spirit and soul intakes. Guard them from what is detrimental and unpure. Keep them presentable to God. Ask for His help and guidance with your nourishment. Keep your soul and spirit by giving them the things they need.

Suicide is different. It is usually a result of starvation – no love, not enough love, malnourished spirit and soul. It is the permanent solution to a temporary situation. The biblical evidence is sketchy. I decided that suicide is wrong but forgivable. But mostly, it's a cowardly act. When someone commits suicide, that person is saying to God that his situation is bigger than God and His power. Suicide insults God because He promised several things that adamantly argue against suicide as a solution. God said that He would not give us more than we could bear and that He would never leave us or forsake us.

Memorized and learned scripture become extremely important when times seem desperately dark. You may feel that the road has no way through but God will make you strong if you seek Him. Hard times come so that we develop a more intimate relationship with Him and a testimony that we can share when other's days don't seem so bright.

Suicide is not the answer. God is the answer to everything.

Lord, help me forgive those who've murdered. Lord, forgive those who've committed suicide.

JANUARY 7

[14] You shall not commit adultery.

Exodus 20:14

The seventh of the commandments is one that pierces households regardless of ethnicity, socioeconomic status, educational background, or Christian leadership. Adultery is the act of sex with another person other than his/her spouse. This act interrupts the marriage and once found out, disintegrates the trust that marriages are built upon. Most often the severity of the act is overlooked.

Adultery doesn't normally start in the bedroom. The actual act happens after a relationship develops. There is something that is lacking in the marriage. The missing component fulfilled by another person leads to that relationship where adultery can result.

The severity is missed because the root of the problem is normally overlooked. The root of the problem is the couple's love language is not being compatible. The Five Love Languages by Dr. Gary Chapman explains the different languages and how to use those languages to love our mates and the results of not loving your mate in these languages. This is what I term emotional adultery. There is an emotional involvement with another person other than your spouse. Either way, adultery tears up the very fibers of any family. Adultery also violates your commitment to God.

Lord, help me honor my commitment.

On This Journey

JANUARY 8

¹⁵You shall not steal.

Exodus 20:15

Theft is dishonorable. In certain small countries, they cut off your hand for stealing as a lesson. Although that seems harsh to some, others want to know why it doesn't happen everywhere. Some people may say that losing a hand is not fair, but that implies that theft is fair or somehow justifiable.

Stealing is wrong if it's chewing gum or if it's the savings and loan scandal.

My question is: why do people steal? One reason is because people want what others have. Another is people cannot afford all the things they want. Still another reason is that people are intimidated by possessing objects.

People seem to place great importance in the possession of material things. This prompts one of two reactions. The first reaction is to possess more than they need because of the status they feel that possessions provide. The second reaction is to steal what they see because they don't think they'll ever have that object(s).

Although I can reason why people might steal, I then wonder if their overrated confidence of accomplishment overruns considering the consequences of their actions. The consequences are greater than the accomplishment.

Final note on theft: some youth steal to impress their friends, or as initiation into a group. Neither of these are reasons to steal. If you have "friends" who are impressed by stealing, reconsider that friendship. They would not be my select group based on character. Remember, if your peers pressure you, are they truly your peers? Probably not. If this is an initiation of some kind, then just walk away. Both of these actions could cost you your future life because of what you did once because of pressure by a group to fit in.

Remember, you already belong to the greatest group there is: God's children.

Father, forgive those who have stolen.

JANUARY 9

¹⁶You shall not give false testimony against your neighbor.

Exodus 20:16

The ninth commandment suggests not to speak untruths of your fellow Christian and man. In this scripture, neighbor is synonymous to fellowman and false testimony translates into a lie. "You shall not lie on your fellowman (or anyone else)."

This simple command honors the other person. You also respect the other person. Everyone has the right to be honored and respected. No one deserves to be falsely accused. Jesus was lied on, persecuted, falsely accused, and doubted each day of His 33-year walk on Earth. So we can expect the same to happen to us. How we handle it differentiates us as Christians versus non-believers.

What do you do when you are falsely accused? How do you handle your accuser(s)? Why were you chosen as the accused? Will someone be saved because of your reaction to the accusation? These are critical components in your Christian walk. Your answers to these questions exhibit your Christian maturity and your trust in Christ and His plan. Situations such as these are designed to bring you closer to Christ. During this "season," Christ reminds you to lean on Him rather than your own understanding. And He uses you as an example of Christian behavior. You are the example of what Christ can and will do in your life because of your circumstances.

Our role is to submit to God's plan, follow Christ's example, and realize the outcome is as God designed. Lastly, consider the golden-rule: do unto others, as you would have then do unto you. Remember to avoid the temptation of falsely accusing others, for one day someone may falsely accuse you. While never doing it doesn't guarantee the likewise from happening to you, the reap/sow rule nearly guarantees that what you've done will show up again. Avoiding the false accusation removes the need for asking God for forgiveness while living in fear of an eventual false accusation.

Lord, guide my tongue such that I don't falsely accuse my neighbor.

JANUARY 10

> [17]You shall not covet your neighbor's house. You shall not covet your neighbor's wife, or his manservant or maidservant, his ox or donkey, or anything that belongs to your neighbor.
>
> ***Exodus 20:17***

To understand the last commandment, we need to define covet. To covet means to desire (another's property) inordinately or wrongfully; to wish for eagerly. Let's spend a moment on covet or to wrongfully desire. Covet means to desire another's property in such an aggressive manner and such a full desire that one might wish the neighbor were not blessed. Further, envy is the basis for one to covet another's blessings or belongings.

With some clarity, we proceed. The scripture commands us not to wrongfully desire your neighbor's house, his wife, his servants, his livestock, or any of his belongings. How does this happen, to covet I mean, you ask? Again, envy, which is greater than jealousy, causes most covetous behavior. Some people want what others have so desperately that they commit crimes to obtain the possession(s). Either they "steal" one so that they have one as well or they "steal" from their neighbor so that the neighbor won't have it anymore. There is also the possibility that one might purchase or acquire the possession legally but at what cost.

The outcome of a covetous attitude is cost and consequences. We have to pay when we envy. Covetous and envious behavior is costly. This cost is a sacrifice of blessings that God has planned which we may forfeit because we are so busy wrongfully wanting what rightfully belongs to someone else. How do we avoid being covetous? Pray for favor, that's my advice. In the process, my prayer partners and I remind each other and I will share with you our thoughts: "What God has for me is for me." This is a reminder that we don't have to envy for what others have because God will bless us as He has planned. Most often, these blessings are better than what we can imagine or covet. It has taken some adults several years to realize that nothing good can come from such behavior.

Remember, "What God has for me is for me."

JANUARY 11

[24]The Lord bless you and keep you. [25]The Lord make His face shine upon you and be gracious to you. [26]The Lord turn His face toward you and give you peace.

Numbers 6:24-26

Scripture memorization is key in your toughest times. When your day is in the dumps, your best tool for recovery from your day is the scripture that uplifts. This is one of my scriptures because it has gotten me through my rough times. Read it again. Doesn't it make you give up your rough times?

Scripture memorization also enables us to minister to the needs of others. If someone around you or a total stranger need some encouragement, you have just the right words to share with them. Often we don't have a second chance to help someone overcome whatever they are enduring. We have to be ready.

We are destined to meet people with whom we will need to share our testimony. Our testimony is us sharing where we are now based on our experiences. My testimony relating to this scripture is that a friend read this to me over the phone when I called her to tell her that my dad died. I had taken a discipleship class with this couple and we became friends. She wasn't home so he read that scripture to me and I cried and cried. I kept that scripture in my heart during each day during that dark time in my life. Each day that scripture meant more and more and the loss of my dad got a little easier. Don't misunderstand; I still miss him, but the tears don't come as often. I realized that God had a plan even in what seemed to be my despair – I wrote two poems, which I published, where I discuss our love and my loss.

Most importantly, I was able to share this experience – my testimony – with others who've lost loved ones. Ones I know and ones I don't know through my poetry. I hope my testimony helps you.

Lord, thank You for Your blessings.

JANUARY 12

[16]When all our enemies heard about this, all the surrounding nations were afraid and lost their self-confidence, because they realized that this work had been done with the help of our God.

Nehemiah 6:16

Most people who don't know Jesus personally still manage to respect Him. They have no idea of who they are or why they are here because they have no relationship with Him. That seems judgmental but it is realistic. There is a void in our lives until we acknowledge Him as our Lord and Savior.

Non-believers will seek you as a believer as a tool to reach answers and solutions. As a Christian, you may be the only connection to God they have. Treat that responsibility with care and respect. The Lord may have chosen you to bring that very person to Christ.

God has a plan for each of us, saved and unsaved. It is up to us to seek that plan and obediently serve Him according to that plan. God chooses events such as this one, where the walls were completed and the enemy did not believe, to show proof of His very existence. These are occasions where God uses us to accomplish what others perceive as the impossible or the unrealistic.

The issue of faith and belief and trust come into play. We as Christians have to believe, too. He uses these very instances to prove to those who don't believe and those of us whose faith has wavered, that He is doing His perfect will.

He provides this as a mechanism to join souls and remind us of who He is.

Lord, they may not have accepted You personally, but they respect Your power even from afar.

JANUARY 13

⁶You alone are the Lord. You made the heavens; even the highest heavens, and all their starry hosts. The earth and all that is on it. The seas and all that is in them. You give life to everything, and the multitudes of heaven worship you.

Nehemiah 9:6

Worship is the highest form of praise to the Lord. Just from this brief description, He deserves all your worship and praise. But in addition to these magnificent acts, He created each person and each animal and each living and breathing entity. Then above all else, He forgives us daily of our sins. He loved us enough to save us, even though He could've created another world; one without sin. But instead He gave His Son and saved us.

I was in a Christian Education class and the facilitator asked us what would we pray for if God was only granting for tomorrow what we prayed for today.

Some people prayed for cars and jobs, while others prayed for their children and family. We were all engaged in what we would pray for when our facilitator broke in, praying aloud for breath; the proper functioning of his organs, life, mobility of his limbs, the ability of speech, the senses, and peace of mind. After he said Amen, I was crying. His follow-up statement was; what good is all of that if you are not here?

It reminded me that the basics are what we owe thanks to Him.

We owe Him praise and worship for all things.

Thank You, Father God for presence and authority over this world. Thank You for my life.

JANUARY 14

[13] You came down on Mount Sinai; you spoke to them from heaven. You gave them regulations and laws that are just and right, and decrees and commands that are good.

Nehemiah 9:13

God is our Father. He asks us to be obedient. He provides for me in spite of my disobedience. That's love – unconditional.

One of God's many attributes is omniscience. Because He created it all, He knows it all, which is inclusive of knowing the outcome of situations and circumstances before they occur.

My mom used to tell me things I had done and I spent hours trying to figure out how she knew what I had done. One day, she revealed her secret. She told me you are my child and I know you. She meant that there was a pattern of behavior that I exhibit that was consistent enough for her to draw a conclusion about my future behavior. Her other clue was the fact that I had left evidence in some instances.

Just as it is with God. God knows even my thoughts, my fears, my dreams, the desires of my heart and everything. He allowed them to be there. He's God. My mother observed me out of love. She cares for me so this was important to her. Both she and God know when I could possibly disobey. They both know what I'm passionate about.

They both love me.

Last thing: if you were/are a curious child and you touched the stove. When you touched it your mother immediately corrected you. She exclaimed, "Hot." She did this in an effort to stop you from hurting yourself. She has a foresight for things that may cause you harm. I would bet though that she had to tell you more than once not to touch that stove. That was because while the stove may not have been hot when you actually touched, she never wanted you to actually be hurt.

If parents can stop the potential for pain, it will only be through our obedience.

Lord, help me follow Your laws and decrees. I will obey because of my respect and love for You.

JANUARY 15

⁴To the Lord I cry aloud, and he answers me from his holy hill.

Psalm 3:4

Have you asked someone a question and they ignore you? You know they hear you but don't respond. Not now, not later, not ever.

The Lord is not that person. As a matter of fact, because He knows us and our thoughts, He knows our prayers before we ask so He already has an answer prepared. Don't give confused with Him not giving you what you ask for immediately. He has three answers: Yes, No and Wait, not right now, maybe later.

The point is that He answers us. The question is do we always recognize the answer? No is the answer to that. As I said earlier, the answer may not be what we anticipate. I asked for my birth parents to get along better. The answer was for them to divorce. There are a lot of reasons why this was the best answer but I was angry because it's not what I wanted. But what makes it all the best is God knows what is best for us. He does what is best for us. Always. We have to examine a little further and sometimes wait for the whole picture. Now that I'm older, I understand why the divorce was necessary. I also learned more about them individually. At which point, I agreed with God entirely.

Faith is important here. There will be times when you may wonder what is He doing but faith is the key. Two scriptures are very important in your walk with God. Deuteronomy 31:66 reads, "I will never leave you nor forsake you." Romans 8:28 reads, "And we know that in all things God works for the good of those who love him, who have been called according to his purpose."

These scriptures are a commitment from God to us about faith and believing and perseverance.

He will answer you. But are you prepared for His response? He said He will do exceedingly and abundantly more than we can imagine. Are we ready?

Lord, thank You for answering my plea.

JANUARY 16

[1]O Lord, our Lord, how majestic is your name in all the earth! You have set your glory above the heavens.

Psalm 8:1

When I first heard these words at the opening of a prayer, I cried. The awesomeness (if that's a word) took residence over my spirit and I haven't been the same since. I immediately asked for the scripture and read the verses over and over. It was already in my heart so memorization wasn't an issue.

Since that time I recite the scripture as a part of my prayer to God. As I pray this scripture, it is hardly routine. Each time I say it aloud, it reaches new heights and depths. I reach a new height with God. A new closeness.

This scripture exercises the very objective of prayer: to acknowledge His power as creator; the awesomeness of His name, His being. When I acknowledge His greatness, I am humbled and grow closer to Him. For most of my life as a Christian, my prayer has been "Lord, I want to grow closer to You." Acknowledgment of Him was my first step toward that closeness. That didn't stop with the first time. I didn't pray the scripture just once. Each time I pray it, I grow closer to Him.

As soon as we acknowledge Him, then we would be further along than we are. The mature Christian acknowledges Him and this separates the mature from the babes in Christ.

Acknowledge Him and His powers and His attributes daily.

Lord, thank You for Your overwhelming presence.

JANUARY 17

[1]God is our refuge and our strength, an ever present help in trouble.

Psalm 46:1

I have had two encounters with suicide in my life: a young man who wanted to die but lived and one who died at his own hands. This was not God's design. God has a plan for our lives and suicide is not on the agenda. Nothing is too much for God to handle. Nothing is too big and certainly not too small for you to ask God for His leadership and guidance.

Troubles and problems happen in your life to do several things:

1) bring you closer to God;
2) be able to share your testimony on the outcome of that issue with others who may experience the same or similar issues; or
3) get your attention.

We will have trouble in this life. God reminds us that He is there for us. We are to depend solely on Him for each of our needs and our wants.

Refuge is defined as shelter or protection from danger, trouble, etc.

God promises that he will be that refuge, where we can find shelter and peace. He is our strength. He is never weak. We can always depend on Him. "An ever present help in our times of trouble."

All God asks us to do is to seek Him. He will do the rest.

As for my friends, I pray that they are made whole. Suicide is a terrible and permanent solution to a temporary problem. If you know of someone who has considered suicide, pray for them and tell your parents so that they can be helped. Let them know their issues are temporary.

Lord, thank You for Your strength and Your refuge.

JANUARY 18

¹⁰Be still and know that I am God; I will be exalted among the nations, I will be exalted in the earth.

Psalm 46:10

God created the Heaven and the Earth. He created you and me. I am moved by the words He speaks.

I take these words literally when I need comfort, strength and answers. As young people, we are approaching maturity in Christ. This maturity brings knowledge of Christ. This knowledge fosters an understanding of Christ, His powers, His creation, His love and ability. When we remember who God is, then we can recognize Him for His power. "Be still and know that I am God." There is an overwhelming awesomeness attached to that statement. In eight words, He explains everything. When you are troubled, "Be still and know that I am God." When you are hurt, "Be still and know that I am God." When you are sad, "Be still and know that I am God." When you are happy, excited, proud and simply okay, "Be still and know that I am God."

I became a Christian in perfect timing with my parent's divorce. I felt these words before I knew these words. The entire process affected me, however deep down I knew it was the best thing for everybody. The time I spent on the whole ordeal was time that was shared with others. In other words, I talked about it because others wanted to.

During all of this, God never let me forget that He was in charge and had the plan. He let me know through this experience that nothing is permanent and He is the master over all things. "All things work together for good to those who love God, to those who are called according to His purpose." Romans 8:28.

Keep in mind and in your heart that He is the answer. "Be still and know that I am God."

Lord, help me be still and to seek Your face.

JANUARY 19

²Hear my prayer, O God: listen to the words of my mouth.

Psalm 54:2

King David is the speaker in this passage of scripture. David submitted at all times to God. God granted David tremendous favor. God empowered David to slay Goliath. God allowed David to be king, passing others by that thought they should've been king. He allowed David to find favor repeatedly when David sinned and then sought God's forgiveness.

David had a model relationship with God. Bible scholars, pastors and others refer to David as a man after God's own heart. They had an awesome relationship.

The awesomeness comes because of these very words. David pleads God to hear him. He boldly asks God to "listen to the words of my mouth." David exhibits great reverence for God and a unique boldness that allows me to understand that David approached God according to his relationship.

God allows us to determine the tone of our relationship with Him. It is up to me to take what God has given me and use what I have to achieve a deeper and bolder relationship with Christ. You and I can ask just like David for Him to hear us. However when we do this, we must expect our responsibilities to increase. "To whom much is given, much is required." When God gives you more, He expects more of you. I consider what God gives us as an investment. When you make an investment, you expect your original investment plus a return on your investment. Interest, if you will. He expects us to invest in others and to be obedient and on and on. He expects us to do in accordance with what we've asked.

I take the Lord listening to me seriously. It is an exhibit of His love for me. He loves me in spite of myself and my sins. Yet, He hears my prayer.

Lord, listening to the words that come out of my mouth is a powerful demonstration of Your love for me. Thank You.

On This Journey

JANUARY 20

Fear and trembling have beset me; honor has overwhelmed me.

Psalm 55:5

Beset is defined as to attack on all sides and to surround. The writer is telling us that fear and trembling has surrounded him. This leads me to question why would a Christian allow something that is not of God, like fear and trembling, to attack on all sides and surround us. Certainly this is not a rare occurrence. We do it all the time. We allow ourselves to be fearful without asking God to remove that fear of whatever it is that we fear. God will remove that fear if we ask. "You have not because you asked not." (James 4:2c).

The author continues with horror overwhelms him. Again, I ask why do we let this happen. But more importantly, we allow temporary circumstances to let us become estranged from God because of that fear. Fear, trembling, horror, and other similar emotions separate us from God. We are separated because we take our focus off of Him in order to ponder these issues and circumstances which leads to fear of their possible outcomes. That lack of faith in Him furthers the separation making it that much harder to return and believe.

When fear, trembling and horror overcome us, we have to confront our fears and pray that God will remove that fear.

Write down your fears and pray over that list, that God will remove each of them.

Lord, I fear that I will disobey and sin beyond Your ability to forgive me. Lord, calm my fears, I pray.

JANUARY 21

¹⁶But I call to God, and the Lord saves me.

Psalm 55:16

I call to God in my joy because He is the source.
I call to God in my pain because He is my comforter.
I call to God in my grief because He is my strength.
I call to God in need and He is my provider.
I call to God because I love Him.
I call to God because He loved me first.
I call to God when I succeed, when I fail, when life favors me or when life doesn't favor me.

God is not fair. He is better than fair. He loves us. He cares for us. He provides for us. In my case, He does all of this in spite of me, my behavior and my disobedience. God is merciful. He is gracious. He treats me better than I deserve. He saved me when I didn't deserve to be saved.

He saves me when I call on Him. Even when I call Him to save me from my own disobedience. He saves me despite my negative endorsements of myself.

I have learned to call on Him. Earlier in this life, I wouldn't call on Him for everything but have since learned to call on Him for everything. He wants to know He can trust me with things I should give to Him and let Him keep.

As you learn to call on Him, you will see changes in your life. You will see and experience a oneness with Christ that you only heard about.

Lord, thank You for saving me when I call, especially from myself.

JANUARY 22

[3]When I am afraid, I will trust in you.

Psalm 56:3

When a wise woman said to me that the Lord did not create the spirit of fear, she had my full attention. The only fear we should possess is fear of the Lord. Everything else is circumstantial. What are you afraid of? What scares you? Why? This is something that stands between you and God. You may ask why I say that. Let's take tests as an example. Suppose you fear taking your history exam. Ask yourself why? Some of the reasons may include you don't like the subject that much, you don't have a good understanding of the material, or you haven't reviewed enough to maintain the material. Whatever the reason, you have to pass this test. It determines your future.

Now the important part: Ask God. Ask God to remove your fear and anxiety in order to pass this test. Take your time to consider each question. When you sit to study, ask for clarity of thought for understanding. This is an exhibit of your trust in Him.

When we are afraid and act out of fear, we make mistakes. Some are bigger than others but mistakes all the same. He can fix them. He will fix them. This requires our trust in Him.

My prayer today is "Lord, I will seek You, when I can't see." It sounds like I will only seek Him when I don't know something but we must be careful to understand that we don't know anything. He knows everything. I can never see what He knows or has planned unless He allows me to see. We are to seek Him at all times, especially when we think we know.

Seek Him. Do not be afraid. Trust Him.

Lord, I will seek You when I can't see.

JANUARY 23

¹My soul finds rest in God alone; my salvation comes from Him.

Psalm 62:1

Contentment has as many definitions as there are people. Each individual has her own contentment levels and method by which that is achieved. Contentment leads to rest. This rest, or unrest in some cases, comes from God alone. Our soul seeks God. It is up to us to experience that rest. It is up to us to understand what that rest means.

It means that He provides the rest we need for the struggles we face. When we face trials and struggles, and we seek rest from God, we will persevere through that struggle better. I have learned that once I have been obedient and give whatever problems to Him, then I will experience rest.

The source of rest and salvation is the same: God. Salvation, as well as rest, is a gift. These gifts are only functional if you accept them. Acceptance means use of the gifts. Translation: use of gifts means sharing your gifts. Sharing how to achieve rest for the soul with others who need rest. Sharing how to achieve salvation with others whom have never experienced God's love by way of salvation.

The most important words in this scripture are: God alone. We often need to be reminded that God alone created us. God alone created this world and each and every thing in it. God alone grants His love and mercy and grace. God alone comforts us and loves us. God alone loves us without condition or circumstance. God alone meets our needs and grants us the desires of our hearts. God alone answers our prayers and soothes our fears. God alone is the grantor all peace and rest. God alone is the source if every solution.

God alone.

Father, thank You for rest.

JANUARY 24

[2]He alone is my rock and my salvation; he's my fortress, I will never be shaken,

Psalm 62:2

Teach me how to love and adore You.
There's no burden You can't see me through.
Never a worry, never a care.
Always on time. When I'm alone
You lift my spirit by Your touch
You make my day bright
Precious Lord
With my whole heart I will bless You precious Lord.

Songs inspire me frequently. When I praise the Lord, certain songs pierce my soul and call me to surrender all to Him. Those words are the lyrics to one such song. This song is all about praise to Him. When I praise Him, I experience peace – the ultimate experience – peace. When we praise Him, we express our love and adoration for Him.

These words of faith encourage the believer and provides proof for the unbeliever. "There's no burden You can't see me through. Never a worry, never a care. Always on time." The impact of those very words move me into instant submission and obedience. No one other than God can see you through your burdens. Not your parents, nor friends, not anyone. The difference between us, (humans and God) is panic. Burdens bring panic to humans. God has never panicked. And will never panic. He has a plan and has ultimate power of execution of that plan.

"He is my fortress." A fortress holds back the enemy. In the days when cities were protected by walls of brick and mortar and surrounded by a moat or swamp, your entrance was permitted only by lowering the drawbridge. This detailed protection plan is what God does all the time without your help.

When I learn to stand behind Him, obey His direction, submit to His will and understand His commands, then I know that I will not be shaken.

God, thank You for salvation and stability.

JANUARY 25

[1]O God, you are my God, earnestly I seek you; my soul thirsts for you, my body longs for you, in a dry and weary land where there is no water.

Psalm 63:1

In our youth, we are closest to God. Our youth is our purest time. Our innocence is still in tact. Honesty is the utmost for a child. As a child, we are the most honest, especially when we ask questions. And we want answers. This is the time in our lives when God is closest and we seek Him most easily. Our prayers to God are most sincere. We have love for everyone, including perfect strangers.

As we grow older, we have to work to maintain, preserve and sometimes recapture that youth, honesty and innocence. As a child, we instinctively came to God. As an adult, we have to remember and then we have to set aside time.

As an adult Christian, I too have to have quiet time with God where we can commune. Where He can talk to me and tell me what is on His mind. This is a time when I seek Him and realize that I was thirsty for Him.

As a maturing Christian, I know when I have been away from my time with God too long. You too will know. I act quickly when I realize that I have not spent my appointed time with God. I have a favorite spot I go where I know He can reach me. I don't want to be disturbed. I need that fuel only He provides. I want His guidance. I sit at the base of His throne knowing I will be fed and nurtured. And when we are finished, I am revived, recommitted and am often convicted but most importantly loved and forgiven. I leave no longer thirsty but full and satisfied.

Master, I come humbly seeking You for rest of my soul, peace in my thoughts, and rest for my body.

JANUARY 26

⁸My soul clings to you; your right hand upholds me.

Psalm 63:8

The soul is the deepest and most misunderstood part of our persons. Your inner most feelings originate in your soul. Everything that is real is in your soul. It is often misunderstood by even our own selves. It is the place where your zeal and passion resides. It is designed after God's own being. It is special. It is to be protected and cherished.

When I discovered that God was my true life line and my existence depended solely on Him, our connection strengthened. I cling to Him because He is my source and is ultimately responsible for everything within. He made me.

Those three words made it clear to me that all that He had ever said and done was true and real. That is such a revelation.

He made me.

He knows all about me and loves me anyway. That's awesome news. Nobody else is that way. Nobody. He loves us unconditionally, without any strings attached. He loves us when we don't even love ourselves. That's real love.

I had a youth pastor that talked to us about sex. One of the examples we said that people used to get us to have sex was, 'prove it.' His response was one that I repeat regularly and it was this: "If you love me prove it and don't ask." I have since added to that and my message is: "If you love me prove it and don't ask. The last time someone loved me so much, He stretched out His arms and died. Do you love me like that?"

It may seem extreme or corny but it's real. Jesus died so that you can live. Cling to Him. Don't sacrifice.

Father, my soul clings to You because it is of You and is not subject to flesh.

JANUARY 27

⁷In your distress you called and I rescued you, I answered you out of a thunder cloud; I tested you at the waters at Meribah.

Psalm 81:7

How many times have we said, "Lord, if you just get me out of this, I promise…" He has proven Himself over and over again. He has proven His power, His love, His omnipotence and His ability to forgive.

There is a time in our lives where we only call Him in distress. We have to swiftly move past that phase. To quote a pastor, "God is not our cosmic bellhop." We owe Him our time and attention and our love through our obedience.

This is just one of many examples where God upholds His end of the promise. He does so over and over. Let's examine our distress. If you've ever disobeyed your parents, then you'll easily identify with my testimony. When we do things they don't approve of, I learned the hard way that if it doesn't turn out as planned then we need to go back and ask them to rescue us from our mistake. Because they love us, they bail us out. Our responsibility is to not to abuse that gesture. In our youth and sometimes our immaturity, we take their graciousness for granted. It is because they love us that they do the unimaginable for us.

As with our earthly parents, our heavenly Father deserves the same respect. Wisdom counts for understanding why they lead and guide us the way they do.

Lastly, we need to be thankful for that rescue. Ungratefulness kills the spirit of God and our parents to the point where they may regret saving us. We want to avoid that. We need to honor, respect and obey them because they love us and they do save us when we are distressed.

Master, thanks for Your power and authority to rescue me in my distress.

On This Journey

JANUARY 28

^{10}I am the Lord your God, who brought you up out of Egypt. Open wide your mouth and I will fill it.

Psalm 81:10

Although we won't thoroughly review the history of Abraham, his people and their escape from Egypt, we will discuss how monumental the event is. First of all, let's broaden our definition of Egypt. I usually refer to anything which is oppressive, cruel and is a platform whereby I cannot freely express my views as Egypt. This is of course, not to be misquoted to include home or school. This was a lifestyle dictated by a power hungry king. Your Egypt may be a number of things, places or circumstances but most importantly it is not pleasant and does not allow you to worship God freely. Egypt could also relate to an addiction which borders on worship. This would include food, drugs, alcohol, cigarettes and spending.

This scripture spoken by God firmly states that He is our God and our Lord. He reminds us of His role which would include His power. When I read this I am reminded of what God has at stake. He created us and made many promises because of that. He reminds us that He brought us out of Egypt, a significant event where God saves us yet again from our enemy.

For the record, just in case we may have forgotten the impact of the occasion and the events surrounding the departure from Egypt, including crossing the Red Sea, He explains that He is that same God. So based on His history of being God, we should not doubt Him or question His word.

Then to conclude, He says to open your mouth wide and I will fill it. As young Christians we could wonder with what will He fill my mouth. As maturing Christians, we might decide that God could decide what He needed to fill us with and we needed simply to cooperate. Certainly we wouldn't all be filled with the same elements or the same amounts but He did promise to fill each of us.

Lord, my God, thank You for deliverance; and being my God of love and truth.

JANUARY 29

³Who forgives all your sins and heals all your diseases.

Psalm 103:3

Forgiveness has to be one of the hardest things we are commanded to do. In the Lord's Prayer, we pray, "Forgive us our trespasses as we forgive those who have trespassed against us." In your quiet time, make two lists. Title one: "People I haven't forgiven" and the second, "What I haven't forgiven myself for." Don't spend a lot of time on it. When you're done, fold it and pray and then discard the lists.

Now reconsider your prayer, "Forgive me as I forgive others." When you think of the prayer, you have to remember what you said. You have committed to forgive. You've asked for forgiveness based on the commitment to forgive others. Have you ever asked yourself 'what if God took me seriously and did not forgive me because I haven't really forgiven _____?' You complete the blank.

God commands us to forgive because He forgives us. He forgives us because He loves us unconditionally. There have been things and there will be many things that we will do in our lives. Admit to yourself that for each of these sins, you expect His forgiveness. God forgives all our sins and heals all our diseases. Only He can. Often I am confused why more people don't accept His forgiveness for the gift it is. I did learn that people that don't expect His forgiveness are usually not forgiving. As I grow, I have learned to not forgive is a sin, too.

As I continue to mature, I pray that I am always able to forgive no matter what. I continue to thank Him for His forgiveness, as should we all. His forgiveness gets you through the rough spots – those times when you think what you've done is unbearable. Nothing you've done is unforgivable. There is only one unforgivable sin which is blaspheme of God. But considering that you wouldn't blaspheme the Lord you love anyway.

Father, thank You for Your forgiveness.

JANUARY 30

[10]He does not treat us as our sins deserve or pay us according to our iniquities.

Psalm 103:10

With God as the head of our lives, the great news never ends. As youth, we often tell our parents that our punishment is not fair or the way they treat us is not fair if we don't get our own way. I certainly recall saying that a few times. But the fact of the matter is that they could be a lot stricter, couldn't they? Sure they could. Instead of not letting you drive for a week, or two or a month, for driving after curfew or backing into something while you were driving after curfew, consider their options. You could never drive again until you bought your own vehicle and/or you could have to pay for the damages. If they were being fair, that could be the punishment or the payment for what you did. Is that worse than not driving for a month? Yes. Is it what you truly deserve? Yes. But did you get what you deserved? No.

Similarly with God, He does not treat our sins as we deserve. Instead, He forgives and offers us another chance. The wage of sin is death. Yet we don't die when we sin. Should we? According to the Bible, we could. According to His forgiving temperament, we are offered life and forgiveness.

I am grateful daily for His forgiveness and love. I am certainly thankful that He does not pay me according to my wrong doing as so often I want to do to others.

He is certainly more fair to us than we are to one another.

God, thank You for not giving me what I just deserve.

Daily Devotional for Young People

JANUARY 31

¹²As far as the east is from the west, so far has He removed our transgressions from us.

Psalm 103:12

When I read this scripture or when I'm reminded of it, I am moved. As we mature as Christians, we get excited about this awesome news. As you study, and really understand that the globe is round and east never meets west, your excitement will increase.

Removing my sin is one feat but to remove them at such a distance is a different one all together. The best news is that those things that have happened have been removed. Remember when you broke Mom's favorite coffee mug – you've been forgiven, even though you glued it back together and didn't think Mom would find out.

You lied about your grades, you hid your report card, forgetting that the next report keeps a cumulative record of each grading cycle, just so you could go out with your friends – you've been forgiven.

You said ugly things to your grandparents – you are forgiven.

You were jealous of your best friend's stuff and her life – you are forgiven.

Whatever your situation is or has been, God has seen it; somebody did it before us. The important point is to ask for His forgiveness, accept it and turn away from that sin, never to commit it again. Some of those steps are hard but each important. You have a small process to His instant forgiveness. As we grow, we experience the value of His timing and infinite wisdom. When we do this, those steps to His forgiveness become less and less hard.

Father, thank You for Your grace and mercy.

On This Journey

FEBRUARY 1

²For great is his love toward us, and the faithfulness of the Lord endures forever.

Psalm 117:2

Love is based on action, true love is anyway. When you are deciding whether or not someone loves you, examine their actions, rather than their words. A short examination of God's actions will prove the greatness and the extent of His love: (1) He created us; (2) He sent His son, Jesus, to teach us to live; (3) He sacrificed His Son so that we can live with sins forgiven; (4) He has a plan for our lives from birth to death; (5) He listens to us when we want Him and when we don't; (6) He answers us; (7) He provides for us – He ensures we have our needs met; (8) He protects us: most often from ourselves; (9) He guides and orders our steps; and (10) He sacrifices for us.

Through all of this, He exhibits His true love for us. Compare His love to the armor He describes in Ephesians 6. Once you put on the whole armor, you will never want to take it off. His love is within us through Christ who dwells in our heart. Consider that each decision we make, we choose to be Christ-like or not. We have the choice to be as He would be or we choose the flesh's nature. This knowledge of choice is determined by our relationship and our source of love from Him. Even when we don't choose His example He doesn't stop loving us. That's the best news. He is still faithful to us even though we actually depart from His love. Sometimes faith is too hard to understand and even harder to explain. Our understanding of faith deepens with our life experiences. So yes, one day you may say, "Oh Lord how great is thy faithfulness" and it will mean something so different, it will be hard to understand why you didn't get it before. You will know one day beyond all concepts of doubt that He is faithful to us.

I referred earlier to Him answering us as we talk and pray to Him, I have countless examples of prayers I've prayed and I got answers years later. That is His faithfulness. He taught me that I was not always ready when I asked for "stuff" and what He has for me to come on His time, not mine. Another exhibit of His love is preparing me for what I ask so when I receive it, I don't mess up. We practice for the big test or for the game or for the date, so likewise in life we must prepare for the next stages.

Your prayer journal should be an account of your conversations with God such that you can go back and read what you've asked for so when you receive that gift you can pray the prayer of thanksgiving and acknowledge His faithfulness. I keep my prayer list in my planner so that I can review it daily. As my prayers are answered, I check them off.

Reflect on His love and His faithfulness and your relationship will deepen. Ask Him to show you when He has been faithful and loving to you. He will.

Father, thank You for Your great faithfulness.

FEBRUARY 2

¹I lift up my eyes to the hills – where does my help come from? My help comes from the Lord, the maker of the heaven and earth.

Psalm 121:1

Help is defined as to contribute strength or means to; render assistance to; cooperate effectively with; aid; save; rescue.

As you define help in your terms, it may look differently. And that's okay. I define help as who responds and how they respond after I say I need help. If they can assist, then they are part of the solution; if they can't, they are not. When I find myself needing help, I stop and think about why do I need help. Any number of answers may surface. I use that information to develop my choices. Usually that list of who will respond is short. The most important thing I do is to ask if this situation is only designed to draw me closer to Him; is this situation designed for me to only lean of Him. If the answer is yes, then I stop and pray; pray for order and guidance – order my steps and guide the right people to me or vice versa. After that prayer, I wait for Him to work. I know then that I've been helped.

Everything we are belongs to God, we are the results of His creativity and overall ability to do whatever He wants. So quite naturally, He knows us better than we know ourselves, so He knows what will make us call on only Him. This serves as our reminder of exactly where our help does come from. A word of wisdom, don't ignore Him – He will persist until He gets your attention.

Master, all of my strength and help comes from You. I am blessed.

FEBRUARY 3

¹⁰My son, if sinners entice you, don't give in to them.

Proverbs 1:10

Often our friends will attempt to persuade us to do things that are simply not right. They will use all available tools to convince you that you should follow their lead. What exactly makes you decide to give in or not?

On the other hand, what makes us entice others to sin? What influences us to do wrong and not only us but to persuade others to follow us into fulfilling the temptation?

There are various reasons why we are tempted and why we involve others in our activities. Most importantly though, we have instructions not to do so. What God tells us in this particular verse is that we are not to be enticed by sinners. What we don't know is who the sinner is nor the sin. What we do know is that God has made provisions for us and these very provisions keep us from failing and faltering into sin repeatedly. Our heavenly Father provides us with wisdom to overcome such obstacles as sin, in all forms. This wisdom coupled with His provisions translate into His love for us. Your earthly parents and people close to you tell you how not to get into trouble all the time. Often you listen, but sometimes you don't.

What I grew to learn was that they who spoke to me about such things, spoke out of love for me and wisdom gained from similar experiences. Sometimes I ignored their advice even though I knew that it was for my own good. At the time I didn't realize all of the reasons why they told me certain things. Obviously I couldn't know what they knew or even anticipate the outcome of ignoring their advice.

Similarly with God, we cannot anticipate the outcome/consequences of our sins and disobedience. His plans for us (Isaiah 25:1) depend on our submission/surrender to His will and our obedience and His forgiveness when we do sin (Ephesians 1:7). He shares with us that His thoughts are not our thoughts (Isaiah 55:8). We are to follow His command, which includes this proverb.

Lord, let me not entice anyone to sin. Grant me the wisdom not to sin.

FEBRUARY 4

⁵Trust in the Lord with all your heart and lean not on your own understanding; ⁶In all your ways acknowledge him, and he will make your paths straight.

Proverb 3:5-6

God's direction: while it is so plain and simple, it seems so difficult to obey.

These two scriptures will impact you spiritually for the rest of your life.

First of all, trust means to give authority. As soon as I realized that I didn't know anything, life was better for me. I wanted to figure it out when there were things that I didn't understand. But as soon as I ask Him to explain it to me or show it to me, then I was better. I was a better Christian.

Our understanding is not always based on truth or fact. God's guidance will lead us into a better understanding of what His plans and desires are for us (Isaiah 55:8). God said it best when He said, "My thoughts are not your thoughts. My ways are not your ways." And although we were created in His image, we spend time at certain parts of our lives trying to get back to an image He may approve.

Secondly, acknowledging Him is a form of praise. Seeking God's face and guidance will provide you answers to all of your questions like what should you do, where should you go, or what's going on.

If you first seek the Source, answers will be easily accessible. Imagine what happens when you ask a question of someone who doesn't have the answer. That is a waste of time. Seek God for answers about yourself, then wait on His response. All He asks is for acknowledgment. All He expects is obedience. Submit to His leadership.

Lord, with all of my heart, which You made, I will trust You to guide me and lead me.

FEBRUARY 5

[12]You will say, "How I hated discipline! How my heart spurned correction! [13]I would not obey my teachers or listen to my instructors.

Proverbs 5:12-13

As a teen, I would've liked to be able to say those words and exhibit that behavior. Sometimes I'm sure that you do, too. You've thought that surely the authority doesn't know what you need and certainly not what you want. They don't listen to you and they don't understand. Several years ago, Will Smith wrote a song, "Parents Just Don't Understand". This tune detailed where teen's and parent's paths diverge. It is a snappy tune and became quite popular. This idea that nobody understands your plight or pressures is not new nor is it true.

First of all, we have all been a teenager once. Our experiences are all different but the lessons learned are similar. I will grant that some adults don't possess the compassion they once wished their adults had. Mostly, this is because we are ashamed of some of things we did as teens. While I wish that we could tell all the gory details to teens in an effort to stop the same mistakes, I realize that there are a few instances when the same mistakes cannot be prevented.

Secondly, adults are under the impression that they are expected to have all the answers. They don't know how to address issues where there is no clear answer. Because of this, they typically avoid such subjects. While this may not be most effective form of communication, it is what some of us can do at this time. Learning how and when to approach your "adult" is valuable. Certain topics, we can't handle. Be sure to find out what those topics are.

Thirdly, listening is key. They, like you, will be cautious to disclose if they are not comfortable with how you have received their information.

Attempt to understand their reasons for disciplining you. 98% of the time, discipline is a result of love.

Father, remind me that discipline is a result of obedience which is directly related to love. Lord, help me to increase my love by obeying more.

FEBRUARY 6

⁴Lazy hands make a man poor, but diligent hands bring wealth.

Proverbs 10:4

Let's start with the fact that all wealth is not related to money. In this instance, it is most related to knowledge and wisdom.

Laziness is the result of not seeking knowledge and not desiring more and not yearning for more. Laziness as it relates to work cannot be overlooked, though. Work fosters responsibility and people-skills and challenges. Without those things, you will lack some of the skills needed to successfully matriculate through the workforce and college. This laziness directly includes studying and the acquisition of knowledge. **D.I.R.T.F.T.** means **Do It Right The First Time.** You only have one chance at high school. You may as well do it right and move on.

Your diligence rewards you. Just as your perseverance. Each stage of your life impacts the next stage. No level stands independent of the other. Doing well where you are now will influence your next level. Your best is required now. If you are already doing your best, then great. If you are not, then start today doing your best. Life requires your participation. You determine at what level.

I measure my efforts by whether or not I'm ashamed to discuss the outcome of my actions. I can always adjust my efforts to achieve or maintain my best. The person you let down the most when you don't do your best is God. He knows when you've even cheated yourself.

Your altitude is determined by your attitude. What you give, you get.

Father, keep me diligent in all my efforts. You have already given me the tools to achieve what I have asked.

FEBRUARY 7

[12] Hatred stirs up dissension, but love covers all wrongs.

Proverbs 10:12

Dissension is defined as strong disagreement; discord. It is the opposite of harmony.

This unrest and unsettlement existing between people stems from several reasons. The verse mentions hatred as a reason for dissension. Consider why hatred exists. Jealousy and envy breeds hatred. Anger and bitterness breed hatred. Lies and gossip breed hatred. Wanting something that belongs to someone else breeds hatred. Now, hatred is not Christ-like nor is it healthy. Hatred breeds contempt. People who concentrate on hatred allow hatred to become a normal attitude. Nobody wants to be around people who harbor hatred.

The good news is that love covers hatred; love combats hatred. Love dissolves dissension. Love dismisses unhealthiness. Love survives storms. Love overcomes the gossip and lies. Love disintegrates jealousy and envy. Love comes in forms hatred cannot comprehend.

Love saves each of us. "For God so loved the world that He gave His one and only son that whosoever believeth in Him should not perish but have everlasting life." John 3:16

Love is an essential to your spirit. Without love, your spirit suffers. Remember, love is a two-way highway. Your spirit suffers when you don't love just as much as when you are not receiving love.

Love is a deep emotional commitment. Love is best defined outside of Jesus' exhibition as found in Paul's letter to the Corinthians in Chapter 13. Paul eloquently describes love and details its attributes.

Because love forgives, love covers all wrongs and dismisses hatred. Jesus set the example and demands we follow His lead.

Love one another is His only command that is not listed among the infamous 10.

Lord, unconditional love is the start of my Christian maturity. Thank You for my growth.

FEBRUARY 8

¹⁴Wise men store up knowledge, but the mouth of a fool invites ruin.

Proverbs 10:14

Wise and older people often say, "Nothing hurts a duck but its bill." The true confirmation of a fool is when he opens his mouth and says something foolish. There will be days when we seem more foolish than others. The key is not continuously be foolish about the same issues. Foolish people refuse to learn and they speak without facts.

Wisdom comes in various forms but all wisdom comes from knowledge and experience. Let's not confuse knowledge with education. Knowledge stems from observation and absorption of information. Wise persons are more powerful than educated people. Wisdom without education goes farther than education without wisdom.

Wisdom is usually associated with the elders of family, community, and church. They achieved this esteemed title because of the behavior they exhibit, the decisions they made and continue to make. They are acknowledged for the wisdom they possess because of the wisdom they've shared. Wisdom is also gained by knowing when to share that very wisdom.

I am only wise enough to know to sit at the feet of the wise people around me. I observe the leaders around me and select mentors accordingly. I have to remind myself that I am young and my experience is mostly academic. My life experiences are limited, so as not to be foolish, when I have little or no experience in an area, I seek the advice of someone who does.

As a youth, we need to be careful about listening to those around us, starting with our parents. They have wisdom we don't have – again starting with the fact that they are our parents. Consider what would happen if we listened to them more often. Consider what would also happen if we asked for what we need from them. There is a statement which says you have one mouth and two ears, use them in proportion.

Lord, thank You for showing me how to speak and listen in proportion to the mouth and ears I possess.

FEBRUARY 9

^{13}A gossip betrays a confidence, but a trustworthy man keeps a secret.

Proverbs 11:13

One of the most powerful traits you can possess is trustworthiness. The one thing that people hate the most about other people is gossip.

You are gossiping when you share information about other people that they shared with you in confidence. Repeating things that you overheard is also gossip. Anytime you participate in gossip, you are not being Christ-like. Not only is gossiping wrong, the results could be quite horrible.

It takes awhile to be considered trustworthy, but it only takes an instance to be considered untrustworthy.

If you have a hard time keeping secrets then you may need to ask yourself why that is. You also need to be honest and tell people you consider friends that you can't keep secrets.

By the way, bad news usually follows: "Don't tell anyone that I told you this …" or "You didn't hear this from me, but …" and "If I hear this again, I'll know where it came from …"

Just consider how you would feel if something happened in your life and you shared it in confidence, such as a low test grade or divorcing parents, and the next thing you know someone asks you about it. You immediately feel betrayed. There is hardly an answer to this issue.

Once someone close repeated something about me that I considered private, personal and not public—I walked in on the conversation where my "stuff" was being repeated. I decided from then on that I would never tell anyone anything I don't want to be repeated. Not sharing other's information requires a mature person, indeed, but it is a choice you make.

Father, I want my family and friends, my loved ones, to know that I am as trustworthy as You.

FEBRUARY 10

[14]For lack of guidance a nation falls, but many advisors make victory sure.

Proverbs 11:14

Consider the United States in this scripture. We have 3 branches of the government. One president. One Vice-President. Nine Supreme Court justices. 564 congress persons (100 senate, 464 in the House – of course it varies based on population.) Approximately 575 people make decisions on a national level; not to mention the countless number of advisors starting with the cabinet members, which influence each decision made. My point is the dictatorship which survives is the one where God is in charge. No dictatorship is led by God. That seems absolute but consider carefully all of the places where there is a failed government or people in unrest or upheaval. Cuba is a good example. There exists no council of advisors. God is not in charge.

Just as the nation has counselors so should we. I have a group of people in my life who mentor me in various areas of my life, especially spiritually. I seek guidance because I don't know everything. Also, outside guidance is typically more objective. My advisors seek my best interests and my well-being. They are interested and invested in my success and accomplishments. Keep this in mind for your endeavors.

There is a separate entity in my life called prayer warriors. They pray for me and intercede for me to God.

These are things to consider as you go forward. There are people who love and care about you and will want the best for you.

Master, thank You for allowing me the wisdom to seek counsel and advice.

FEBRUARY 11

¹⁶A kindhearted woman gains respect, but ruthless men gain only wealth.

Proverbs 11:16

I don't know if the difference in gender is paramount at this time. Respect is an interesting encounter. Reflect on who you respect. Spend a moment noting why exactly you respect him or her. Is it their spiritual lifestyle? Was it something that they said or did? Did they just happen to be there to help you when you needed an ear? Have they offered you some sound advice?

Why do others respect us? Is it what we do or say or how we do or say it?

Respect is earned, not simply given. Hard to achieve, easy to lose.

Kindheartedness will afford you some respect, certainly. People respect kindness. People respond to kindness. People give into kindness.

On the other hand, ruthless people push others away. Camaraderie is hard to build with ruthless people. They are seen for their business savvy and often viewed as manipulative. The perception of manipulation breeds distrust and hampers the ability to build healthy relationships.

This business savvy does give them the advantage of securing wealth. This is not to say that kindhearted people can't be wealthy. It does however speak to the issue of the length of time will be different and certainly the method will be different to gain this wealth.

Ruthless behavior will relate to lack of integrity in the eyes of some. Integrity is related to character. Lack of integrity and questionable character do not warrant respect from most people.

Either trait is a choice. You govern your actions according to what you want to be known for. When you choose remember the Golden Rule: Do unto to others as you would have them do unto you.

Prince of Peace, help me gain respect, for to You I owe all of who I am.

FEBRUARY 12

[1]Whoever loves discipline loves knowledge, but he who hates correction is stupid.

Proverbs 12:1

The one topic that was always difficult for me in my youth was how discipline related to love. I didn't believe it was possible that love related to discipline in any manner. Now that I'm older, I know that love is directly related to discipline. Let me help you understand the relationship.

Discipline implies that there was something done wrong – disobedience, even.

When you love someone you don't continue to let them continue to remain incorrect or to be disobedient. Instead because of love, you correct them; you show them the error and help to correct it. This discipline is related to knowledge. Knowledge is the solution to disobedience and correction. It takes love to discipline someone. You don't normally discipline a stranger. You are disciplined by persons who love you. You discipline people you love. You accept discipline from people you love. People accept discipline from people they love and from people who love them. This mutual love promotes communication where discipline is simply part of the total relationship.

The opposite of discipline is lack of correction. Rejecting correction is stupid because it is a rejection of love.

Rejecting love is insensitive. Love comes from the heart. Rejecting ones heart can be hurtful of the other person. So now that you have the relationship, be careful when you question the discipline rendered when you make a mistake or are disobedient. Keep in mind that discipline starts out of love.

Master, thank You for allowing me to escape stupidity.

On This Journey

FEBRUARY 13

[10]Pride only breeds quarrels, but wisdom is found in those who take advice.

Proverbs 13:10

Wisdom is gained from experience—yours and others. Wisdom is also about judgment. Judgment is knowing when to seek advice. Great judgment comes with wisdom. Also, wisdom comes from knowledge acquired directly or from others.

When you can seek the advice of others, wisdom is there.

Pride on the other hand doesn't allow us to depend on others nor to seek others. Pride is the source of many mistakes. Not much good can come from pride. Pride usually is heightened by boasting and stems from a showy nature. Pride often involves hurting others in order to be better, rather than allowing merit to stand for the person or situation.

In this scripture, pride is said to breed quarrels. Pride also provides envy because of boasting. Pride promotes unhealthy competition which results in quarrels. These quarrels are not a result of wise actions. The presence of wisdom is evident in many instances, inclusive of knowing when to share certain information and details.

Wisdom is also evident when you decide against putting others down in order to lift your own cause. Wisdom is knowing that you can talk about your good qualities or attributes without talking about others at all.

Wisdom is seeking information about an issue whether you know about the topic or not. Wisdom is not gained early but you can gain it easily by patiently waiting on your experience to provide a spring board for knowledge.

Remember, misused pride can hurt, even if you don't intend for it do to so.

Be wise.

Lord, take any prideful thing from me.

FEBRUARY 14

[30] A heart at peace gives life to the body, but envy rots the bones.

Proverbs 14:30

Most people cannot honestly say that they've achieved peace in their heart. Sadly enough, many never will. Christians, however, have an advantage over the rest. We can achieve that peace by simply submitting to the will of God. It's easier to read and write, but harder to understand.

A heart at peace is of God. Peace is achieved and maintained when you envy no one, when you are patient, when you are kind, and when you actively seek God's will, among other things.

A heart at peace gives life because the heart is the control center of the body. The heart sets the pace for the rest of the body. This peace allows the eyelashes to move well; the limbs move freely; the eyes to see clearly; the brain to function properly; the creativity to flow; the blood to reach each area of the body; the strength to do what God has for you to do; the breath from the lungs that go in and out without notice and the heart to love.

Envy is not love and it is not peace. Envy creates negative energy. It involves too much time spent on the wrong things. Envy means that we worship or desire the other person's possessions, personality or gifts. Most of the time people envy the intangible. Someone may envy another's vocal ability. Concentrating on their talent and wanting to acquire that talent is envy. The results of envy are harmful. The difference between envy and jealousy is action. When envy is present, most of the time there is action taken in order to achieve similar status or discredit the talent of that person. The action is designed to prevent the other person's success or from meeting their goal, so that envious person can't achieve his/her goal.

Nothing good comes from the envy of another. Envy of another will cause you to lose focus of your purpose. Further, it can cause you to lose your talents. Greed usually follows envy if there was success in acquiring or sabotaging the other's talent or object.

If there is something that someone else has and you want it, then ask the Gift Giver for it. Don't seek it from the individual. They are only the recipient. Be a recipient. Ask God, more importantly, thank God for your own "stuff." Then do what you are supposed to do with it. Only then can you ask for more.

Father, let me not envy. Thank You for Your peace.

On This Journey

FEBRUARY 15

⁷Where a man's ways are pleasing to the Lord, he makes even his enemies live at peace with him.

Proverbs 16:7

"Forget about yourself. Concentrate on Him and worship Him. Worship Christ the Lord." These words came from an old song we sang in our choir.

"If I could live in such a way that I am pleasing in your site" is my prayer.

We are here to please, obey and to worship Him. If I please God, I've done my part. I've done my job.

It is sometimes hard in our ways to please God. However, it is harder to repent when our ways don't please God. I feel worse when my ways are against God's will.

God knows that "His ways are not my ways." Isaiah 55:8. So He already knows that we will not do just as He would do. However, that does not excuse our disobedience. He compensates through repentance of us not to mention, He already planned for our shortcomings by redeeming us through Christ's death and resurrection.

Now, prayer will accomplish the pleasing ways we need to achieve. Asking God to mold your thoughts and actions such that they may pleasing to His sight is one such request. God honors that because it is submission to Him. This action is in obedience to Him. This action is out of love for Him.

Your enemies will recognize the Lord's presence in your life. They will respect that. It may not cause them to not be your enemy but it will cause them to understand that you are not moved by their behavior. Part of obedience to God is praying for your enemies and anyone who is against or stands between your relationship with God.

Recognize and reorganize where you can be more pleasing to God. Concentrate on that which pleases God so there is no time to worry about an enemy. God will honor those efforts which please Him.

Lord, let my ways be pleasing to You.

FEBRUARY 16

³The crucible for silver and the furnace for gold, but the Lord tests the heart.

Proverbs 17:3

"With my whole heart."

A crucible tests the metal through high temperatures. It heats then the silver is shaped for consumer use. The furnace melts gold for blending and shaped for consumer use.

The Lord however molds and tests our hearts for His use and His glory. He uses a process to design each of our hearts to serve Him as He chooses.

He does this in several unique ways. Recently, my prayer warriors, a group of women, and I were praying. When it was my turn to pray, I poured out my heart to the Lord about a friend of ours that lacked love and wasn't able to love. While I prayed for her relationship with the Lord, I shed so many tears. The significance here is that love for another is our Christian duty. It is my responsibility to pray for others who need prayer for healing, for love, for forgiveness or for anything else.

God's test for me is that even if that individual hurts me is whether or not I will pray for them in spite of my hurt.

God tests our hearts to determine that we will be obedient and will love others. He wants us to respond according to His will. He wonders what will we do in certain situations.

Basically, He wants to know if we will cleave to Him and "lean not on our own understanding." He wants to know if we will tell Him everything on our hearts even though He already knows what exists there.

Bottom line, He melts, molds, and makes us into the Christians who love Him and submit to Him unconditionally.

Thank You, God for testing my love for You.

On This Journey

FEBRUARY 17

⁹He who covers over an offense promotes love, but whoever repeats the matter separates close friends.

Proverbs 17:9

This scripture addresses the difference between wisdom and foolishness.

"I told you so" and "if you had just listened to me" are indeed hard to avoid. Wisdom and maturity are required to avoid those phrases as well as cover an offense.

He who does this does two things:

1) Show his maturity and wisdom; and
2) Show compassion for others.

When I try to hold a grudge against someone or remind another of a wrongdoing, I am immediately reminded that God could do the same to me. If that's not what I want done then I won't do it to others. God forgives because He expects us to forgive as freely as He. God does not keep records of wrong. Once He forgives us, He forgets the sin. God loves us, but not some of our thoughts and actions. The phrase, "God hates the sin, not the sinner," pops into my mind.

A person loves for many reasons. I have discovered though that if you overlook someone's shortcomings or faults, they will align themselves with you. They realize that your relationship has a deeper meaning. They grow closer to you. The mutual investment in one another's lives increases. The mutual respect builds. At this level, they decide never to disappoint you again. They exercise every technique within their power proving they deserve your continued respect and love.

By not reminding your close friends of their errors, you build a bridge between the two of you, rather than a wedge which would be easier.

Love allows close friends to grow.

Thank You, Father for the wisdom of love and of Your will and sacrifice.

FEBRUARY 18

⁸The words of a gossip are like choice morsels; they go down to a man's in most parts.

Proverbs 18:8

Ribeye steak is a great source of iron and eaten in moderation is a great source of nourishment. Too much beef will not digest quickly and will deposit in the body. This deposit aids in weight gain and too much of this deteriorates your health.

Gossip has two rules:

1) never gossip, and
2) never gossip about your friends.

Gossip hurts, plain and simple. Gossip demoralizes and demeans and is always negative, never positive. These negative, degrading comments rip away the very lining of the soul. Gossip is hard to recover. Gossip is a lie most of the time. No one who gossips really cares about others. Gossips are selfish. Gossips don't seek the mature, accepting approach – communication, open and honest.

Gossip has infected you or someone you know. Please consider if you were the subject of the gossipers. Could you handle it? Would you be able to handle it? Does it seem fair then?

The worse scenario imaginable is one where you overheard someone who you consider to be a great, close friend gossip about you and your family. She is sharing all of the details of a conversation that her mother had with your mother. You've never heard this information before it appears to others, at their lockers, where they are certain you are out of ear shot. You learn some scary things about your father as a result of gossip.

The last rule of gossip appears on several levels of life: you reap what you sow. It could happen to you.

Remember gossip costs. So how do you decide who pays?

Thank You, Lord for my soul's wisdom and understanding.

FEBRUARY 19

¹¹A man's wisdom gives him patience; it is to his glory to overlook an offense.

Proverbs 19:11

Wisdom is key to your success in life. Wisdom is knowledge plus experience, both of which foster maturity. Wisdom cannot exist without maturity and maturity exists because of wisdom. Wisdom brings about patience, a critical trait which often offers a path to love. Your patience with someone could make the difference. Love and compassion are expressed through patience. People feel loved and cared for when you are patient with them.

"Patience is a virtue" is a phrase I always heard but was older when I finally understood what that meant. Virtue is moral excellence. Patience is an option you want to be able to exercise at will. Patience is a character trait you need to possess. Patience factors into wisdom. Wisdom is a combination of several character traits, so of course, wisdom doesn't come immediately.

Now the second half of the scripture. According to this scripture there is honor or glory for the man who overlooks the offense of another. Forgiveness becomes key as a tool to successfully overlook another's offense. Keep in mind these two actions, forgiveness and overlooking another's offense, prove Christian maturity and a unique closeness to Christ.

The most important of these actions is that if you sow such behavior, the more assured you are to reap the same treatment. I pray fervently that God will treat me better than I treat others. I consider this each time I want revenge on someone. I recall that I should not be doing God's job. So I stop and sometimes I repent and ask for guidance.

Remember wisdom and maturity is essential to Christian growth. All of which come from God.

God, instill in me the ability to overlook anger.

FEBRUARY 20

[7]The lamp of the Lord searches the spirit of a man; it searches out his inmost being.

Proverbs 20:27

The spirit of man is the good and pure part. The spirit is the part of you that keeps everything even. Your spirit is the very crux of you. It is from this place that your deepest feelings exist. It is with this spirit that you love the deepest and care the most. It is with this same spirit that you love God the fullest.

The Lord created your spirit. He designed it to love Him deeply and fully and unconditionally. The Lord's lamp seeks that inmost being to determine if it is the original creation. God is a jealous God and wants total commitment and full love and a yearning spirit. God seeks the pure parts of the spirit so that you serve Him with that spirit.

Your most passionate responses come from the depths of your soul. God wants you to respond to Him better than we do to our favorite color or favorite car or favorite song. When you respond to God, remember God created you and that passion to serve Him. We often reallocate the passion and spirit He created to serve Him to other areas of our life. When He searches, He seeks that passion again. In my spirit, I ask God to cause me to yearn for Him and His teachings. I ask Him to renew my passion for Him. He answers my prayer each time to higher heights.

He reminds me when He does anything for me that He loves me and just wants me to love Him more than anything or anyone.

"With my whole heart, I will love you, precious Lord. Teach me how to love You." This is a song that my church's praise team sings and although these are the only words I can ever remember, they seem to be the most important ones of the song.

He demands my love for Him. He seeks to occupy my entire focus and He starts within the spirit He created.

God, thank You for searching my heart and seeking my spirit.

FEBRUARY 21

There is no wisdom, no insight, no plan that can succeed against the Lord.

Proverbs 21:30

When I first read this scripture, I was so excited. I truly rejoiced. When I heard mature Christians say "the fight is fixed," I would wonder what assured them. This is one such scripture that removes any doubt that all fights are fixed because God decides the outcome of everything.

I still rejoice in this word.

Now understand this implies two things: the first affirmation is my enemies cannot succeed against the Lord through me. I realized that they could not succeed because God would not let them. It is as simple as that. Your enemies are enemies for various reasons, but whatever those are, they are not enough to succeed against God.

I find great comfort knowing that God will fight my battles for me. I rest assured knowing that Christ is in charge of all things.

Have you wondered why people stand "against God" when He created each of us? I wonder. It's hard to envision success against someone you've never seen. This is also applicable to situations which are not Christ-centered. As soon as it lost order, you should've lost interest.

The second issue is our own schemes, good, bad or indifferent cannot stand against God either. God planned each of our lives when He created each of us. If I plan to be a schoolteacher but God plans for me to be a rocket scientist, I know that His plans for me will prosper over my own plans. That seems a far-fetched example but God's divine plan prevails each time. So even you as a Christian cannot succeed against Him. The joy is that He has plans for me which are better than what I can conceive or plan for myself.

Lord, remind me that it is by Your grace that I am granted the desires of my heart; not by my own plan.

FEBRUARY 22

[1]A good name is more desirable than great riches; to be esteemed is better than silver or gold.

Proverbs 22:1

All of my life I have received compliments about my name. People tell me how pretty it is. They ask me what it means and where did I get it. I feel great when people ask me about my name. In our family, we have a naming tradition where we are connected by first or middle names in some fashion. I'm proud of that tradition.

Further, I decided a long time ago to make a good name for my family. I lead a life such that I don't bring shame to my family and more importantly my Creator. I make decisions based on the consequences of my potential actions. There are certain goals I have that I know would be ruined if I didn't avoid certain behavior.

I won't try drugs no matter what peer pressure because I know the effects on my person as well as the persons around me and my future. When I drink alcoholic beverages in moderation, so that I am not intoxicated. I made a commitment to abstinence and purity to become closer to Christ.

I have seen what the use and misuse of drugs, alcohol and sex can do to people and their families. This abuse can ruin the trust of the family. This will definitely shake the foundation of a family.

I always wanted to make my parents proud and never wanted to disappoint my family. They love me and they want the best for me. This love elevates my esteem. This esteem is what the scripture says is better than silver or gold. This esteem is the difference between accomplishing my successes and overcoming my failures.

The love of your family will see you through your triumphs and tears, your failures and fears, your successes and set-ups. That love will see you through the good and the bad. This love will also steer you to make decisions with a different attitude.

Keeping a good name coupled with that esteem will aid in maintaining God's joy.

I cannot impress upon you enough the importance of good decision making and how it affects your future.

Lord, thank You for my name.

On This Journey

FEBRUARY 23

¹⁵Folly is bound up in the heart of a child, but the rod of discipline will drive it far from him!

Proverbs 22:15

Children are naturally playful. Some more so than others. However, there is a time for everything (Ecclesiastes 3:1). There is a time in your life when you will move away from child-like activities and behaviors. (I Corinthians 13). Most of us retain some of our childhood lives but we know when that's appropriate. Proper discipline prompts the appropriateness of that discretion. Folly is a youthful trait and should be employed at the proper occasion and subdued at the proper time.

Folly needs to avoided at all times if it results in unChrist-like behavior or hurts someone. Practical jokes also need limitations.

At each point in your life, you should start employing discipline into your life. This discipline influences the persons around you and others who observe you. This discipline places you in an opportune position to more quickly accomplish your goals.

Although I sometimes want to retreat into the security of childhood, I realize that I am unable to do so. Discipline, adulthood and maturity calls for my rational behavior and logical leadership. With all of this follows respect from your peers and family.

Following is a list of activities I like to do and sometimes still do because youthfulness is a state of mind that could be materialized really easily:

Here's that list:
- play jacks
- play cards
- jump rope
- swing
- play scrabble
- blow bubbles

I also have the mature list:
- chess
- golf
- horseback riding

Just remember why folly needs to be guarded. Keep in mind that there is an appropriate time for this display. Take advantage of your childhood. These days will never return.

Lord, thank You for Your discipline because of Your love.

FEBRUARY 24

> ¹⁷Do not gloat when your enemy falls; when he stumbles do not let your heart rejoice.
>
> *Proverbs 24:17*

This has to be one of my weaknesses. It is hard not to derive some semblance of retribution when your enemy falls or stumbles. This may even be God's way of addressing the issues, which made them an enemy. We have to be sensitive to that lesson. It is not of God to gloat about the learning experience.

Your excitement will exist but pray that it is contained to understanding the outcome of the lesson rather than the actual fall or the stumble. Also, remember God uses our enemies to teach us lessons simultaneously. The first lesson is to keep our sight focused on Him and to give Him the glory in all that we do and accomplish.

My challenge is to pray for my enemies and then to pray that if they should fall or stumble that they submit themselves wholly unto God; to ask Him to not let them break but to return to Him.

I know that sounds formal, but essentially you may want to ask Christ to have your enemy respect you and seek knowledge about you. It may just mean that you ask God to stop them from being mean to you. Explain to God how the interaction or the lack thereof, with your enemy feels. Although He knows, He wants you to share it with Him. He will hear you and already knows your heart.

Lastly, remember not to gloat because we are not in a position to laugh at someone else's misfortune. It could be you.

Lord, thank You for sparing me from failure. Let me remember Your commands.

On This Journey

FEBRUARY 25

¹⁵Through patience a ruler can be persuaded, and a gentle tongue can break a bone.

Proverbs 25:15

As you mature, this scripture will be one that will come in handy. My grandmother always said that you can catch more flies with honey than vinegar. This cliché translates into your niceness delivers greater results than rude behavior or an unpleasant attitude. People are resistant to sour attitudes and rude behavior rather than pleasant and warm attitude.

This scripture speaks to the power of prayer as well. It is through prayer we are able to remain patient. Coupled with God's already well made plan, a "ruler" or anyone in leadership over you, your patience with them proves rewarding. This includes your parents, too. I wasn't mature enough as a teenager to pray for favor from my mother for the things I wanted. I prayed for her and our provisions and our safety but never prayed for the favor of my mother.

Prayer is essential in your life and to your spiritual growth.

Equally, a gentle tongue is an asset which cannot be replaced with anything of more value. A gentle tongue has abundant power. I continue to pray for a gentle tongue. The power of a gentle tongue with the intervention of God can break a bone. Gentleness can break something strong better than strength breaking strong things. Strength combats strength with strength; rather than strength being broken by gentleness.

The Lord makes these things possible. I strive for these abilities. This is powerful for your spiritual growth.

Father, I seek a gentle and loving tongue.

FEBRUARY 26

¹⁶If you find honey, eat just enough – too much of it, and you will vomit.

Proverbs 25:16

We as Christians must learn to avoid greed. Too much of anything is harmful to you. It causes any number of consequences to result, including material worship, physical illness, gluttony (overeating), and other sins. Anytime you overindulge in anything, it's a sin.

The writer of this scripture uses honey as an example because it's sweet and too much of a sweet thing will make you sick. Honey is a unique example because you probably don't use much honey. You may be more accustomed to honey being used as a sweetener in hot tea or to add flavor to baked ham. Even for those uses, too much honey will ruin the flavor.

This scripture is called words of wisdom which we may not consider until it's too late to do so. The entire book of Proverbs is designed to impart wisdom on us. This wisdom influences our Christian growth tremendously.

We need this wisdom in order to move beyond our current position. My goal is to always achieve all that I can at one level such I may move to the next level.

Now for you, honey may just be a substitute for things you really enjoy, such as sports, cheerleading, etc. Keep in mind life requires balance at all times.

Too much "honey" leaves you unbalanced and consequently sick.

Father, dismiss the desire to overindulge in anything.

On This Journey

FEBRUARY 27

[21]If your enemy is hungry, give him food to eat; if he is thirsty, give him water to drink. [22]In doing this, you will heap burning coals on his head, and the Lord will reward you.

Proverbs 25:21-22

Behaving as Christ would in the presence of my enemies is a difficult area of my life. The human side of me wants my enemy to get exactly what she deserves for treating me so poorly. The Christian I am and the Holy Spirit which dwells within me knows that is against God's wishes. So here's what God calls us to do:

1) Do not gloat when the enemy falls or stumbles (Proverbs 24:17)
2) Love one another (John 13:34-35)
3) Feed the enemy if hungry
4) Quench the enemy's thirst
5) Take no vengeance on your enemy as vengeance belongs to the Lord

Now let us be reminded that God loves me as well as my enemies, so I have to be ever mindful that He blesses us both, provides for us both and most importantly, He loves and created us both. This in an act of obedience and consequently love (John 14:21).

One victory is certain, which applies to each of us, is the Lord deals with us individually and fairly according to His measure for us.

One more important point: consider the place you occupy when you suggest what someone else deserves. You have assumed a role in which you don't belong: God's. I ask God not to judge or discipline me as I deserve because I would be worse off. If I ask for God's favor, meaning asking for better than I deserve, then I should allow God to bless others in the same manner.

New cliché: "Do unto others as you would have God do unto you." Sound fair?

Father, giving to my enemy may be hard but it's harder not receiving from You. Create within me the desire to give.

FEBRUARY 28

¹⁷As iron sharpens iron, so one man sharpens another.

Proverbs 27:17

Each of you represents the church. As a member of the church body, you have a responsibility of fellowship at worship.

Christian fellowship is the duty of Christians. This fellowship facilitates several activities:

1) Spiritual growth among believers
2) Familial bonding
3) Spiritual accountability between believers
4) Prayer partners
5) Your duty as Christians
6) Being an example or source of inspiration for others
7) Serve as a resource

It is our duty to educate and uplift one another. Everyone in your life is there for a reason. You have crossed paths for a purpose: a God ordained purpose. It is also our duty to seek God's guidance on that reason and then act on it as soon as you know that purpose.

Fellowship is not to be confused with anything especially gossiping. Fellowship requires spiritual growth and education and compassion during the interaction. Further, there ought to be a trust that exists when the fellowship transpires.

In short, if God is not the center of the fellowship, it becomes dysfunctional. God leads and orchestrates spirit-filled fellowship, just as He does everything else. He uses us to sharpen each other in His words. We all need to surround ourselves with persons with whom we are able to share our issues and receive a Godly response.

If no one is in your life that does that job, then pray that someone is sent to fill that role.

Father, send me friends who will "sharpen" me in Your word.

FEBRUARY 29

[8]*Speak up for those who cannot speak for themselves, for the rights of all who are destitute.*

Proverbs 31:8

Imagine life for a moment where you could not speak for or defend yourself. It wouldn't be great, would it? Consider who may fit this description. A person who is deaf may fit. A person who needed a wheelchair for mobility may fit. A person who couldn't speak may fit into that category. Any person who does not fit the societal standard may fit the description. Consider how they feel to be considered outcast. Consider how you would feel if it were you.

So with those thoughts in mind, speaking for those who cannot speak for themselves is our responsibility, our duty, our charge. The fact that they can't speak for themselves is not a reason for their rights to be denied overlooked or ignored. Their inability to speak is the best reason for us to speak for them.

I consider this as an opportunity to do my responsibility of completing God's will. Further, the golden rule is significant at this point. It may not occur to you but it is important that I do unto others as I would have them do unto me. One of the teachings of His word is that you will reap what you sow. I don't want to reap bad seed.

Finally, I don't want my request to ever fall on deaf ear for assistance when I am in need as these people are.

Keep these people also at the front of your prayers. They need your prayers, too. Remember that kindness goes a long way to build a kindred spirit.

Lord, thank You for my example of Christ.

Daily Devotional for Young People

TRUE LOVE WAITS

True Love Waits (TLW) is a program which encourages young and single persons to remain abstinent (not engaging in sexual activities) until marriage. TLW also offers support to those who have committed to abstinence. TLW includes a commitment ring and ceremony.

I committed to TLW in December, 1998. In February, 1999, I committed publicly with 25 young people and 3 other adults. TLW was an amazing journey of self-discovery for me. I committed to not having sex because God wanted me to be dedicated to Him. I knew that pre-marital sex was a sin. I knew that sin limited my relationship with God. My indiscretions prohibited me from approaching God with the honesty required to have a fully intimate relationship with Him. So I decided to stop.

The commitment to abstinence wasn't hard. The commitment forced me to realize that sex with persons who weren't my spouse has negatively affected my self-esteem. When I told men that I was abstinent, I never heard from them again or they stayed around to attempt to convince me that they were different, but they weren't. I learned the hard way that who I am was not defined by the arms of a man who was not committed to me through God for the rest of our lives. I also realized that sex was delaying the arrival of my husband. Because I hadn't commit to God, then I wasn't able to handle a wife's responsibilities. When I committed to abstinence, I committed my body and myself to God completely. He answered my prayer—He restored my self-esteem through His word and He filled me with the Holy Spirit.

I used this time to study more and pray more and became more intimate with God. I read books that addressed womanhood, ministry, prayer, and wifely duties. I read enough to know that I had no idea of what I had asked. When I moved closer to God, I accomplished much of what I prayed for. I grew as a Christian. I was renewed and revived.

At the same point, I decided that I was happy focusing on God, His word and His work. I started this journal and devotional during this time. He blessed me to publish The Blue Print: Poetry for the Soul. He blessed me to complete my novel, Promises, Promises. He blessed me with sound judgment and discernment so I could continue to say no when storms came my way.

Finally, when I wasn't thinking about it and was no longer focused on it, He blessed with my husband. When my husband found me, I waited on the Lord to send confirmation. He sent confirmation several ways. When it was God's timing for each of my blessings to come to fruition, I was grateful for my obedience.

TLW is your commitment to stop having sex or not to have sex until you are married. TLW is a commitment to God for purity and to Him for study and service. TLW is worth your commitment. Just a note about TLW: if you have already had sex, TLW will renew your purity for your marriage.

On This Journey

You have heard or said, "if you love me, prove it." The response should be "if you love me, prove it and don't ask. The last time someone proved His love for me, He stretched His arms out and dies. Are you willing?"

TLW realigns you to the love of God and God's definition of love and God will lead you back to the path of love He designed. True love does wait.

MARCH 1

[1]"Cast your bread upon the waters, for after many days you will find it again."

Ecclesiastes 11:1

Based on our capitalist economy, most Americans hoard goods and resources, especially money. We treat success like a game: those who reach the finish line first, wins. Our world revolves around slogans very similar to that, such as; the one who dies with the most toys, wins. We teach this mentality early on as well.

I remember vividly around November 1st of each year, I would browse the wish books from Sears and J.C. Penney for my toy list for Christmas. At Christmas, I got everything on the list. As an adult I ask, "Was that really necessary?" and "Did I play with all those things?" Was I just trying to have the most? Is that how it will always be?

I forgot that children and teens compare what they have to what others have and this is so serious that deaths have occurred behind tennis shoes. This is jealousy and low self-esteem resulting from what someone else has at his or her home. Do parents know or have they forgotten as I had? When are we going to tell them that material possessions are temporary? But most importantly, how do we get past this issue?

One of the most important lessons I ever learned was to share. Often you find that what you have will brighten someone else's day better than your own. How valuable would that be if we could do that all the time? This behavior doesn't support a capitalistic society but it would support Christ.

If you have something, you should be free to give that to someone else and not know regret. The Lord blesses whom He can bless through. If you know you should share something you have – spiritual or material – give it up. He will replace it, and that may even be better than what you gave up.

Master, You have given me confidence not to worry about anything. You promised to return to me what You gave to me as Yours.

MARCH 2

[10] So then, banish anxiety from your heart and cast off the troubles of your body, for youth and vigor are meaningless.

Ecclesiastes 11:10

God has made so many promises, all of which He has kept. Throughout His word there are illustrations of His Promises. But an important one is that He will give you rest from your burdens. Being anxious or having anxiety equates to worry. Worry is a sin. So you ask, "I am to give all my troubles over to the Lord?" The answer is a resounding YES! "Why?" you ask. Because He is God and He said so. More importantly, He has the answers to those worries and anxieties. Banish means to send away unmercilously, I might add. When we learn to give God all of our troubles, anxieties, and burdens, we can fully focus on Him and His will for our lives. That was a mouthful. Anything that has you figuring and calculating and reasoning can be classified as a burden, anxiety and/or trouble. Give it all to Him and He will give you rest. What a trade-off. But we reason and say "this" is too little for God or "that" I can handle myself. Ask yourself, "During the time I spent worrying, did the situation get better? Was there a solution reached? Could I have been serving God? Could I have been talking to God? Could I have been listening to God?" The answers are no, no yes, yes, and yes.

All means all. This includes tests, relationships with people you like, your parents, your siblings. EVERYTHING. My dad was ill and hospitalized and I wanted so badly that he come home. He was in the hospital 5 weeks when I had my 27th birthday. I saw him on my birthday and I sang to him and I realized during that song that God's will had to be done. Not mine. When I gave my anxiety up, I better handled his passing. I had to give up EVERYTHING I felt and wanted about him, and for him, but mostly for myself. The best thing that God reminded me was that He would keep my secrets and my fears and my desires to Himself. God is the one to whom we never have to preface what we say with "I have something to say but you can't tell anyone!" Besides, when I realized that He knows our thoughts, our everything, it did me no good to keep it myself. He just wants us to tell Him.

GIVE UP keeping those things to yourself. I have to remind myself that He is the solution and until I stop trying to deal with it on my own, He can't do His work. But more importantly, I have to be able to give Him the glory and praise. It is incredible what He can do when we let Him do His will.

All means all.

Lord, thank You for allowing me to release my anxiety, my burdens, casting them on You.

MARCH 3

[8]"For my thoughts are not your thoughts, neither are your ways my ways", declares the Lord.

Isaiah 55:8

When I first read that scripture, I wept. This declarative scripture announces several things. We are not God. We have no conception of what God has to do or be. We do not know what He knows. Considering all that, I became thankful. He distinguishes Himself from us. Although He is God, He said it so eloquently. Simply put, "You are you and I am the Lord." That whole attitude breeds one of reverence and respect. It also functions as a reminder that we have shallow views versus God's global perspective. His view of just our individual life alone, He knows more than we do because He has the plans and He created us. Those two facts support the differences.

If we knew what He knows, we would not make some of the decisions we've made to this point. On the other hand, do we actually possess the wisdom to have even a fraction of this knowledge to do as He instructed? I beg to differ. We have His words – the Bible – and still don't follow them to the letter at all times. This example of disobedience supports our inability to handle more.

Further, my ways are not His ways. First, God doesn't hold a grudge; I have. He's quick to forgive; sometimes it takes me a long time. He loves unconditionally. I love with stipulations. He keeps His word and is trustworthy; sometimes I'm not. He has plans for me and He takes care of me; better, of course, than I take care of me.

With all that has been said, I know that this is His gentle reminder for me to remember my role. But better to remind me of what He is capable of. I am not God, not even to myself. What I mean is He treats me better than I treat myself. One day this will mean more to you than ever before as it did with me. I love the difference between God and me, but I still cry.

Lord God, thank You for Your higher thoughts.

MARCH 4

[5]"Before I formed you in the womb I knew you, before you were born I set you apart: I appointed you as a prophet to the nations."

Jeremiah 1:5

"When I made up my mind to create you, I decided what you would look like, what you would do in your lifetime, if and who you would marry, what would inspire you, what you needed to be content, what things would make you unhappy. I know you. Before you arrived, I separated you from others I have created. Although you have similarities, the differences are extraordinary. I have special plans for you – things even you won't understand immediately. But because of our relationship, you will understand as necessary." This is God's message to us.

How often do we forget that we are not in charge of ourselves – not even a little bit. God knows exactly what He wants from us and exactly what He wants us to do. Deviations from the original plan – His – only delay the outcome, also His. When I consider my mistakes and detours I've taken instead of following His voice and His plan, I get angry because I know I could be closer to the results of the plan. I don't stay angry because I would lose focus and I realize that He has made allowances for my interference.

Further, I realize that because He knows me He has allowed for my mistakes and already forgiven me for those mistakes, errors, and delays.

Lastly, this scripture reminds me that I'm special to God; that we all are. We are special to God. That's really important to me.

Thank you Father for having a destiny preplanned for me.

MARCH 5

⁹The heart is deceitful above all things and beyond cure. Who can understand it?

Jeremiah 17:9

The heart has two functions:

(1) it is the central station for our blood which keeps us alive; and
(2) it is the emotional harbor for everything that happens to us – good and bad. The heart remembers the events and the details of our lives. It keeps an account of what is said and our reaction to those words. It usually records more negative than positive. It's usually the first part of us to hurt. When we hurt, it retreats then it retaliates – the deceit then sets in. That doesn't heal it though – it is then beyond cure. Healing is growth; growth cures.

Deceitful is the heart? That sounds harsh because the heart is pure. The heart is the place where we love others. It is where we love ourselves. How can deceit come from the love source? The scripture reads "Blessed are the pure in heart for they shall see God." Does that lead us to believe that one is wrong and the other is right? No, rather Jeremiah speaks to the issue that the heart is capable of deceit. This deceit usually follows hurt for which there is usually no cure. The good news is that there is no cure for love either. Further, the pure heart discussed in Matthew speaks to our ability to come to the Lord with the purest heart giving all you have to Him. The stretch for some of us is to actually be pure with others.

Love is wonderful no matter what the outcome. The heart is the source of the love, pure love that is unlike anything in this world. Indescribable at best, love is one of the best things that can continue to happen to us. I Corinthians describe it best.

So the heart is deceitful? Sometimes, but usually not continuously so. Strive for the purest of hearts.

Lord, help me with my heart.

MARCH 6

¹⁰"I the Lord search the heart and examine the mind, to reward a man according to his conduct, according to what his deeds deserve."

Jeremiah 17:10

As the Lord does this, how does each of us rate? What reward does our conduct render us and which of our deeds render us deserving of God's favor? We don't know at what hour the Lord will search or examine us, but what we do know is that He will.

My mother would ask me: "if Jesus returned right now, would He be pleased with your behavior?" She posed this question to remind me that even when she was not looking, Jesus knew my every move. I had to decide whether or not He was pleased.

So when God searches and examines, He gets the luck of the draw. He could get great thoughts or not so great ones. Have you ever said that you've hated your parent(s)? At that moment when you did, if God happens to examine your mind, what then would He do according to what you thought? While we don't have an answer, we do know that He was not pleased.

Giving of your time and talent and even your money to entities and people who are of God and benefits God and His people are the deeds that will yield the most returns when you compare those deeds with others. Also, we need to consider how we do those deeds. We need to address them with cheer and excitement rather than begrudgingly. "God loves a cheerful giver" is often used to relate to money but also applies to your time and talents as well. We ought to be glad to give to God, especially when we are glad that He gives to us.

Father, show mercy when You reward according to my deeds and conduct, for I am not worthy of much.

MARCH 7

⁶"O house of Israel, can I not do with you as this potter does?" declares the Lord. "Like clay in the hand of the potter, so are you in my hand, O house of Israel."

Jeremiah 18:5-10

A prayer that I have heard spoken and often wonder if we know what we are asking for is "mold me, make me, shape me, O Lord." One might refer to it as an old time prayer. Our parents pray it and our parent's parents - grandparents - prayed it. That is such a powerful request, one to which we may not know the magnitude of when we start praying it.

A potter makes clay pots from dry clay. This process involves wetting the clay and making that clay thicker to form a solid vessel free from impurities and designed exactly as the potter envisioned. They spin the formed clay to help smooth and form the vessel. Then after that, the potter fires the pot, which means that the vessel is hardened by fire, heat or baked, is a great comparison. After the firing process, out comes a wonderful vase or vessel that is ready for use.

The Lord has to treat us in the same manner – He has a process by which He makes us into who He wants us to be. He shapes our hearts and minds the way He wants them. He forms our souls and spirit with what He needs in them. He molds our outside to His design. None of this can we request. However the request that we spoke of earlier, one where we ask to be in His will. When I ask God to make me, mold me, and shape me, I mean for Him to transform my thoughts into His thoughts and turn my heart towards Him and bring me spiritually closer to Him. When I ask for a transformation of that magnitude, I know that I must turn away from my sin, sinful choices and/or ugly ways and allow the Holy Spirit to direct me closer to Him and in line with His desires. When you kneel with that prayer, you will rise with a new disposition.

Lord, thank You for molding and forming me. For I am Your piece of work.

MARCH 8

[11]"Now therefore say to the people of Judah and those living in Jerusalem, "This is what the Lord says: Look! I am preparing a disaster for you and devising a plan against you. So turn from your ways and your actions."

Jeremiah 18:11

Scripture is timeless thus applicable to each day. If I were to replace Judah with Americans and Jerusalem with United States, this would directly address us. On September 11, 2001, there was a tragedy in our country that changed each of us immediately. This disaster struck our country at a time when we were comfortable and complacent and only worried about the value of money and how that value affected our retirement plans and college funds. Then came the onset of biological warfare.

This is our chance every day to turn away from our evil ways and reform our ways and actions. The outcome to the September 11 disaster would've been just as God planned in at least one fashion: it sparked a call to pray. Businesses proudly displayed slogans reading: 'God bless America,' 'Pray for our country,' and 'Pray for our lost Americans,' and others. The point was that we had not really discussed prayer openly in over a decade. Prayer was banned in schools and lawmakers found themselves reviewing the decisions. However, schools were saying the Pledge of Allegiance with new zeal.

For me, the most rewarding part was the unification of a nation that had previously neglected the awesomeness of our freedom that God provides. We owe God a debt of gratitude for His grace and His mercy. We have no idea from day to day what God actually protects us from. The things that could happen to us don't happen because God is in control.

Consider the bad things that happen to you – now consider that it could've been worse or it did prevent something else from happening to you. But the bigger issue is that God gets the glory. Many things that could happen don't but we are not always mindful about thanking God for that very protection He provides.

Thank You for offering me the opportunity to reform before casting punishment on me for my deeds.

MARCH 9

³⁹But I tell you, do not resist an evil person. If someone strikes on the right cheek, turn to him the other also.

Matthew 5:39

There were days when I didn't understand this. But I reflected to my school days and realized that this grooms humble behavior. Your enemy will examine your behavior to determine just how far he can go. You don't want to influence that behavior. You want him to understand that you stand firm and tall and will not be defeated but not by mirroring his behavior. Rather you will be victorious by being an example through your own behavior. People will continue to focus on their perceptions of your weakness(es). Your response needs to remain Christ-like and meek. Your behavior can lead to their change. Whether that change was simply to stop bothering you, to as serious as accepting Christ.

Let your walk and talk be your witness. Your behavior and speech can easily lend as a tool to lead your peers to Christ. This is how Christ intended it to be. You need to use all of yourself to lead others to Christ.

Taking the scripture literally may seem ludicrous, but consider that you will recover. And the reward for obedience is far better than any level of sacrifice for disobedience.

Thank You God for providing examples so we can have godly combat.

On This Journey

MARCH 10

[44]But I tell you: Love your enemies and pray for those who persecute you.

Matthew 5:44

I once believed that it was important for everyone to like me. Then I discovered that some people were going to despise me anyway – no matter what I did, they still hated me. But even worse than them hating me was that I had no idea why they hated me. Enemies often develop reasons we are not aware of. How we respond to an "enemy" is what separates us from non-believers.

First of all, you have to decide when someone is considered an enemy. Then how you treat them is important. You must treat them kindly and honestly. Jesus instructed and demonstrated to us how to handle our enemies.

Typically, an enemy is one who doesn't share our interests or they don't have our best interest in mind. People hated Jesus, the person who came to save us all, so I expect that some won't like me either. How do we determine that we have an enemy? How do you decide that someone is an enemy? What did they do, or didn't do, to be placed in the category of enemy? How do they act?

Jesus handles enemies in quite a peculiar way. He still loves. (Mark 14:18) Consider Judas. Jesus predicted the betrayal, shared it with the disciples, which they each denied. Later because of Judas' betrayal, Jesus is persecuted and crucified. Now who was the true enemy, Judas or the king (Pilate) who placed the orders? Or both? Humans take action quickly, but Jesus is slow to act.

I have glazed over the story so let's go back. Compare Judas to Peter. The same Jesus said that Peter would deny Him three times before the morning. (Mark 14:30-31) This is the same Peter who walked on water with Jesus. (Mark 14:66-72) Did this denial make Peter an enemy? Why did he deny Jesus? Now with all of this, there are a couple of details missing. One was that He predicted His betrayal before He ate with the disciples. How often do we eat with our enemies? And still serve them as if they were our friends. Now later, as well, Judas kills himself. He suffers significantly between the two events but more importantly, Jesus never attacks him as an enemy. But we would.

This type of love is uncommon and best described as unconditional. The love with godly characteristics. The love to embrace everyone, especially our enemies. (The scripture that addresses love for our enemies being the real test.)
   1) Can we love our enemies the way Jesus loved Judas and others?
   2) Can we expect Jesus to love us without strings when we attach the most strings to our relationships with others?
   3) When will we reach that level of love?

Thank You Lord for the wisdom to love my enemies.

MARCH 11

⁶But when you pray, go into your room, close the door and pray to your Father, who sees what is done in secret, and will reward you.

Matthew 6:6

Prayer is the communication between you and God where you get to do some talking. You tell God all of your problems, fears, anxieties, triumphs, trials, and wishes. You tell your heavenly Father what you tell no one else. You reveal you heart's secrets and desires. You don't pray in front of everyone, though. You pray the longest prayers when you and God are totally alone.

God knows when you are sincere and when it means the most. He also knows when you are insincere. Bring your heart to God and He will reward you for your honesty and sincerity.

Have you ever seen your parents pray? You may want to ask them to pray in your presence one day. Compare how they pray with your prayers. This comparison is only designed to show you the differences. You should remain autonomous in your prayer.

I also suggest you offer to pray over your family meals. Special occasions may be reserved for the eldest but you most certainly can offer to pray. I was 25 years old before my family let me pray over a family meal on a special occasion. I have never forgotten that experience.

Prayer is very important. It is the time when you thank, praise, petition, and intercede all at once or one at a time. This time should be protected. It is special.

Thank You, Lord for the reward of prayer.

MARCH 12

[13] And lead us not into temptation but deliver us from the evil one.

Matthew 6:13

God's promises are clear and true. I have asked God to lead me away from temptation. Time after time, He delivers me. He eliminated obstacles and roadblocks from my path.

These are two monumental requests in one sentence. We ask God for the ultimate: lead me not into temptation and deliver me from any evil. For me personally, I need God to totally remove me from a situation for me to avoid some temptations. I decided years ago that the best way to avoid temptations is to not be there – not be in situations that compromise my ability to say "no". The scripture may read better if it had said, "Lord lead me away from this tempting situation I've gotten myself into."

This is often the situation. So let's address the issue. If your friends drink, avoid going to their homes when their parents are not there. If they do drugs, avoid settings where they use the substances. If your mate is pressuring you for sex, then be sure to stay away from surroundings where there is little supervision. In these situations, you need as much help as you can get to be saved. The first step though is recognizing your weak areas.

Asking God to remove these as weaknesses may be one solution. Asking God to assist you in controlling your temptations is another solution.

Whatever method you use, God requires your commitment to Him. He has promised in His word to "never leave or forsake you."

Thank You, Lord for the power of deliverance from evil and temptation.

MARCH 13

^{14}For if you forgive men when they sin against you, your heavenly Father will also forgive you.
Matthew 6:14

"Forgive us as we forgive those that trespass against us…"

If only God will continue to disregard that portion of my prayer when I speak the Lord's Prayer. How often do you hold a grudge for even a moment? That is against God's will, especially when we don't want God to hold a grudge against us for even a second. We want to be forgiven immediately, even without asking. I know that I do.

Likewise, we must forgive others when they wrong us. It is as simple as that. When I want to let my anger linger, I consider what would happen if God let His anger linger when I lied to someone to save myself? Or if He held on to that disappointment when I cut off someone on the freeway?

What if He decided not to forgive you for that test where you cheated? When your best friend misplaced your favorite pen. You stopped talking to her for several weeks. This behavior is not as God planned. It is certainly not how you would want God to behave. We have to ask for the ability to forgive if we are having trouble. Keep in mind that you want to be forgiven so you need to be forgiving.

One lesson I learned was that it takes more energy to remain unforgiving than to forgive and reach a peaceful agreement. Wasting this type of energy could prevent your progress and growth.

Forgive and be forgiven.

Thank You, Lord for the promise of Your forgiveness through our deed of forgiveness of others.

On This Journey

MARCH 14

^{25}Therefore I tell you, do not worry about your life, what you will eat or drink; or about your body, what you will wear. Is life more important than food, and the body more important than clothes?

Matthew 6:25

God is very secure in His ability to supply our needs and the desires of our heart. He is aware of His ability to fulfill each promise, those written and those unrealized. Why is it so hard for us to simply understand? When I was in school, I often wondered why my mother never bought the designer jeans and such. This was before I knew this verse. I wanted the same things other kids had. I wanted to be popular because of the clothes I wore. I once thought that it was because she didn't want me to be popular or that we couldn't afford designer clothes.

The truth is that those were two of her reasons but most importantly she wanted me to remain focused on being a child, a teenager, having fun and not be misguided. School is most important and success there is paramount. Clothes and popularity can prove distracting for some youth. My mother wanted the best for me. She didn't want me to lose focus by spending time keeping up with the fashion trends instead of keeping my focus on my grades and my future.

Likewise, God wants what's best for us and from us so clothes and food are least important when we deal with life's issues. Our trust in Him becomes paramount.

I was never resented because of not wearing designer clothes. My grades were great. I made friends with ease. I was popular because of my personality, my knowledge and how I treated others. I still don't require designer labels. They don't influence my person or my future.

Thank You, Father for commanding me not to worry and placing ease in my spirit.

MARCH 15

[33]But seek first His kingdom and his righteousness, and all these things will be given to you as well.

Matthew 6:33

God states repeatedly that He is a jealous God. He commands us to seek His kingdom and righteousness FIRST. He seeks to be first. He desires to be first. He demands to be first. He is determined to be the most important being in your life.

He created you. Does He deserve to be first? He has plans for you. Does He deserve to be first? He protects you. Does He need to be first? He loved you first. Does He beg to be first? He loves you unconditionally. Does He fight for first? He gave His Son for you. Does He negotiate for first?

What does it take for God to be first in your life? What will influence you to keep God first? What does it mean for Him to be first?

I ask myself these questions often. I need Christ to be first always. My spirit cannot afford to be without His leadership. I yearn to hear from God. My spirit thirsts for Him. Remember the phrase: seek and ye shall find.

This is so with God. All you have to do is ask Him and He will show you His kingdom and righteousness. He fulfills His promises. You, too, will yearn to be in His presence and experience His kingdom and righteousness. He will honor your desires and commitments to commune with Him.

Stay focused and don't be afraid to admit that you need His guidance.

Thank You, Father for showing me Your kingdom and offering me the privileges of Your kingdom and righteousness.

MARCH 16

³⁴Therefore do not worry about tomorrow, for tomorrow will worry about itself. Each day has enough trouble of its own.

Matthew 6:34

When I first experienced this scripture, I could hardly contain myself. I was at a point of worry about things that were not in my control, which most things are not. I read this scripture and remembered that worry was not created by God. Neither was fear, by the way. They usually occur simultaneously or in succession; one ushers the other in.

We can only live successfully one day at a time. He blesses us sufficiently each day and will provide for tomorrow when it comes. I sometimes want to know what God has as plans and solutions for some of these things we create for God to fix. Yet I know I can't handle knowing some of that because I can't handle what is happening today.

Today's the day we need to praise and worship the Lord, forgive others and request forgiveness from Him. Not tomorrow. Tomorrow belongs to Him, not to us. The cliché: don't put off for tomorrow what you could do today. Often, adults are reminded through death that tomorrow is not promised, but as a young person, you should capitalize on the benefit of other's experiences and just take my word for it. We recently buried a church member who we had been promising to have dinner with he and his wife. We never had that dinner and I regret that because we had many opportunities to meet for fellowship. This behavior proves critical for success with God.

Do it today. Love yourself today. Obey today. Finish your project today. Love others today. Love God today.

Father, thank You for reminding me that You didn't create the spirit of worry.

MARCH 17

[1]Do not judge, or you too will be judged.

Matthew 7:1

This passage brings a mirror to my face and probably yours, as well. It's direct. It's simple. It's true. We as a people are critical of others. Yet we don't fare well under that same criticism. We don't want to endure that same scrutiny or observation. We want to point fingers and forget about the three fingers which point back.

Whatever someone wears or how they wear their hair or what they eat for lunch is not for us to discuss. Likewise their behavior is off limits as well. Of course, it goes without saying that whether or not they drive and what they drive is also unacceptable.

Two things that deserve consideration:

1) One day it may be me being judged by others. How will I stand under that scrutiny? We don't realize how delicate an ego is or how easily feelings are hurt until they are our own.
2) Do you want to be judged by your own standards? Can you sustain being judged by your own standards? Are your standards of God?

Keep in mind the scripture: let he who is without sin cast the first stone. This speaks directly to us not having the authority to judge another.

"When you live in a glass house, you should not throw stones." Be careful not to throw stones when you yourself live in a glass house.

However we phrase it, the bottom line results in avoiding judging others for you too will be judged. I have decided to commit to treating others with as much forgiveness and mercy as I possibly can. When I can't, I need to go in prayer and ask for God's intervention.

Father, I come asking You for forgiveness for judging others that I may be spared from judgment by my own standards.

MARCH 18

⁷Ask and it will be given to you; seek and you will find; knock and the door will be opened to you.

Matthew 7:7

God promises repeatedly to provide for our needs and to grant us the desires of our hearts. This is important to some but what does that really mean? As God gives to us, we still have requirements to fulfill.

God expects our love, loyalty, respect and honor. It is important that we understand that God blesses us because of His love not because of what we do. However, God will not tolerate continuous dishonor, through the same sin(s), conveniently worshipping and praising Him. God will not tolerate this behavior and will ignore our requests.

God wants us to have what we need and want but He won't give us anything we can't manage. If He suspects misuse of a blessing will occur, then He will certainly reserve that particular blessing for some other occasion.

Parents are similar in that manner. My mother didn't allow me to drive until I was 17. She wanted to feel confident that I was able to handle such a responsibility. At 17, it never occurs to you that irresponsible driving can costs lives. I wanted her to trust me and eventually she did. One day though, I really wanted to go somewhere and she wasn't home. Without her consent, I drove across town to see a friend. Without considering the consequences, I drove there and back. Fortunately nothing happened but that action proved to her that I couldn't handle such responsibility. Likewise with God; He will reserve certain things until we have consistently exhibited the maturity to handle what we desire.

Father, thank You for the privilege of asking You anything and knowing that You will answer my prayers.

MARCH 19

¹²Do to others what you would have them do to you.

Matthew 7:12

How fair is that? Some people treat others so poorly, yet they themselves are never treated poorly. Does that make it right? No. Does that mean that they will never be treated poorly? No. But you need to remember that the Golden Rule will always be in affect.

This doesn't mean that you need to let others treat you poorly. It doesn't mean that you are the enforcer of the Golden Rule. It does mean that we cannot rightfully mistreat anyone and never expect to see a similar action (or worse) in return.

I have learned that if you treat others justly, then you can sleep without worry. It doesn't matter how they treat you in return. Let the Lord handle them. If you've done what you can do then you don't worry about the rest. Sure, their mistreatment may hurt or bother you but you must not retaliate in a manner that sheds a bad light on you. You never want to look bad as a result of that type of situation.

This includes how you treat people when they are serving you in some form (i.e., retail store, restaurant). Remember you may one day be on the other side of the counter. Wear those shoes and the treatment will look much different.

My mother always stated the Golden Rule and sometimes her words fell on deaf ear, but I try to always govern myself by those words. I've imagined some of the things I have said coming back to me in double strength. I didn't like the thought, so I know I won't like the reality.

God, thank You for treating me better that I treat others.

MARCH 20

[26]He replied, "You of little faith, why are you so afraid?" Then He got up and rebuked the winds and the waves, and it was completely calm.

Matthew 8:26

Believing God is sometimes impossible, but a consistent and complete blessing. Faith is an exhibit of the Christian you are when you don't have each item of your wish list. Faith is who you are when no one is looking. Faith is evidence of your Christianity when you feel God is ignoring you.

In this text, Jesus is in the boat with several disciples and they were worried about a storm. Jesus sleeps through this storm. When they wake Him, He seems angry. He proved to them who He was again. Faith is when God doesn't have to continuously remind us of what He is capable.

How much faith do you have? In what situations do you have faith? In what situations does your faith fall short? Why is that?

Why is it so hard to have faith in God? Has He not proven He is worthy of our faith? Why do we continually want Him to prove to us when we continually fail Him including the area of faith? How do we gain more faith? How do we communicate to God that we are faithful?

He considers our faith when He acts on our requests. He honors our faith when He fulfills our requests.

Jesus also reminds us that God did not give us the spirit of fear, so we need to work to avoid adopting fear.

Lord, help me to increase my faith as I walk with You for this journey.

MARCH 21

[20]Just then a woman who had been subject to bleeding for twelve years came up behind Him and touched the edge of his cloak. [21]She said to herself, "If I only touch His cloak, I will be healed." [22]Jesus turned and saw her. "Take heart, daughter," He said. "Your faith has healed you." And the woman was healed from that moment.

Matthew 9:20-22

There was a song we sang when I was in the youth choir. The words were these:

> It's Jesus
> Yes, it is Jesus
> It's Jesus in my soul
> For I have touched the hem of His garment
> And His blood has made me whole.

I don't remember if there were more words but I didn't need any more words then. I really don't need any more now. I was convinced at age 8, or thereabout, that "His blood had made me whole." He demands our faith and confidence. He wants us to believe that He will keep each of His promises and He will answer each of our prayers. He is our Father and He loves us (John 3:16). Consider this: You have faith in your earthly parents. I grew up in a blessed environment where I never wondered whether the lights would work when I got home or not. But as a Christian, I worry God to death about things He has already provided for and for which He has a plan. We are supposed to trust Him and believe in Him, just like most of us come home and flip that light switch without worry.

I can only imagine how awesome it was for that woman to realize that Jesus was her source of strength. Then to decide to seek that source of strength for His healing power. She exhibited perseverance. Her faith and determination was so strong that she recognized the power in His cloak. She is an awesome example of the power of our faith delivering us from ourselves.

We need to operate out of faith that exists not so deeply within. Our faith is very accessible. When I start to worry and doubt now, I sing to myself:

> Teach me how to love
> And adore you
> With my whole heart I will love you
> Precious Lord
> You make my day bright
> When I'm alone
> Then I am reminded that I am whole.

Lord, I find myself looking for the hem of Your garment.

MARCH 22

[39] Whoever finds his life will lose it, and whoever loses his life for my sake, will find it.

Matthew 10:39

I didn't understand this scripture for a long time then one day a pastor preached a sermon and referenced it.

I wanted so badly "to find myself"; "find out who I was." During this search, there were times when I ignored God, His priorities and His commands. I still went to church but my investment level was low. I went when it was convenient. I was late when I went. I wasn't involved in a ministry. No one was benefiting from my Christian experience. I was not sharing Christ with anyone. I was a lukewarm Christian at best.

This quest for "me" still left me empty. I returned to Christ completely, yet not complete. I returned to Him and He made me whole. He revealed my strengths, my weaknesses, my power, my gifts, my passions, and most importantly, Him. Everything I was looking for I found because I am a Christian, a committed, whole Christian. As soon as I sought Him, I was at peace. I had no more questions about "me." Christ showed me who I am. He also showed me who I need to be. I no longer sought the approval of others. I sought God's approval and found it. I found all the things I was missing from the world.

I put God and His commands absolutely first. I gave up my life and my priorities that contradicted Christ's. He showed me a new life. When I stopped putting myself first, I then truly experienced His favor, His love and His grace.

I truly don't know where I would be if I had kept "searching for myself."

Lord, thank You for saving my life.

MARCH 23

^{28}"Come to me, all you who are weary and burdened, and I will give you rest."

Matthew 11:28

There are moments in your life when the walls are caving in and tumbling down all at once. For you, there is also rest.

For the moments when you are not certain how many tests there are, how many more you can endure, how much longer you can stand, there is rest forth coming.

There are many experiences in your life but there is a distinct few which distinguish themselves as defining moments. These moments may be great ones but some will be terrible. Those are the moments to which God refers. He promises to offer you rest from your weariness and burdens. He promises to provide you peace. He promises not to give you more than you can bear.

My dad died and I wondered why the world hadn't stopped because I thought it should've. He had been ill and hospitalized for several weeks. One night I couldn't seem to sleep and that was the night he died. When I woke and called my mother, she shared the news. I wept. I called one of my best friends and they read to me the following:

> May the Lord bless you and keep you
> May the Lord shine the light of His countenance upon you
> and grant you peace
> May the Lord bless you as you go out and come in
> rise early and settle late
> in your labor and in your leisure
> in your laughter and in your tears
> Until that day when you shall stand at the feet
> of Jesus where there is no sunrise or sunset

These scriptures provided peace and soothed my spirit. He delivered peace through His words that morning. The words didn't replace my dad nor did it stop my tears, but it did help my pain.

Thank You, God, for Your comfort.

MARCH 24

²⁷But Jesus immediately said to them: "Take courage! It is I. Don't be afraid."

Matthew 14:27

When Jesus speaks to us, He expects us to take heed. In this particular passage, Jesus has just joined the disciples who were in the boat. He approached them walking on the water. When they first saw Him, they thought He was a ghost. This is when He lets them know that it is He.

One of the things that consistently happened with the disciples and Jesus is that Jesus was always reminding them of who He was and of what He was capable.

At this point of the scripture, Jesus addresses the faith of the disciples. Jesus empowers us to believe in Him however He decides how He shows up, and what He does for us. Our faith in God is directly related to our relationship with God, the Father and Jesus, the Son. Our faith and the proclamation of our beliefs inhibit us from being afraid. God did not give us the spirit of fear. So when He says to take courage, not to be afraid and "it is I", then He expects us to do what He has commanded.

He has provided for us such that we can call on Him. Further, in His awesomeness He made himself available to us in the human form so that He could have true compassion for us in our walk. Then He allowed, granted us access to Him through intercessory prayer. Then on top of all of that, His Father, our God, proclaimed through Jesus that we could not get to the Father but through the Son.

So, from now on, when the Holy Spirit tells you something or confirms what you've sought or answers your prayers, there is no need to be afraid or to be fearful. Do what God has charged you to do: with courage.

Thank You for coming to me Lord, especially when I fear.

Daily Devotional for Young People

MARCH 25

²⁸"Lord, if it's you," Peter replied, "tell me to come to you on the water." ²⁹"Come," he said. Then Peter got down out of the boat, walked on the water and came toward Jesus.

Matthew 14:28-29

Testing God. Is that wise? I don't think so, but we each will do this at least once in our life. Well, Peter did it on several occasions, but this was one of the most profound of the requests.

Peter impressed me with his boldness and his courage. (He asked Jesus what I don't have the nerve to ask.) He asked for proof of the Lord's presence. He asked that question with doubt. Jesus answers assuredly, "Come." This is affirmation of Jesus keeping His word. He grants us the desires of our hearts.

Peter already had proof of Jesus' presence, but what really arrested my attention was the magnitude of the request. In one question, Peter asked Jesus to prove His miraculous power and His power to grant what seemed impossible.

Jesus met Peter on his level of understanding for several reasons. One reason was that Peter asked. There was more to gain by granting Peter's request than to deny it.

A second reason was an addition to the witness of miracles. Jesus was standing on the water when Peter makes this request. If I were Peter, I may have asked a little differently. I would've simply asked Jesus to let me walk, too. The "if" is a clear exhibit of a lack of faith and somewhat disrespectful. I'm not sure what the results would've been but the experience was impactful al the same.

Thirdly, and most importantly, Jesus calls for Peter's faith and his belief. In a single word, Jesus confirms His presence and demands that Peter increase his faith. Peter asks with doubt. Jesus honors the request and removed the doubt.

Jesus calls for our faith. Be careful of testing God. Your faith and belief in God does not rest on God performing last minute acts and miracles. The bottom line is God's plans for you has nothing to do with mini-miracles we perceive will serve us or prove anything. This testing, which can also be considered an ultimatum of God, does not prove God's love or anything. If God fulfills your test, then He planned for that. If God does not fulfill your test, then it means that God loves you and the timing of that fulfillment is not God's timing. Remember, He loves us and wants the best for us. Also, don't abuse the power of God.

Even when I don't deserve to be shown, Lord, you continue to show me that You are here as my Savior.

MARCH 26

> ³⁰But when he saw the wind, he was afraid and, beginning to sink, cried out, "Lord, save me!"
>
> *Matthew 14:30*

Fear, False Evidence Appearing Real, steals your joy. Fear disturbs your relationship with Christ. God did not give us the spirit of fear. Instead, He gave us the means to increase our faith. Faith in Him and in ourselves.

His lack of faith caused him to sink. As with all of us, our faith wanes. However, we are not to panic. Peter panics in this verse. In Matthew 14:28-29, He basically says, "Lord show me." Now he says, "Lord save me." I had to consider when he asked God to save him, was he really in trouble? At first glance, it appears that he is in trouble but on second thought, why would he be in trouble when he was there walking on water by God's invitation? Peter is on the water with God in his sight. Peter saw the wind.

Peter took his eye off God. This is what happens to us when we get distracted by our own desires and STUFF. I have to keep my focus on God. I get distracted. When I notice this, I stop, fast, and pray and regain focus on Christ. I have to say to myself, if I keep my eye on God, I will not see the wind. If I concentrate on listening to God, I won't hear the wind.

The same with fear. I will mention it again: Christ does not honor fear. If we concentrate on God, we can't be in trouble. Everything that happens, God has control. He proved that He is God. What we perceive as trouble can easily be factored into God's plan. And it will all work to accomplish His desired outcome. The part we play is one of participant. We should remember that we are here because God invited us. Poor decisions result when we panic. I pray that God keeps me in His hand and in His care. I know that prayer is to remind me of where I am versus praying to convince Him to let me stay in the wrong place. He has no plan to leave or forsake me, but I still ask.

"Lord, save me," Peter cried out. I feel certain that God wasn't prepared to let Peter drown. More importantly, I feel that if Peter had taken a moment to refocus on Jesus, then these words would've never been needed. I do this: I start on my own path and then need God to fix and save and repair. If I remain with His plan and concentrate on my focus then I will not need to say these words. However, I do stray. I do say these words. I do regain focus. I do follow the plan. He continues to love me. He continues to save me. He does so without a grudge but with His usual unconditional love.

Jesus, thank You for allowing me access to call You when I deviate from Your plan.

MARCH 27

Daily Devotional for Young People

³¹Immediately Jesus reached out His hand and caught him, "You of little faith," he said, "why did you doubt?"

Matthew 14:31

When you find yourself doubting God, how do you feel? I always feel a little guilty. God promises that He will provide for all your needs at just the right time, in just the right amount and exactly what He decides.

Under what circumstances do you doubt God? How often? Why? These are all questions you may need to consider when you decide to doubt God's ability.

I remember when I was six years old my parents were divorcing. I thought that God had abandoned me. I was wrong. He stood even taller in my petiteness than I could ever imagine. I relied on Him to see me through this ordeal and He did. He also gave me the wisdom to emotionally support my mother in her time of despair, as well.

We will experience many situations in our lifetime. You have to trust God has already planned the outcomes for these encounters. The scripture reads, "Trust in the Lord with all your heart and lean not on your own understanding."

Jesus' disciple challenged Him by saying: "if it is You then call me to You." Jesus allowed him to walk on water. This type of exhibitionism is exactly what we need to avoid. Challenging God at this level may not be a great idea because what you've asked for as proof may not be what's best for you.

Imagine if I had asked God to mend that broken relationship between my parents to show me His love for me. What God could see was two people who were unmatched as a couple but I could only see my benefit. God actually planned it so that I saw my mother become saved. In all of this, I realized God's blessings as better than what I could've hoped or asked for.

Also, you have to be firm in your faith that God is right there and won't let anything happen to you. You must trust and not doubt.

Thank You for coming to me Lord especially when I fear.

On This Journey

MARCH 28

¹⁵"If your brother sins against you, go and show him his fault, just between the two of you. If he listens to you, you have won your brother. ¹⁶But if he will not listen, take one or two others along so that 'every matter may be established by the testimony of two or three witnesses.' ¹⁷If he refuses to listen to them tell it to the church; and if he refuses to listen even to the church, treat him as you would a pagan or a tax collector."

Matthew 18:15-17

I must confess, I avoid potential or developing conflicts. However, I learned through Christian maturity that conflict is not avoidable however, the most important thing about conflict is how you reach a resolution. Reaching an amenable resolve to issues is crucial to your relationship. Conflict resolution is essential as a life skill. Relationships will contain conflict. The best ones survive conflict and continue to grow.

Reaching resolve for me involves God. I have to seek God so that I resolve conflict by communication rather than the lack thereof. I usually shut down and avoid any further contact. What I learned was that I was wrong. So I sought scripture to solve my problem. The scripture is clear about your course of action. As soon as I opened myself to be receptive to scripture the sooner I was better able to address conflict.

Another thing I discovered about conflict is that most of the time your perception of the conflict and that of the other person's may not even match.

Conflict Resolution Hints:

1) Remain calm
2) Pray for clarity
3) Seek to understand the other person; then seek to be understood
4) Pray with that person
5) Learn to agree to disagree
6) Learn to disagree without being disagreeable
7) Remember God made them too
8) Weigh the cost between the importance of making it right and remaining friends with the person with whom you've developed conflict
9) In 20 minutes will you really remember the importance of what you are arguing about
10) Love conquers all 1 Corinthians 13

Remember these even when it's the school bully or a teacher with whom you don't see eye to eye.

Lord, teach me to avoid conflict but when I can't guide me as I attempt to resolve conflict in my life.

MARCH 29

[19]"Again, I tell you that if two of you on earth agree about anything you ask for, it will be done for you by my Father in heaven. [20]For where two or three come together in my name, there am I with them."

Matthew 18:19-20

God offers His power and love at each turn of our lives. He is there through everything and He offers us Him and the most important gift we will ever receive – Eternal Life. So if He offers us anything else, to me it is simply extra.

In these scriptures, He promises to grant two or more believers who gather in His name whatever it is you ask. These have to be two of the most important scriptures impacting family prayer. Prayer, an essential element for communication with Christ, is where you address your needs to God, praise God, and admire God. Family prayer bonds your family. As you plead your cause to God in the midst of your loved ones, you will fully be moved closer to one another. Prayer changes minds, circumstances, and situations. Prayer bridges gaps. Prayer is powerful.

Let's investigate the triangular relationship:

The closer we both grow to God, then the closer we grow to each other. Prayer causes that relationship to happen. Prayer will join hearts and provide peace to relationships.

You show your respect and submission and fear to Jesus through prayer. For that respect and submission and reverence, He has promised to give you what you've asked because you have joined and agreed. Most importantly, He promised to be there with you. His presence is essential to your spiritual growth. So He has promised His presence for you gathering together in His name. He is gracious enough to reward us for doing what He deserves.

Lord, thank You for granting me the requests of my loved ones and myself through group prayer.

On This Journey

MARCH 30

³⁷Jesus replied, "Love the Lord your God with all your heart and with all your soul and with all your mind."

Matthew 22:37

This degree of love for God is the ultimate in love. Your heart, soul, and mind is all of you. With your total self, love the Lord. Your total self.

That seems easy. But is it really? Love is an action. We know that people love us by what they do, not by what they say. God is no different. How will the Lord know that I truly love Him with my total self, you ask?

Well, let's see. Let's examine some issues.
Does God know you love Him when:

- You clean your room (complete chores)?
- You complete your homework?
- You are engaged in church?
- You succeed in your activities?
- You are obedient to your parents?
- You misbehave in school (cut class, disrupt class)?
- You lie (even just a little bit)?
- You cheat (tests at school, plagiarize a paper)?
- You steal (significant others included)?
- You have sex?
- You do drugs?
- You come in after curfew?

While these examples don't seem to fit you exactly, consider the ones which do. Your obedience is key to communicating your love to the Lord (John 14:23). Several of those examples could be answered either way, meaning that you may do these things but lack consistency.

Several examples are directed at disobedience. These all depend on choices. It is simple. If you have chosen to serve God and you want Him to know you love Him then these are actions and choices you need to employ in order for that to happen. Show Him you love Him – obey His commands.

Oh Lord, this the step that leads to a total love of You.

MARCH 31

[39] And the second is like it: "Love your neighbor as yourself!"

Matthew 22:39

We as people often get caught up into our own lives and own schedules and we forget to be compassionate to others. We forget that our friends as well as our neighbors have problems or conflicts. Those persons need our love and compassion. They need a shoulder to cry on or perhaps a listening ear. Often we don't reach for those around us because we don't make time for them. Resolve in your mind to allot time to spend with your loved ones and your neighbors.

One thing is certain is that tomorrow is not promised to anyone. Loving someone is a privilege and should be cherished and not taken for granted. I have also learned not to take people for granted whom I love. These people are not promised to always be in my life; nor am I promised to them.

Our love for one another must be pure and genuine. It must be cherished. Love of this kind could only be what Paul speaks of in I Corinthians 13. This wasn't something I fully understood in my youth but now I understand it better. I realized that pure and unconditional love is built on your relationship with Christ. Your relationship with Christ is crucial to how you love or don't love others. Your ability and desire to love others develops out of your ambition to please Jesus.

Loving others is not easy by any stretch of imagination but it is rewarding. Consider this fact: when you love others, you then have loved God. Loving others is essential to loving God. To love God, we have to love each other, His people, His creation.

It is simple to love others when you consistently remember that first, Christ loved you.

Lord, teach me to always love my neighbor as myself.

APRIL 1

³⁵'For I was hungry and you gave me something to eat, I was thirsty and you gave me something to drink, I was a stranger and you invited me in, ³⁶I needed clothes and you clothed me, I was sick and you looked after me, I was in prison and you came to visit me.'

Matthew 25:31-46

I first heard the scriptures related to a parable where the lady heard that Jesus was coming to town. She cleaned and cooked and prepared for His visit. She was so busy preparing for Jesus that she missed Him. Three different persons came to her door each needing food, drink and clothing respectively. She denied each of them. When Jesus knocked on the door, she answered it saying that she had waited for Him all day. He responded that she had missed three times. He was referring to the others who He sent before Him. In order to serve Him, we have to serve others.

I am often convicted when I don't help others who are <u>perceived</u> as less fortunate than I. The people who sit on corners with signs reading: "Homeless" are one such example. I don't give when I have it to give. Some people say that they will never give to those people because they will not use it for food. That's not for me to judge for two reasons.

One reason is that I don't use the money that God blesses me appropriately all the time. One might argue that I earned it. While this is true, I am still blessed through God to earn that money so I too need to use it appropriately.

Secondly, what would happen if I were that person? I would want people to help me and trust me with what they give me. Christ trusts us with what He gives us even though often we are not trustworthy.

On top of all that, Jesus is our best example of how to treat others. There are countless stories of how Jesus reached out to others to heal, to comfort, and to love them. The woman with the issue of blood, Lazarus' resurrection, Jairus' daughter to name a few, describes Jesus' grace and His mercy.

Lord, thank You for showing me how to help those labeled "least of these brothers" when I really know that the "least of these brothers" could easily be me.

APRIL 2

³⁹"My Father, if it is possible, may this cup be taken from me. Yet not as I will, but as You will."
Matthew 26:39

The Lord has plans for my life. He has lessons planned; events planned; success planned. He has our life planned from beginning to end. When bad things or not so successful events happen, although it may not have been as you have planned, He will watch your reaction through the end of the situation. These life lessons He requires help us make it to next spiritual level. Although we may see this as a set back, it should be viewed as a set up for success. View all set backs as a set up for our success. I believe that it has been proven that pruned trees grow successfully during its season.

God did not promise that all of my days would be easy. He did say that He would never leave me or forsake me (Joshua 1:5). He promised to provide strength. He already provided the adequate love to support all of His promises.

I have to consider the lesson I may miss when I ask to be removed from a situation when I can't see the end or because I don't know the entire plan.

Jesus, on the other hand, knew the plan and prayed this prayer to His father. He prayed this prayer because of what was to come rather than what had past. Needless to say even though He wanted to save my sorry soul, He wasn't exactly excited about having to die to do so.

Be careful when you ask to be relieved of your life lesson or experience. You may miss the very lesson God has in store for you. Your spiritual growth depends on these lessons. Measure the growth against the cost before deciding to ask out of some difficulty.

God is right there in the midst of each circumstance, each experience and each encounter.

Lord, thank You for showing me Your will for my life. Father, thank You for sharing with me that my will is secondary to Your will. Always remind me that Your will be done.

APRIL 3

[42] He went away a second time and prayed, "My Father, if it is not possible for this cup to be taken away unless I drink it, may your will be done."

Matthew 26:42

Ultimate submission to God is our mission. We are to allow, submit to, His will to happen in our lives. Jesus moves me in this passage because He was asked to give the ultimate. Still, He submitted to His God and Father, even though He really didn't want to. It also made me wonder why didn't He want to. What made Him not want to? But then again what would make you want to make that sacrifice. Serving God is about sacrifice and service.

"To whom much is given, much is required." Part of this requirement is yielding to God and His will, thus reaping His love, His reward and His approval. When you actually measure the sacrifice compared to your reward, you soon realize that the reward far outweighs the sacrifice. Keep that thought in proportion.

The Lord inspires me to keep my vision and focus. Keeping my vision is important because it is God inspired and influenced. It is a direct answer to my prayers. My focus is important because it is a direct reflection of my discipline and maturity. Focus should not be a challenge to a mature Christian. One reason is that you have the attention of Christ. This reason alone is enough to dedicate yourself to something such that you can reach the desired end result.

God wants to give you the desires of your heart but He also wants your heart – your whole heart. He had Jesus' whole heart.

Lord, thank You for assisting me in submitting to Your will.

APRIL 4

²⁹And then twisted together a crown of thorns and set it on his head. They put a staff in his right hand and knelt in front of him and mocked him.

Matthew 27:29

Often we think our situation is the worst. We forget that our situation is not the worst. Whether we've been pushed around by the bully at school or at work. Or maybe our parents have been hard on us recently. The problem with all of that is that there are people who are in far worse situations and circumstances than we.

Consider why bullies become bullies. They are bullies merely because they want attention and they don't get enough love. Imagine what it would it be like if you receive less than the love you desire or need. We would attempt to attain that in any way possible.

Consider also that the other people whose circumstances are worse than our own.

The Homeless – people with no place to live
Parentless – people without parents or families
Disabled – people who are incapacitated and unable to care for themselves
Diseased – people who have incurable diseases and don't know how long they will live
Victims – people who have been tortured for reasons beyond our comprehension

Last of all Christians. Those who suffer because we proclaim the God we love and serve who sent His Son to save us from our sins.

There are people who have less and some with more. Either way, we cannot complain about our plight at this time in this life. We have to consider two things: (1) our situations could be worse and (2) they mocked our savior first.

Lord, remind me when I complain about outsiders ridiculing me that they persecuted You first.

APRIL 5

²⁹But whosoever blasphemes against the Holy Spirit will never be forgiven; he is guilty of an eternal sin.

Mark 3:29

Blasphemy is the act of insulting or showing contempt or lack of reverence for God, according to Webster's Dictionary. All Christians ask at one point in their growth whether or not there is an unforgivable sin. Each Christian I've ever answered has been surprised when this is my response. They expected the unforgivable "one" to be based on some other activities, but it's based on an activity that we never considered.

Showing contempt for God is problematic. While I can't possibly imagine and am not interested in knowing that information, this scripture was written for anyone who could have contempt for God.

Insulting God or lack of reverence of God is likewise something I advise against. The scripture is self-explanatory. Why should God forgive us if we insult Him, act contemptuous towards Him, or lack reverence toward Him? You wouldn't forgive for those same instances. As a matter of fact, we hold grudges and are unforgiving for much less.

He will forgive you for everything else provided you ask and don't abuse His forgiveness. The follow up question I hear posed most often: will I be forgiven for suicide? While the answer is yes, why would you want to commit suicide? If you ever consider or considered or know someone else who did, I ask you to consider this and share it with your friends. If God is merciful enough to forgive you for the sin of killing yourself, don't you think that God can bring you through your storm? Isn't He powerful enough to hear your cries and your plea and to save you from yourself?

Lord, I always want to be forgiven. Thank You for Your graciousness.

Daily Devotional for Young People

APRIL 6

³⁶What good is it for a man to gain the whole world yet forfeit his soul?

Mark 8:36

My soul is the deepest, most true part of me. The soul is where my secrets and ambitions hide because they are protected there. Most importantly, it is the place God created for Christ to dwell. I protect that entity viciously. In that place, God speaks to me.

Let's examine the cost of goods. We love stuff – material possessions and social status. We want that stuff. We wish for them. But what do we sacrifice and pay for them? What does this cost us? In order to gain status, do we deny God? In order to have material stuff, do we sacrifice God? In order to have things, does it cost us our relationship with God?

Judas sold his soul to the devil for 75 pieces of silver, then later committed suicide. Judas thought that the value of the silver was worth the life of Christ. Judas betrayed Jesus just as Jesus said someone would. Judas thought his world was worth that silver but he gave his soul away.

How can we avoid these temptations? Seventy-five pieces of silver was a lot then. Money will make you do things that you may regret. Forfeit of the soul is not worth not even a fraction of a penny nor all the money in the treasury. Your soul is not for sale.

Consider that if you sell or forfeit your soul then you've given away Jesus' home. So you've rendered Jesus homeless.

You can spend as much time on this as you would like, but the soul is not negotiable. My rule is if it doesn't require me to have a relationship with Christ, then I'm absolutely not interested. If I can't relate it back to Him or His word, then I'm simply not interested. Make this decision early and then there is no discussion.

Just a thought: Why do you think Jesus' killers approached Judas versus the other eleven? Could it be that they knew who was truly committed and who was negotiable? Decide what you need to do so that your disposition doesn't read negotiable.

Lord, protect my soul from temptation which would forfeit my soul.

APRIL 7

[46]For whoever is not against us is for us.

Mark 9:40

In boxing, both the opponents have a corner. In that corner, there is the manager, the trainer and someone who medicates the boxer's wounds. There is also someone who wipes the boxer's face and removes and replaces the mouthpiece. In total, there are 5 people who are there to support, motivate and coach the boxer. On the other side of the ring, there are the same number of people doing the same thing for the other boxer. But they are against each other, the two boxers that is. In this example, there are people in the crowd rooting for each boxer and against the opposite boxer. This is easy to distinguish in a sports arena but harder to determine in life.

My prayer partner and I discussed the spirit of her son and myself at his age. He was accustomed to people always loving him. When he finally met people who actually didn't treat him kindly, he didn't understand how the children at his new school didn't treat him as he had always been treated - with love. I shared with his mother that his spirit was unprepared for that mistreatment. He asked her why they didn't love him. My answer is that his meek spirit intimidates some. They are ill equipped to love him because their love for him may challenge their self-love.

There is a simple formula for determining whether someone is for you or against you. Use the following questions:

1) Is this person invested in my life?
2) Does this person support my goals and dreams with genuine interest?
3) Does this person remember the important details of my life?
4) Does he/she love me unconditionally?
5) Does he/she lift my needs before the Lord for His consideration?
6) Does this person attempt to understand my needs and the desires of my heart?

The answers will allow you to understand their motives.

I don't like it that some don't like us but consider it this way: if everyone liked you, then I wonder if I'm completely in God's will because after all, some people didn't like Jesus. It is okay for people to be against us. For just as many are against us, there are more for us.

Jesus, thank You for helping us to distinguish who is for us and against us.

APRIL 8

⁴¹I tell you the truth, anyone who gives you a cup of water in my name because you belong to Christ will certainly not lose his reward.

Mark 9:41

A wonderful scripture about giving to others. Often times we are so concerned about not having enough to give to someone else in their time of need. This, however, is not so. No one has ever been without when they've given what they have to help another Christian or because it is the Christian's duty.

Christ rewards our generosity and selflessness. God loves a cheerful giver. God blesses who He can send blessings through. It is not rocket science but it does take us a while to sometimes understand that everything that God gives us is designed for us to bless others. Our resources have never been sacrificed because we've given to someone else.

Where would we Christians be if people had not opened their doors to let Christ eat, bathe and sleep? As He traveled, He didn't have homes in all those places. He stayed with Christians and He blessed them. There are several Biblical passages about what happened when He visited people's homes. I was engaged in a discussion one day about the people who stand on the corners with signs announcing their need for help. The major issues were "why should you help someone like that" and "why can't they work like us?" A Christian posed those questions along with others, such as what if they spend the money I give on liquor or drugs or cigarettes. My response was this: we don't know why people stand on those corners. We don't know how many doors have been shut in their faces. Our duty is not to decide how they spend the resources you've been blessed with to bless them with. Our duty is to bless them and forget it. Now the other side is should God bless us with money if we decide to purchase liquor or drugs or cigarettes. He doesn't stipulate what we do with our 90% of the resources He blessed us with. Why should we stipulate to others? It's not fair. I also added that resources include but are not limited to money. Offering a job is a resource. I give bottled water if I have bottles in my car. I drink lots of water and even if it's my last bottle, I will lower the window and give it to the person. I have never been refused. I have been thanked and I have been blessed. Just a cool drink of water goes a long way.

What will you give of yourself to bless another?

Thank You for reminding me to give, Lord.

APRIL 9

⁹Therefore what God has joined together, let man not separate.

Mark 10:9

There are two events happening here:

1) don't interfere with God's projects; and
2) what God has joined, we are too weak to destroy. He will not allow us to separate what He has joined. Likewise, He will not let "man" interrupt His plans.

Considering the entities which God joins, this list includes humans with humans, humans with places, humans with things, etc. FACT: The only one who can undo what God has done is God.

I work in an environment that I wish to leave but I can't leave there until I finish His work no matter what happens. Keep in mind, I can't leave and no one can remove me until He says that I'm done and He's prepared the next place for me.

Often, this scripture is used in weddings and other situations relating to marriage. However, this applies to persons including family, marriages and other relationships. The tests which present themselves in relationships are often hard to persevere but that test becomes your testimony about what God did to maintain and sustain you and your relationship.

Wise people will suggest that we follow our first minds because it is usually right. Well that's because our first mind is of God. So that means follow God. God will lead you to your place – what He has planned for you. All detours between you and His plan are short lived. Not even you can sabotage God's plans for you.

FACT: The only one who can undo what God has done is God.

God, I pray not to interfere in Your work.

APRIL 10

⁴³Not so with you. Instead, whoever wants to become great among you must be your servant, ⁴⁴and whoever wants to be first must be slave of all.

Mark 10:43-44

Americans have a problem executing even the thought of serving others. Our attitude about service is poor. We want to be served but don't want to serve. But everything that is great includes serving others and meeting their needs. Consider all the "great" positions: pastor, pope, president, politicians, leaders, authorities, etc. These positions are popular because of the power associated with them. The piece that most people miss is that the power and status costs. The popularity, power and status only comes if the people who appointed and/or elected the leader are pleased with the service provided to them. An effective leader has to be an unselfish servant of the people they lead.

Leaders typically go wrong when they forget they are simply servants with a title. They get too busy or too powerful or too egotistical to serve the real needs of those people. The consequence usually results in their dismissal from the position.

Learning to serve is a great quality but a harder task. Putting others first is the first task. Meeting their needs is the hardest, but next task. It's the hardest for a few reasons:
1) their needs change;
2) the group's needs are not all the same;
3) the leader may not agree with their desires;
4) the leader ignores their needs or desires; and,
5) the leader stops addressing their needs. Finally remember we are simply servants is the last task.

As a Christian, we are committed to service. With Jesus as our example of service, we are shown and taught service throughout His word. When we pray to be Christ-like, we are asking to be a servant to all humankind. He spent His human life serving us so that we would serve others. He is the greatest among us.

Jesus, if I could be ¼ of the servant You are.

APRIL 11

²⁴Therefore I tell you, whatever you ask for in prayer, believe that you have received it, and it will be yours.

Mark 11:24

Growing closer to God requires regular prayer. Honesty is essential during prayer. God wants to hear you speak the desires of your heart aloud. More importantly, you must believe that you have received those desires. Your belief is an exercise of your faith. Your belief tells God that you know that He is able to give you the desires of our hearts.

I keep a prayer journal where I record what I ask God for. When I receive an answer, I take note of my blessing. Also in my journal I detail what I thank God for and all that I speak and all I hear Him say. When I ask, I also thank Him because He is going to give me what I ask.

A word of caution: be wise in your requests. The Lord will give you the desires of your heart. Although I don't believe He has limits, nor do I support that He would deny us, I do believe that wisdom needs to be exercised. Consider your 'wealth' carefully. If you have 'candy' and want more of it, then would it be wise to ask for more? If you've never had 'candy', and you really want it then ask. I don't think that God prioritizes either but I ask for what I need before what I want. If you need new school shoes or uniforms but you ask for a dirt bike, my advice is to speak the truth in prayer by asking for your needs then your wants. That may be me being old fashioned, but first things first. He can and will do it all.

My last note about what you want: God is not going to give it to you until you are ready under His judgment. He is the parent who loves us, but He is not going to let us mistreat His gifts. I ask to be married in 1996. I got married in 2001. God didn't send me to my husband until we were both ready at exactly the same time for each other and what He has planned for us. Let's use a pet for example. If you don't clean you room and clean up after yourself, then why should you have a pet when you haven't exhibited your ability to care for yourself? You would get the benefit of a pet and leave the responsibility of caring for it to someone else, like your parent(s) or older sibling – not fair. With everything we ask, comes benefits as well as responsibility. We need to be prepared for both. We will not get our desires until we are ready for them.

Thank You, Father for giving me what I have asked.

APRIL 12

²⁵And when you stand praying, if you hold anything against anyone, forgive him, so that your Father in heaven may forgive you your sins.

Mark 11:25

New interpretation of the Golden Rule: Do unto others as you would have God do unto you. Scary, huh? Apply this to what you do daily and you will notice a change. It is a powerful moment when you realize that you cannot do to others what you don't want God to do to you.

Bad events have happened to many of us and you may say that you'll never forgive them for what they did or didn't do. While that may help you overcome your immediate pain, that method falls short of your goal to heal and allow that experience to increase your testimony of what God can do. Forgiveness of yourself and others promotes healing. Forgiveness expedites your healing. Praying for your "offender" also hastens the healing process.

Forgiveness requires a pure heart. Forgiving with the motives of being forgiven is no good. Even Jesus forgave His murderers while He was still on the cross. "Forgive them Father for they know not what they do." Many of us would not be able to say those things, especially not during the situation. But Jesus did.

Forgiveness in some situations seems impossible. These situations require God's help. Just ask Him. He promised to give us those things we ask for and believe that we will receive. That includes asking Him for the ability to forgive. That also includes asking Him for healing your hurts. He will do it.

Learning to forgive in the really bad times requires you to spend time with God in prayer. Your event while not comparable to anything else is not really designed for you. This event is a process toward Christian maturity when you will share that event, your ability to forgive, how awesome God is, and how you've grown because of it. But you won't be able to say those things until you forgive. Your testimony blesses others so that if the same event happens or happened to them, they will see what is possible.

Forgive so that others can grow through your testimony. God is the Wonderful Counselor – allow Him to counsel you through your "storm."

Jesus, thank You for showing me how to forgive myself and others.

APRIL 13

[17]Then Jesus said to them, "Give to Caesar what is Caesar's and to God what is God's." And they were amazed at him.

Mark 12:17

Tithes belong to God. Taxes belong to the government. Caesar was unfair to the people, but Jesus told the people to give Caesar what belonged to him. Obedience is the key objective here. Disobedience is not justified by our perception of the fairness of the rules. We will always owe taxes regardless of whether or not we feel that the amount is fair.

Jesus was in support of the obedience factor. He let His Father take care of Caesar and the fairness factor. If you owe, then the Christian pays. Simple as that. There are people, even Christians, who don't believe in tithing, giving a tenth of your income to God by way of the church. Tithing, however, is commanded by God. There are consequences to not tithing. Don't allow your blessings to be blocked by not tithing. It seems like a lot sometimes and doesn't seem like it should be a big deal but it is our exhibit of obedience to God and His commands.

Why would God continue to increase our financial resources when He can't trust us with what we already have? Why do we always think we could manage more in an effective manner? Sure it's possible, but is it likely? That's between you and God.

Keep in mind that you want what is owed you. If you don't pay what you owe, then how can you expect to be repaid? The 'reap what you sow' concept rears it's head again.

Christians are commanded not to be borrowers but to be lenders. We are also not to owe anyone, especially not God.

Lord, let us not be borrowers but lenders. Let us owe no one.

APRIL 14

[32]Love the Lord your God with all your heart and with all your soul and with all your mind and with all your strength.

Matthew 22:37, Mark 12:30

This is one of the simplest and mostly easily understood scriptures written. This is the answer to many questions and dilemmas, such as How do I let God know that I love Him, How do I give Him anything when He has everything, and what do you give the Creator of everything for He created everything.

It is the best thing for you to do. Although this is simple and desirable, it is difficult to accomplish and even harder to maintain. I have to focus on making sure that I don't lose sight of where I direct my energies and consequently my love.

Your love is a reflection of how you spend your money. Your love is also how you spend your time.

Often I feel that my resources (i.e. money, time, heart, soul, mind and strength) are split. They are not always on the same accord at the same time. I must learn to accomplish that on a consistent basis. This is what God requires in this scripture all the time. And why not – why shouldn't He require that. I require a lot of Him. I ask Him for everything. I need everything from Him. I couldn't even breathe without Him.

He created me. He has plans for me. He wants the best for me. He wants the best from me. He thinks of me daily. He meets my needs daily. He loves me in spite of myself. He loves me in spite of my disobedience and character flaws, which I have developed – not ones that are of Him. He offers me some of my heart's desire. He allows my heart to have desires. He is my everything. He gave me the design, desire and inspiration for a project such as this. He hears and responds to my prayers. He is my all and all. My prayers don't go unanswered or unheard. He deserves my love. After all, He exhibited the ultimate love – He sent His only son who died so I might live and have eternal life.

Lord, help me love You with my whole heart, soul, mind and with all of my strength.

APRIL 15

³⁰"I tell you the truth," Jesus answered, "today yes, tonight - before the rooster crows twice you yourself will disown me three times." 31But Peter insisted emphatically, "Even if I have to die with you, I will never disown you." And all the others said the same.

Mark 14:30-31

If you've ever heard the cliché that the road to hell is paved with good intentions, then you will understand why it was the first thing that came to mind. Jesus has just spent time setting the scene for the disciples about His demise and all the related details. So He then shares with Peter that Peter would disown Him. Peter denies Him. However, later, just as Jesus said, Peter disowns Jesus in order to save himself.

While I sympathize with Peter's desire to be noble and didn't want Jesus to be correct, I thought by now that Peter would've known that Jesus was right regardless of the situation. Even when we want Him to be wrong, He's not. I'm glad I wasn't Peter. That had to be heartbreaking.

Could Peter have responded differently? With Jesus in your presence would you have said something differently like why is that going to happen or how can avoid that situation or can He prevent it from happening? I would like to think that I would, based on what we have witnessed.

The major issue comes in the last sentence: "And all the others said the same." Well Judas had already betrayed Jesus. When they heard this statement, they didn't know what else to say. The disciples were at a loss for other words. I wonder if they had become afraid to search for answers from Jesus about the future and its outcomes.

This is a time for preparation for His work. We are always on standby for His work, but if we are not prepared then we miss an opportunity to share our blessings and be a blessing to others. Were they unprepared even though He foretold these moments and taught them what they needed to go forward?

What can we learn from the disciples?

1) Listen for the voice of Jesus.
2) Understand our role in His agenda.
3) Be prepared for what He has planned for us.
4) Remember to ask for help.

Jesus, remind me of Your knowledge and wisdom, especially when I have decided against the truth.

Daily Devotional for Young People

APRIL 16

[1b]"Lord, teach us to pray just as John taught his disciples."

Luke 11:1-4

The Lord's Prayer is powerful and awesome. It addresses each area of concern in our lives. It builds the bridge to restoration for relationships. It is so thorough and complete while concise and compact.

When I say the words of that prayer (Matthew 6:9-13), I enter into a renewed relationship with Him.

Our Father who art in heaven,
Hallowed be Thy name,
Thy kingdom come.
Thy will be done,
On Earth as it is in heaven.
Give us this day our daily bread.
And forgive us our debts, as we
Also have forgiven our debtors.
And lead us not into temptation,
But deliver us from evil.
For Thine is the kingdom, and the power and the glory, forever.
Amen.

You will pray repeatedly this prayer. It will never mean the same thing twice. I learned and meditated on the meaning of some of the words.

Hallowed means holy; Holy is your name.
Your kingdom come; Heaven come to Earth.
Give us today's provision and not worry about tomorrow.
I promise to forgive those who have sinned against me.
Lead me not into temptation. Temptation is different each day.

Consider this as you pray the Lord's Prayer: Jesus taught His disciples how to talk to His Father. Considering the source of the information, I will follow His advice.

Thank You for the power and privilege of prayer.

APRIL 17

> [9]"So I say to you: Ask and it will be given to you; seek and you will find; knock and the door will be opened to you. 10For everyone who asks receives; he who seeks finds; and to him who knocks, the door will be opened."
>
> *Luke 11:9-10*

This is one of God's promises which I hold on to intensely. I have learned what to ask for and what's important to desire just because of this scripture. I have learned with as strong a promise as this one, I cannot afford to ask for anything frivolous. He has promised that what I have asked for I will receive.

Further, He promises that what I looked for, I will find. This includes the tangible, or material, and the intangible. This includes when I seek Jesus I will find Him. Any type of search you start, you will get answers, including when you seek yourself. Again, this is a very important promise.

Lastly, if you knock on the door will be opened. Unlike us, He promises to open doors where we knock. Many of us take a long while to open when others knock. Consider how long it takes for us to open when our friends "knock" and ask us how we are or what's wrong. Consider what happens when our parents "knock" and we may or may not let them in.

Jesus provides for our knowledge, our insight and our peace through these very promises. We can go forth unafraid to ask, seek and knock.

Lord, thank You for Your gifts and blessings.

APRIL 18

Daily Devotional for Young People

[28]"Suppose one of you wants to build a tower. Will he not first sit down and estimate the cost to see if he has enough money to complete it?"

Luke 14:28

In this life, everything has a cost. The basis of economics is that there is no such thing as a free lunch. Or anything else for that matter. As is true with your relationship with Christ. Your commitment to Christ will cost you.

The sacrifice suggests that you need to count the costs involved with being a disciple of Christ. The surrounding scriptures, Luke 14:25-35, support this implication. Jesus tells us that there are several issues that will prevent one from entering discipleship. While He tells us those facts, He never really addresses what it really does take to achieve discipleship. As a matter of fact, I don't know how some of the first disciples were chosen.

As you consider the cost of being a disciple for Christ, you should know some things:

1) Following Christ requires hard work, dedication, sacrifice, obedience and commitment.
2) Witnessing for Christ causes your popularity to diminish.
3) God loves you more than you love Him. His love is consistent and most importantly unconditional.
4) God prefers you hot or cold, rather than lukewarm. A lukewarm spirit or heart means you have not settled on a decision in your heart. He respects hot or cold because you are decisive. If you are hot for Him, He knows He can depend on you to stand in difficult times or uncertain ones.
5) Your decision will change your life. Forever.

When I made the decision, #3 was most important to me. His love is all the reward I need. I realize that it costs. I pay daily for the decision but I reap daily for my sacrifice.

Thank You for allowing the benefits to outweigh the costs of following You and being Your disciple.

APRIL 19

[33]In the same way, any of you who does not give up everything he has cannot be my disciple.

Luke 14:33

Literally, you may ask. To an extent, yes, literally. God wants you to have things, "stuff" if you will. But that "stuff" cannot precede Him or His priorities.

A few things that I know that God will not tolerate and will have to be discarded in order to be His disciple:

- Pride (Lucifer)
- Idol worship
- Blasphemy (the one unforgivable sin)
- Deal making
- Boasting

Let's discuss pride for a moment. Lucifer was an angel in heaven. He became so proud and pride filled that God asked him to leave. When your pride is misplaced, God will not tolerate that and I feel He becomes angry with me because of it. This anger prevents me from being a reliable disciple.

Idol worship simply put is putting someone or something in front of God. God has to be first in order for you to be His disciple.

Blasphemy is the only unforgivable sin. Without any further discourse, if I don't hold God in the highest esteem, then I don't need to be a disciple.

Boasting denies God's work in your life. One such example is Ephesians 2:8-9 which fully explains how we have been saved by grace, not by our works, "so that no one can boast." Boasting is likened to pride.

Deal making is characteristic of adults mostly. Deal making for children is typically learned. Children make deals with their parents. The same with Christ and us. All deals are null and void.

Following God as a disciple requires discipline and sacrifice. These things don't come easily. God is a righteous God. He will offer you all the tools to follow Him. You supply the rest. Discipleship is worth all the sacrifice.

Follow Christ.

Lord, remove the things in my life which prevent me from serving You.

APRIL 20

⁴"Suppose one of you has a hundred sheep and loses one of them. Does he not leave the ninety-nine in the open country and go after the lost sheep until he finds it?"

Luke 15:4

Most of us would probably not look for one sheep or one of anything but some of us definitely would. I would. I remember when my puppy got out of our gate. My mother explained to me what happened. I wasn't satisfied with that explanation. I sought her out. I found her resting on the median. Although we would never play together again and I wasn't happy, I had peace of mind knowing that I had done all that I could for her. If I hadn't gone after her, then I would only speculate of her whereabouts.

Same concept with Jesus and each of us. He seeks us out when we stray away from Him. Our commitment to Him is really important. Our well-being is important to Him. He seeks and keeps us because He loves us.

In my prayer to be more Christ-like, I mature to realize that in order to realize that prayer, I must act as He does. In this particular instance, I must venture to find one while a multitude waits. This is a daily quest. Finding ways and behaviors to model this scripture brings me closer to my Creator and more similar to my Creator. Examining my heart and motives also contributes to my journey for Christ-like mannerisms.

For some it's easy to seek the one, for others next to impossible; yet required. That one sheep you will seek will provide you hope and promise. This will be the one that offers you the most benefit from your effort.

Often times, I feel we do certain things to get God's attention. The mistakes are the action and memory loss. God never took His attention away from you. I decided not to be that straying sheep. However, I also decided that if that sheep appears in my life, I will exercise my Christ-like behavior and go get that one.

Thank You, God, for keeping and seeking each of us.

APRIL 21

⁸Or suppose a woman has ten silver coins and loses one. Does she not light a lamp, sweep the house and search carefully until she finds it? ⁹And when she finds it, she calls her friends and neighbors together and says, "Rejoice with me; I have found my lost coin."

Luke 15:8-9

The message: each one of whatever we have is worthy of our attention and we are responsible for our possessions. Although people aren't our possessions, we are also responsible for the people in our lives and our paths.

If the woman had not searched for the coin, what would you think of her? Would you think she was rich or careless? Would you wonder if it meant anything to her at all? What is important enough to her for her to search for it should it become lost? Was it too much trouble or was it worth it to her to seek what she lost?

We have to care for what God has given us. What we don't care for, we lose. It is simple. God does not continue to bless us or bestow us with gifts if we mistreat what He has already given us.

Have you ever had a toy that you ask for but you didn't take care of it? One day your mother took the toy away. You asked why. If you recall her response, she said because you are not taking care of it.

The same with God. If you lose it, then search for it. He does the same with us. If we move away from Him and become lost, He will come find us. Remember the sheep. If He gives you something, take care of it or lose it. When you seek it again, it may not be available.

Lord, let not my heart be far from You nor worship in vain.

APRIL 22

¹⁵He said to them, "You are the ones who justify yourselves in the eyes of men, but God knows your hearts. What is highly valued among men is detestable in God's sight.

Luke 16:15

Some of what we suffer is at our own hand, meaning it's our fault. We brought it on ourselves. "We are the ones who justify ourselves in the eyes of men…" indicates that we define ourselves by the standards of men rather than of God. When we move our focus to man rather than God, we are headed for danger. This justification is evident when we compare ourselves and our material possessions with that of others. It is further evident through our behavior to gain material possessions and to prefer the more expensive and designer goods, attaching that to status by societal measures.

Now this means nothing to God. I didn't realize this when I was younger and wanted some Jordache jeans, which is comparable to Tommy Hilfiger. I begged and begged. My mother remained unmoved. I never owned a pair of Jordache. But I only wanted them because my classmates wore them. Which, of course, at 8 years of age made the most sense.

God knew my heart and still does, none of which has anything to do with designer clothes or anything else. None of this defines me. You have to reach that point in your life, too. Others cannot always influence you and your decisions. They are fickle and this will lead to your demise.

What society values, God detests. He places no value in that which we place value, if it's not of Him. Why should He? He created it and He can replace it.

I still don't own any designer jeans. By the way, Jordache is not even in business anymore, but God is still God.

Thank You, for being Jesus Christ and sacrificing for me.

APRIL 23

[40] On reaching the place, he said to them, "Pray that you will not fall into temptation."

Luke 22:40

In December, 1998, I vowed abstinence until my marriage. This scripture became quite important to my survival. Jesus speaks to the disciples about the next phase of their journey. They are on the Mount of Olives. Jesus goes to pray for God to absolve Him from duty. While He prays, the disciples fall asleep. They were supposed to be praying.

Jesus never specifically stated what temptation they may encounter, however, He was very certain about temptation. He could stand assured on that due to the fact that He Himself had been tempted during a forty-day fast. He didn't fall into temptation because He prayed, just as He warned the disciples to do.

I took His advice quite personally. When I vowed to be obedient to Christ, I knew everything that could happen would. I knew it would be difficult to do. It is very important to me and to God that I remain obedient. So that this is possible, I have to depend on God for my strength and support.

I had to realize that I must totally give myself over to Him. He knows all and He knows me. Falling into temptation is easy. Temptation is everywhere. Remaining steadfast against temptation requires maturity and a commitment. You will face obstacles and temptation is simply an obstacle. Temptation is what stands between you and what you really want.

I took the vow because I needed to be obedient to God. In exchange for my obedience, maybe He would hear my prayers. I have asked God for tremendous blessings, like a spirit-filled husband, successful marriage, healthy and intelligent children, successful and profitable businesses and a spirit-filled life. With my prayer list being that intense, my obedience is key to my blessings and my rewards. "To whom much is given, much is required."

On top of which, the scripture reads that if I regard iniquity in my heart, He will not hear me. This means that if I continue to sin, He will not hear my prayers. Those consequences encourage me to remain obedient. This should be enough for you too.

Lord, grant me strength to avoid sometimes overwhelming temptation.

APRIL 24

[62] And He went outside and wept bitterly.

Luke 22:62

Jesus cried out of hurt. As do we. I know when I have done wrong, because I weep uncontrollably and bitterly. There is no doubt about it. I usually have a guilty knot in my stomach or I have a burning desire to confess my sin. God does not let me rest until I have addressed my issues with Him.

I know Jesus cries when I sin because I hurt Him. It's similar to being a teen and your parents know that you've done something wrong. They decide to wait until you tell them. Then when you tell them, they react totally different from what you expect. Often that's how God treats us. He waits on us to confess our sins to Him and ask for His forgiveness and then He forgives us. Sometimes we know that we do not deserve His forgiveness but He told us to ask anyway as there is only one unforgivable sin.

God is sensitive and loving so it should come as no surprise that I cause Him to weep when I do wrong. I love God. I strive daily to impress God and try daily to stay away from sin so that I don't further disappoint God. God has saved me from myself enough times for me to recognize that He is in charge of my life.

The only person who will weep for you like Jesus is your mother or father. It is just as important not to disappoint them. They have prayed and prepared for your success. They want the best for you. And just like Jesus, they grieve when you make a mistake or a poor choice.

I decided to make better choices and stop doing the very things that grieves God and my parents. This has proven to be better for me.

Lord, I weep bitterly when I sin against You. Thank You for Your abundant forgiveness.

APRIL 25

[34] Jesus said, "Father forgive them, for they know not what they are doing."

Luke 23:34

In this passage, Jesus is being persecuted and preparing to die. Jesus pleads forgiveness for His enemies. He requests that God have mercy on them. Talk about unselfishness. If I could only be half as giving as Jesus in such situations. Jesus has literally protected his enemy. Now, whether God punishes them or not is not conveyed in these passages, but what we do know is that Jesus was concerned with them just as much as those who love Him. This is powerful. Jesus leads by example. The scripture clearly states to love your enemy. Most of us don't do that. We shun them because we know they don't mean us any good.

I get discouraged sometimes when I have to deal with people who don't like me or don't understand me. But I have to remind myself that they persecuted Jesus without mercy. Nothing that anyone can do to me is worse than what they did to Him. This thought provides me with encouragement when I start to feel defeated by my enemies.

Little did Jesus' enemies know that He saved them and loved them, too. I wonder how He could do it but I realize that when you love God unconditionally and with your whole heart then loving those that don't love you is easy.

In my Christian growth, I anticipate being that mature one day but as for now I pray daily to be more like Christ.

I have learned to pray sincerely for those people who persecute me. That's the answer to our prayer.

Lord, my Father, forgive me for I know not what I do.

APRIL 26

⁴⁶Jesus called out with a loud voice, "Father, into Your hands I commit my spirit." When He had said this, He breathed His last.

Luke 23:46

When a scripture moves me, I feel like a more mature Christian. This scripture moves me.

First of all, I was moved by the method by which Jesus communicates with God. Jesus doesn't use much metaphoric language. He is typically very straightforward and specific with God. We need to address God in the very same way. Specific. Concise. Plain language. Consistent in His message delivery. Consistent in His frequency of His communication.

Secondly, He said some of the most important words to God He could ever say. "Father, into Your hands I commit My spirit." God's hands are powerful. He created the world (Genesis 1) in seven days. He created the land and sea. He created the animals. He created the fish. He created man. Then He created woman. All with His own hands. I pray regularly to God to not let me out of the palm of His hand. In this prayer, I have to be careful to realize that I am the only reason why I would be out of His hand.

Commitment to God is extremely profound and important. It is what He requires. When you commit to God, it is abundantly important to keep that commitment. Your commitment comes from your heart and that is what He requires; your heart.

Your spirit is one of the most important parts of you. God created your spirit to reside and to worship Him in it. Worship in your spirit is crucial to your relationship with God. I find the place I seek dwells in my spirit after I have worshipped Him with my whole being.

You have to decide on a spiritual lifestyle. A lifestyle where you can say with earnest and sincerity, "Father, into Your powerful and capable and creative hands, I willingly commit my undeserving spirit."

Lord, I know that my spirit is Yours and I commit all of it to You.

APRIL 27

⁶He is not here; He has risen!

Luke 24:6

Luke wrote his gospel with a more human perspective. He explores the depth of Jesus as a man. This passage was proceeded by the recount of the crucifixion and the burial and now He has risen.

First and foremost, this is news of monumental proportion. Jesus is missing from the tomb where He had been placed. They did not practice underground burials. They placed their dead in a tomb with a stone to cover the opening.

Jesus is not in the tomb and they realize that rather than being "stolen," He has indeed risen. It takes this passage to realize that they finally believe. They finally believe that Jesus is Jesus and all of what He said to them and all of what they witnessed is real. They revealed their faith through this very statement, which is what Jesus had been working on since His arrival.

This is what Jesus wants for all of us. He wants us to live on strong faith and for us to understand His word. God designed His word to feed us, provide us with evidence of His love and His sacrifice.

Our faith enables us to live a strong life in His name.

At that moment, the disciples realized that their experience with Jesus would be like nothing else in their lives. Any doubt that existed had passed and they were able to share their accounts of what they witnessed with others just as He had intended.

This verse is the most powerful testimony one can deliver. I owe Him at least that, after all, He died for me.

Lord, thank You for rising for me. Thank You for being obedient and sacrificing for my life.

APRIL 28

³²They asked each other, "Were not our hearts burning within us while He talked with us on the road and opened the scriptures to us?"

Luke 24:32

Two of the disciples, Cleopas and another, walked and discussed the events and life and the seemingly untimely death of Christ. Jesus joins them during this talk. After His departure from them, they realized that it was Him.

If it had been me, I know that all of the memories would flood back into my mind. My heart would become overwhelmed by my emotions that would resurface because of the closeness we developed during His time on Earth. Then of course, I would be reminded of all the things I wanted to say if He were to return.

I then know that my faith could never be weak again. Further, I could never doubt God or His motives or His method or His timing.

But it was not me. It was them. Their hearts burned to remind them of the intensity of Jesus' study and teachings.

His reappearance after His death makes His journey complete. They are testimony of the entire process of the death and the resurrection. More importantly, the witness of His life made His whole life complete.

The final visit with them completed the disciples "rites of passage." That visit confirmed their testimony and made them whole. This was the culmination of everything God had prepared them for.

They kept their commitment to spread the word about Jesus' love.

Sometimes I wish I was there. I'm glad that I'm here now. Witnessing now and leading non-believers to Christ now differs dramatically from that time. I know God made me for this time. I have to be sure to be in line with God's plan.

God, the more I know the more I want to know. Father, I love You for increasing my desire to study Your word.

APRIL 29

³⁶While they were still talking about this, Jesus stood among them and said to them, "Peace be with you."

Luke 24:36

He departs from them and offers them His peace. I can only pray for Christ to offer His peace to me. "Peace be with you" is powerful and profound.

> Peace brings you solitude.
> Peace offers you power.
> Peace feeds your soul.
> Peace refuels your spirit.
> Peace fosters intuition.
> Peace gives you rest.
> Peace strengthens your mind.
> Peace invokes and provokes stillness.

When He offers you His peace, He has offered you some of the best of His love and care. His peace transcends all your doubts and fears. His peace supersedes your complacency and your burdens.

Ask the Lord for His peace. Ask when you are burdened or worried about something. Ask when you are unsettled or are concerned about the outcome of a situation. Ask when your mind wanders. Ask when you don't know what to do. Ask when you need direction and guidance.

Ask for peace when you need peace. Your spirit needs a rest sometimes. Ask for that.

Even as adults we need to remember the peace that God can provide and will provide, if we simply ask.

As a youth, I often sought God to get through the storms around me rather than storms of my own because comparatively speaking, I didn't have any problems.

If there is something you need, then ask. If it's His peace you seek, then ask. He will provide it.

Peace be with you.

Father, thank You for granting me Your peace.

APRIL 30

³⁸He said to them, "Why are you troubled, and why do doubts rise in your minds? ³⁹Look at my hands and my feet. It is I myself! Touch me and see; a ghost does not have flesh and bones, as you see I have."

Luke 24:38-39

Jesus is speaking to the disciples when He sees them for the last time after His crucifixion. I wonder why they doubted. Then I ask how would I respond if I had been them. Nothing replaces the actual experience, bearing in mind that the disciples' actual interaction with Christ is designed for them to witness to others about Him. This visit confirms their role as witnesses.

They are provided as an example for us. I decided that I need to always conduct myself as if He had just come or was on His way. Consider how different we would behave if Jesus Himself could tap on the shoulder when we do wrong. He is able to do that through other people, like our parents, friends and pastors. With them, it is impactful but if we learn to govern ourselves as if it was really Him, then we would behave differently.

Our daily living must correspond with the Christian leadership we represent: God. Equally, you need to bear witness with things in your life. You are able to hold others accountable when you are accountable. Without that accountability, you weaken your witness.

Keep your witness strong through your behavior.

Christ, thank You for I know Your word is true.

On This Journey

YOUR PERSONAL TESTIMONY

Why do you need a personal testimony? Better question, why do you need to share your testimony? Your testimony was designed to share with others. This personal encounter with God is designed to elevate them and their spirit to a new level where more growth and development can occur. Don't be surprised when you experience some growth and development, too.

When did you accept Jesus into your heart? When have you recognized God for being in your life and moving you to the right place? When had God done the opposite of what you asked but it was better than you expected? When has God simply provided you His peace?

Spend about 15 minutes writing the answers to these questions, while considering how you would share these answers and with whom you would share the answers.

_____
_____
_____
_____
_____
_____
_____
_____
_____
_____
_____
_____
_____
_____
_____
_____
_____
_____
_____
_____
_____
_____
_____
_____
_____
_____
_____
_____
_____

MAY 1

⁴⁵Then He opened their minds so they could understand the scriptures.

Luke 24:45

God is all knowing and all powerful. He created Jesus to be the same.

Jesus has risen and returns to speak to the disciples one last time. He shares with them what the scripture says. He does something far more powerful though. He allowed clarity in their minds so they could understand. This is very important because their misunderstanding could've easily been the source of their doubt. But in that moment, He cleared up both the misunderstanding of the word and the doubt they had.

It was critical to Jesus and the faith that they understand fully because their witness was instrumental in God's plan. Their witness was designed to lead others to Christ, so it was very important.

This is also a very important example of Jesus' power that deserves our attention. It has never occurred to some of us to ask God to create within us an understanding for those things that surpass our understanding. This is also an example of God's love for us. He loves us enough to help us to overcome any misunderstandings that we develop.

I often ask for Him to increase my understanding, to allow me to understand, for clarity and for practical application. These requests enable me to become closer to Him because He knows I desire His insight and a closeness with Him.

I admire God for offering us an understanding of Him and His word. That is an example of God's humility.

The power and dominion rest in Your hands, Father God such that You do the complex as well as the simple. Thank You.

MAY 2

[26]"I baptize with water," John replied, "but among you stands one you do not know. [27]He is the one who comes after me, the thongs of whose sandals I am not worthy to untie."

John 1:26-27

John presents Jesus to people who have different faith than he. There is a faith that John has that is not matched by any. He speaks boldly of Christ before He anything does anything. I ask myself how it is that John can be so sure and grounded about Jesus' ability and have such faith of who He says He is.

A call to faith is what we need. Imagine the things that God does to prove who He is and to convince us to have shallow faith. Just a little faith.

The faith of a mustard seed is what God requires of us. We have faith but it's conditional and subjective. We exercise faith when it's convenient. That's not exactly faith of which He speaks or asks.

John inspired me to live on faith and believe that He will deliver as promised. John believed and Christ delivered exactly what the prophets said.

Let's not forget that John was also quite meek and humble. He is very direct as he addresses them about Christ.

Our closeness to Christ depends on our faithfulness to Him and our faith in Him. I work on my faith daily and implore you to do the same.

God, I am extremely privileged to be Your child. Your presence is powerful to me. I am so unworthy.

MAY 3

⁷Jesus said to the servants, "Fill the jars with water"; so they filled them to the brim.

John 2:1-11

Jesus is at a wedding and the host depletes the wine. Mary, Jesus' mother, approaches Him and explains the situation. He responds to her that it is not His time. He proceeds to have the vessels filled with water and He turned it into wine. The event's host was surprised as were the guests but the mother only wanted Him to do what she knew He could.

I asked myself when I first read this story why would she ask Him to exercise such a great power over seemingly such a menial task: they didn't have enough wine.

His actions reminded me that no matter what the situation, He has an answer. He has a plan. He will provide. I realized that in all ways and circumstances to seek God. No matter how big or small the matter, we need to ask God for intervention and guidance. We are given permission to seek Him for everything but often we don't because we think that it may be too trivial for God and we can handle it. This scripture reaffirms for us that for every matter God has an answer. Our obedience in this matter allows God to trust us with what we ask for. Remember that He will direct our paths.

Lord, Your divine timing is crucial to my blessings. I realize I must submit to Your timing.

MAY 4

[16] For God so loved the world that He gave His one and only Son, that whoever believes in Him shall not perish but have eternal life.

John 3:16

When you think of all that it means to sacrifice your son or daughter, then you really learn how awesome God is. Imagine what would have happened if your parents had given you to save the world. Imagine if you have children and God ask you to sacrifice one of them or your only one as He did Abraham. How would you feel?

You know your parents love you and know that they wouldn't do anything to hurt you, but the amount of sacrifice they make to show that love is monumental.

I learned early what things cost and soon realized that my mother's sacrifice was beyond what I had imagined. I then committed myself to make her sacrifice worthwhile. I earned good grades and worked at being obedient. I wasn't the best child but I made certain that I didn't embarrass her with our church family or her friends. I tease her now when she discusses my childhood that all I ever did was talk on the phone too much. Which by comparison to others was angelic.

Love is immeasurable and it never stops. Your parents want the best for you just as God wants the best for us which is why He gave His son to save this world.

Remember your parents sacrifice for you to be blessed.

Thank You, God for Your extraordinary love.

MAY 5

³⁴"My food," said Jesus, "is to do the will of him who sent me and to finish his work."

John 4:34

Jesus spoke only what was within God's will. Jesus never attempted to intermingle His desires or designs into God's already well-ordered plan. After one sincere plea, He was reminded of the prophecy His life would fulfill.

Of course, that is exactly opposite of our behavior. We consistently challenge God's power. We intervene and impose on His will. We compromise His plans. All by doing what we want. We do whatever we want to do. Mostly we do the things that He hasn't answered or that we dare not ask. Sometimes I don't ask or pray about things that I'm certain the answer will be no.

I had to decide that I would no longer circumvent God's will. I will not do things, which blatantly disrespect God's love and care for me. I will actively concentrate on being obedient. My obedience influences my blessings and abundance.

As for the food of which Jesus speaks nourishes the spiritual portion of your body. This fills you and comforts you, cares for you and loves you. This food feeds your soul and spirit. Food typically energizes you. The vitamins and minerals fuel your body and offers you an appropriate amount of calories. Doing God's will in accordance to His instructions will complete you. You will be fulfilled. You will be fed. You will never be hungry again in the same way. God's food, although you will still hunger for His word, fills you more and more. It also draws you nearer to Him with each helping.

My statements to non-believers and new believers is always: "The more you know about God, the more you want to know."

His food – His word – is everlasting; never to disappear. His word is true and never will return void. I always want to eat the food prepared by God, so I always want to do His will and finish His work.

What Jesus means is that my nourishment is do the will of Him who sent me. Jesus means that He is fulfilled by doing the will of God. God's will feeds Him. Finishing God's work nourishes Him.

Lord, I pray to always crave Your food.

MAY 6

[35] Then Jesus declared, "I am the bread of life. He who comes to me will never go hungry, and he who believes in me will never be thirsty."

John 6:35

Literally speaking, your spirit will never go hungry nor will your soul go thirsty. Have you witnessed persons who say they feel so empty? Have you wondered why they are empty? This is evidence of a weak or non-existent relationship with Christ. Christ and the Holy Spirit fills you and never allows you to be hungry or thirsty. This seems intangible but imagine life with Christ and all that He is. A smile comes across my face instantly. A warmth comes over my body. A calmness comes over my spirit. Then I look around me and immediately thank Him.

Now imagine life without Christ. I would have to depend on my judgment alone. Bad news. I make mistakes now with Christ. Imagine the amount of damage I would cause without Him. I cannot depend on me for everything. I am not able to foresee all of my needs. I cannot meet all of my needs. With all of those things, I cannot live without Christ. I have never questioned my decision to follow Christ. I have never regretted asking Him to live in and take over my mind, body and soul.

It may be an assumption but a safe one because I have learned how to live with Christ. If He will feed me and I not be hungry, if He will quench my thirst and I am satisfied, then He will do as He says in His word on Earth before in Heaven and provide me shelter, so I will never be homeless. As He dwells in me and I in He, I will never be alone. I will never be without Him.

Father, thank You for allowing me to come to You and offering me Your comfort and strength.

MAY 7

³⁶But as I told you, you have seen me and still do not believe.

John 6:36

One day I realized that I had enough experiences in my lifetime to make me never question God again. Never question His love or faithfulness. Never doubt His ability or His plans for me.

I have lived through so many events where I questioned my own survival. So have you. God and Jesus, in their infinite wisdom, knew that this would happen. They knew we would doubt and not believe. God planned the work of Jesus such that we would see. That sight was designed to prove Jesus' power and His ability.

We have to grow as Christians to believe in Jesus and His power and His plans. God will help you believe and not doubt. God will guide your growth. Keep your focus on Jesus and modeling your life after Him.

Faith and belief are important; critical even. Faith is not optional. **STUFF** is an acronym meaning **Situations That Unravel your Faith and your Future**. You have to protect your faith from your stuff. If you feel your faith waning, just ask God to restore your faith. Certain events occur in your life so that your faith is strengthened. Your faith reflects your strength as a Christian. You faith is evidence of your ability to call on God at any time.

Be faithful and believe.

God, increase my faith such that I can believe without seeing everything.

MAY 8

[37] All that the Father gives me will come to me, and whoever comes to me I will never drive away.

John 6:37

Jesus experienced human life as we do today. Further, Jesus faced the same issues and situations we face. However, Jesus never fell prey to sin. Imagine if you never sinned. For us it seems impossible; we sin each day. Some of our sins we don't even acknowledge, much less ask for repentance. This causes Jesus to grieve, but in His grief He does not turn us away. We hurt Him through sin, especially the sin(s) we continually repeat.

While as a human, people rejected Him, people doubted Him, people hurt Him. In turn, He forgave them, continued to love them and still intercede on their behalf. He could've rejected us. He could be selective about who He lets in and for whom He intercedes. Yet, He does not discriminate against any of us. He loves us all the same, and in spite of our sins. However small or large you perceive, He treats sin all the same. He promises to never drive me away. That's important to me. As a Christian, it should be important to you as well. Knowing God's promises are important to your spiritual growth. God's promises make life best. His promises make life more bearable. His promises encourage me daily. His promises will provide you strength in the difficult and uncertain times.

Jesus, thank You for accepting me and being my intercessor.

MAY 9

[38]For I have come down from heaven not to do my will but to do the will of Him who sent me.
John 6:38

Jesus made a profound statement. He announced and confirmed His purpose. Without shame nor excuse, He stated with conviction that He was on Earth because His father sent Him. He let His disciples know that His will was not important nor was it the reason He was here.

He is here to set the example. He is a leader who led by example. We are here to do the will of He who made us: God, the Father. We are not here to fulfill our own wills or selfish desires.

Life becomes different, not exactly easier or worse. When we do His will, we are in obedience. That obedience brings forth a different attitude and behavior: the one of Christ. God honors Christ-like behavior. God honors our obedience and respect to Him. God designed Jesus to establish the precedence. With the expectation level set, we then have a choice. We either follow God and His plan or we decide not to follow Him. The results of following Him are bountiful, beginning with Him granting us the desires of our heart until we spend eternity with God and Jesus.

I struggle to do His will daily; you may as well. While He knows we are not perfect and does not expect perfection, He does expect us to strive daily to obey His laws and commandments. He demands our best while He forgives us for our shortcomings. His rewards come in many forms but the most important is His love.

Christ, thank You for reminding me of my purpose.

On This Journey

MAY 10

³¹To the Jews who had believed him, Jesus said, "If you hold to my teaching, you are really my disciples. ³²Then you will know the truth, and the truth will set you free."

John 8:31-32

Jesus is the truth, forever. However at the time, He spoke this because there were non-believers, just as there are now, but more importantly, there were believers He needed to address in reference to their roles as disciples. Believers need to be reminded where the truth originated. They also needed this conversation as empowerment.

Discipleship is a responsibility where sharing the truth of Jesus rewards you. If you can recall your first encounter with Christ, you will realize why that experience needs to be shared. At the same time, if you recall the first time someone shared Christ with you, again you will remember how wonderful you felt. I was such an excitable child. I was six years old when I first accepted Christ. I was a very decisive child. When I share my testimony, how I accepted Christ, the tears always well in my eyes as if it were yesterday.

Keep in mind and in your hearts the truths as set forth in His word:

1) He loves us (John 3:16)
2) He will return for us (John 14:2-4)
3) He has plans for us (Hebrews 11:40)
4) He knows our thoughts (Psalm 94:11)
5) He has forgiven us for our sins (Matthew 6:14)
6) He wants us to have abundant life (John 6:35)
7) He promised to never leave or forsake us (Joshua 1:5)

These are truths that we need to share with each of those persons in our lives who are non-believers and with believers who need encouragement.

Lord, thank You for the truth and the privilege to share it with those who don't know You.

Daily Devotional for Young People

MAY 11

[35] Jesus wept.

John 11:35

Jesus cried. He responded compassionately to Mary (His mother) and the Jews because Lazarus was dead. He saw her and "He was groaned in the spirit, and was troubled" (John 11:33). His compassion caused Him to act immediately on behalf of Lazarus. He resurrected Lazarus and Lazarus lived again.

When does Jesus weep compassionately for me and moves on my behalf? One such situation was when my great grandmother died. He wept then. And again when my great grandfather died. He saw me cry and He wept, too. The most recent was when my step-father who I called dad died. My weeping amounted to more than what I would know.

How often do I make Jesus weep? I implore you to ask this question of yourself. Now, I ask that because I also believe there are times when I make Him weep because of my disobedience or other sins. I really want Him not to cry for this but I realize that my sin grieves Him.

Lastly, the Lord also cries when I don't show Him my love and commitment. He cries when I neglect Him. Also when I don't have real faith in Him. He states Himself that He is a jealous God. He grieves when I don't respond to His demands and requests. I am learning to not do this.

As a family we recite a scripture after one of my grandparents bless the food. My sister always says, "Jesus wept." For a long time I thought she said, "Jesus swept." My mother always said a number of other scriptures. I thought that a sign of maturity was being able to recite other verses, so I did. I learned more. One day I read this scripture and the passages surrounding it and I cried. My respect for my sister and her verse increased by leaps and bounds. My maturity is in being able to read and understand the scripture but also feel the same compassion for the scripture each time I read, hear or speak.

Lord, forgive me when I cause You to weep.

MAY 12

>¹⁴Now that I, your Lord and Teacher, have washed your feet, you also should wash one another's feet. ¹⁵I have set you an example that you should do as I have done for you. ¹⁶I tell the truth, no servant is greater than his master, nor is a messenger greater than the one who sent him. ¹⁷Now that you know these things, you will be blessed if you do them.
>
> *John 13:14-17*

I taught a New Member's Orientation class where in one of the lessons I washed the feet of my students as they read the scriptures. Most of them cried as I did so. When I decided to do this with them, I prayed about it such they would receive it as I intended. They did.

Christianity and Christ-like behavior requires service to His people. Serving others is the only way to bring them to Christ. It is also one of the best ways to remind other Christians why they are Christians.

I can only imagine what it must have felt like to be one of the twelve with Jesus washing their feet. Simon Peter didn't want Jesus to wash his feet. Jesus responded by saying if I don't wash your feet, then you will not be a part of Me. He washed each of their feet, including the one who was to betray Him.

Again, Jesus exhibits wisdom, He doesn't discriminate between them. He washes them with the same diligence and spirit and integrity. He doesn't have any ill-will in His heart. He possesses God's peace about His fate. This very occasion provides them with yet one more testimony of what Jesus has done in their presence.

Although He shares with them the upcoming betrayal, He remains calm and continues to act with dignity. I wonder how some of us would respond when we sit and eat with someone who will betray us. Will we respond the same or differently?

I have matured to pray for those people who I feel will betray or have betrayed me. Also, I pray for people who find themselves in envy of me or who hate me. These people really need love, so I want to serve them in prayer.

He has set a tremendous example of service for us that we have no reason not to serve others.

Lord, humble my heart and set aside my ego so that I may obediently serve You through serving others.

MAY 13

¹⁵"If you love me, you will obey what I command."

John 14:15

Love is clearly an action. God continually exhibits His love for us. Several examples of His love come to mind:

1) He created me; each of us – He made me.
2) He created me in His image – we were born Christ-like.
3) God sent His Son to die for the removal of my sins.
4) He has plans for me – He wants the best for me. My joy is important to Him. He wants to give me the desires of my heart. He inspires me. He gives me drive and ambition. Each and every step of my life is guided and planned by Him.
5) He knows everything about me and loves me unconditionally anyway. He is not like the wind or anything that changes often or anything which is subject to perception. He treats me better than anyone I know, including my family.

These are just a few reasons that He loves me and I am able to prove it.

He commands us to have the same love for each other, however this is difficult for some of us to do on a consistent basis. He tells us that our love for others exhibits our love for Him. We rationalize out of this but it's really ignorance of God's command.

Here are a few ways you show God you love Him through your actions:

1) Obey your parents and other authorities.
2) Treat others better than they treat you. Do unto others as you would have them do unto you.
3) Read, study and memorize God's word.
4) Commit yourself to Christ and live in obedience to Him.
5) Pray without ceasing.

Although there are certainly more methods, I will say that these are where I have had the most success.

Lord, teach me to obey You so that when I say that I love You, You will hear me.

MAY 14

[18]"If the world hates you, keep in mind that it hated me first. [19]If you belonged to the world, it would love you as its own. As it is, you do not belong to the world, but I have chosen you out of the world. That's why the world hates you."

John 15:18-19

I tried to imagine life independent of Christ. It was impossible. He is who I confide in when I can't tell anyone else. He is who I know is there whenever I call. He is my best friend because of His unconditional Love for me. He cares for me. He restores my spirit. He nurtures my soul.

He saved me.

The world will not do any of those things. They have a special definition of love that doesn't match up to God's definition or His ability. The world changes its mind from day to day, whereas God doesn't ever change. The world doesn't chose us to do anything worthwhile.

However, Jesus chooses us out of the world because He loves us. That love prompts actions to share that love and protect us from the world.

The world is often more attractive than the Word but is that temporary appeal worth our lives? The world has no plan for me that can compete with God's.

They do hate me for His love but they could have it too.

I have to remember when the world mistreats me that they mistreated Him first.

Jesus, they haven't done anything to me, which they haven't done to you first. Thank You for taking me out of this world.

MAY 15

⁷But I tell you the truth: It is for your good that I am going away. Unless I go away, the Counselor will not come to you; but if I go, I will send him to you.

John 16:7

The Counselor is also the Holy Spirit, to whom Christ intercedes on our behalf. I can only imagine what the disciples were feeling when they realized He would die because of betrayal. As I am when my loved one died, I am certain they were somewhat distraught because of the upcoming circumstances.

However as He explains, His departure is crucial. The Counselor is crucial to our spiritual well being and growth.

Now, the Counselor brings us to Christian maturity through study, reading, meditation, prayer and listening. Our communication with the Counselor enables us to seek the Father and He hears us. This is critical to our relationship with Him. Imagine if Jesus were not crucified and resurrected. That is selfish and not good news. I would have loved to meet Him personally, however I have measured the costs of being there then and being here now. I determined we have the best of both worlds. He has already saved my soul and redeemed me of each of my sins and I benefit from my ancestor's experience. I want to hold His hand and I will. In the meantime, I must follow the instructions in the Bible. More importantly than holding His hand is holding a mirror now. The mirror of accountability. We must live such that others know that God is holding our hands. As we walk with Him, our communion is key.

Christ, thank You for sacrificing so that I may have communion with the Father.

On This Journey

MAY 16

³³I have told you these things, so that in me you may have peace. In this world you will have trouble. But take heart! I have overcome the world.

John 16:33

Confidence. Peace. Power. Protection. Reassurance. Jesus was sent to save our souls and lives. He has the obligation to intercede on our behalf. His presence here bridges the gap between who we actually are and who we need to be. His earthly experience offers Him the ability to have empathy, which means He understands because of His experience. Jesus wants us to have peace knowing that He can be trusted with our issues, our needs. He, being omniscient, knows that we will have trouble. Further, when He was here as a man, He too had trouble.

He gives us the confidence to seek Him and to believe Him. He offers peace through His experiences as a man. He offers us His power because He has all power. He offers us protection from the world, which often means us harm.

He offers us reassurance that He is on our side. Jesus clearly reminds us that He is all-powerful. He encourages us because He has overcome the world. So surely He can overcome the daily issues we endure. Although it seems huge – our issues – comparatively speaking are small. So we need to let Him handle the big and the small in our lives. That relationship builds trust.

Christ, thank You for Your spirit and promises.

MAY 17

⁴I have brought you glory on earth by completing the work you gave me to do.

John 17:1-5

God has plans for us. He determines the talents we will possess. He has designated the talents we will possess. He selects the people in our lives. He plots a plan for our lives in respect to every detail. He designed the color of our eyes, the shape of our lips and nose.

He also has work for us that will glorify Him. Just imagine if God left us a list each morning on the refrigerator of the things He wanted us to do and know for the day.

I imagined it may look a little like this:

1) Pray and thank Me for forgiveness, breath, strength and life.
2) Apologize to sister for hurting her feelings.
3) Help that woman in the wheelchair cross the street.
4) Let your parent(s) know that you love them. Don't be mad if they don't say the same in return.
5) Go to bible study tonight.
6) Smile at those who mistreat you.
7) Read My word.
8) Pray before you go to bed.
9) Be obedient to Me and your parents.
10) Obey My word.

If that was the list for one day, could we complete it? Would this list indicate we were clearer about God's wants and what time God wanted it. We would be a lot better off, right?

Well truth be told, we have that list. It comes in two forms: reading His word and praying to Him. He outlines both what He wants and what He demands and expects in those two places.

With that said, why do we find it so hard to make the list of what God wants us to do each day? We need to make a concerted effort to establish such a relationship that He is able to talk to us and tell us what work we need to accomplish.

At the end of the day, I try to reflect on the day's events hoping I did everything that was pleasing to His sight. I find that most days, it's hard to say yes. I also reflect on my work for the day and what I've accomplished. Sometimes I can say yes. Sometimes I can't. I believe those whose work is complete, sit with Him now. When our work is complete, we will sit with Him, too.

Lord, if only I could ever say, "Lord, I have done the work for which You sent me."

On This Journey

MAY 18

¹⁷For in the gospel a righteousness from God is revealed; a righteousness that is by faith from first to last, just as it is written: "the righteous will live by faith."

Romans 1:17

"We've come this far by faith." This line from an old-time gospel reminds us that each day is a walk of faith. How strong is your faith? The answer comes daily with each new test and new trial and our reaction to those tests and trials.

There are people we know personally or by association who have attempted suicide. Suicide, attempted or successful, translates into disbelief or lack of faith. Suicide communicates to God that faith is imaginary and disbelief in His plan and His ability to help overcome this situation. Suicide is an escape with coward written all over it. Further, suicide also gives the triumph to the devil.

Suicide says that you believe your situation is permanent and you can't bear to see it through to resolution. What is actually permanent? Nothing really. God provides an escape even from suicide. He will help you stop your attempt. He will put you in a place at the right time to stop someone from a success. He will give the signal to call and talk to someone just as they were thinking of suicide as an option to solve their situation. We just have to pay attention to the signs. Listen for His voice.

Suicide saddens God because He doesn't get to give us our gifts He has planned. Further, His love for us is deep and genuine and didn't want this to happen. My question is why do some succeed? Do their efforts exceed God's plan and ability to save them or is it a choice He makes? I don't have the answer but what I do know is that His love is permanent and everlasting – forever.

Suicide doesn't solve anything. Consider the consequences of such a death. No insurance covers a suicidal death, which means your parents have to pay out of pocket for your burial. Do they have that money saved or will it put them in bad financial shape? Your friends and church members will miss you. Your classmates, church members, family and friends will cry a lot. You will miss the opportunity to grow, graduate from school, get a degree or two, get married, have children and travel among many other things. You may not achieve all these things but if you are not here, you don't even have the option to try.

Living by faith and righteousness requires work but not anymore work than planning a failed suicide attempt.

Lord, help me to be righteous and faithful.

MAY 19

²¹For although they knew God, they neither glorified him as God nor gave thanks to him, but their thinking became futile and their foolish hearts were darkened.

Romans 1:21

If you know God but you give no praise, no thanks, no glory, you make a choice to live outside His will by not obeying His command. More important by than His command, if you know Him and don't do these basic things, you don't love God. Further, offering Him glory, praise and thanks expresses our love for Him, accompanied by our respect and honor of Him.

When you have to do something out of obligation or when you owe someone, you may resent it, but when you do because of your love then it's a joy. So do we not praise because we resent praising Him or do we not like to praise Him or are we not full when we praise Him? Whatever our excuse, we need to stop excusing ourselves from giving Him His true praise, glory and thanks. Using excuses are foolish tools, which block our blessings. We are blessed when we praise, glorify and thank Him. 'How', you may ask.

When I surrender to Him in praise and thanksgiving I am able to take in all of His love and His peace and His mercy and His grace. Also, I experience His love. His love pours over me and saturates me. Saturates exceeds fullness. Consider that 'full' is equivalent to a glass being full. Saturated is water on the outside too.

Glory to God for His goodness. Praise be to God for His forgiveness. Thanks be to God for His love.

If anyone deserves anything, God deserves our attention in those areas. If you really think about it, only our pride stops us from offering Him glory, praising Him and thanking Him. Why does our pride stop us from praising, glorifying, and thanking He who lifts us, loves us and cares for us?

By the way, there is no glory in being foolish.

Lord, thank You for keeping me grateful.

MAY 20

[11]For God does not show favoritism.

Romans 2:11

Unlike humans, and the proverbial 'teacher's pet', God has no favorites. He does not treat us any differently than our fellow Christians. This means that we are treated the same as our parents and vice versa. In that there's good news and bad news.

The bad news is that what He does to one He will or can do to another. That's also good news if you view it as blessings. But the important part of all this is God's fairness.

Often we question God's fairness when something goes opposite our plan. For example, when a grandparent, parent, sibling or friends dies, we ask 'why me, God' or if something happens to us such as injury or paralyzation, then we ask 'why me, God?' We don't ask this question and often it's the better one: 'Why not me, God?'

The next best question is 'what do you want me to learn from this situation, God?!' The next question: 'who is to see Your magnificence and glory through my praise, behavior and actions?' The answers to these questions alone will give us new motivation as Christians. I feel that He trusts us when He tries us.

God's fairness is not to be questioned. If God wanted to be fair, He could've started over after Eve ate the apple. He could've kept His only Son for Himself and didn't have to save us. So be careful when we tell God He is not being fair because fairness is relative. Besides when He blesses, is that really fair? Is it what we really deserve?

The best news about God's lack of favoritism is that He loves us all the same. His love is equal for each of us. That is awesome.

'Jesus loves the little children. All the little children of the world. Red and yellow, black and white. They are precious is His site. Jesus loves the little children of the world.' The good news is that we are those children. Although we grow up, we are always God's children. God promised to always love His children.

Thank You for loving us all the same.

MAY 21

²³For all have sinned and fallen short of the glory of God.

Romans 3:23

ALL means ALL. Me. Our parents. Our teachers. Our friends. Our siblings. Our grandparents. Our family. Our clergy.

This is not first thing that comes to mind when we start to pass judgment on someone. When others do 'wrong' we are quick to judge their actions. We persecute them for their wrongs as well. We shake our heads in judgment because they have sinned. But when it is us who has committed an indiscretion, we don't want to discuss further our wrongdoing. Not to mention, we don't want any questions asked because even we can't explain why we have committed certain wrongdoings. My most reliable answer as a teen was, 'I don't know.' This was my answer because I really didn't know why I did some of the things I did. I had no idea why it was so important to talk on the phone long after my curfew. I couldn't explain why I didn't readily do my chores. When I neglected my schoolwork, I was speechless.

ALL have sinned. ALL of us have done wrong and lacked the glory of God. ALL of us have missed God's mark. ALL of us have fallen short of His glory.

The best thing about falling short of His glory and having committed sins is that we are forgiven. God forgives us when we sin.

Sin is not new but forgivable. There is nothing new under the sun, so there's nothing new that we can do. There's nothing we can do that will surprise God. However, there are a million things you can do to surprise yourself and others around you.

Growth and maturity are measured by choosing to walk away from sin. The more maturity we acquire, the more complex the sin which will be presented to us. The growth is being able to continue to walk away from sin.

Lord, I know I embarrass You. Thank You for forgiving me anyway.

MAY 22

⁷"Blessed are they whose transgressions are forgiven, whose sins are covered.

Romans 4:7

Who are 'they'?
What is 'blessed'?
Why are 'they' 'blessed'?
When are 'they' 'blessed' with His forgiveness?

'They' is us. We are 'they'! We are God's children. He cares for us and He forgives us our transgressions. He wipes the slate clean. He forgives as we forgive others. We have been selected because He loves us.

We are blessed through His forgiveness. We are blesses because of His forgiveness. In spite of our unwillingness to forgive others, He still forgives us. Despite the fact that we don't deserve forgiveness. This blessing means gift. Our forgiveness is a gift.

'They' are blessed because of His love and His grace and His mercy. 'They' are blessed because He wants us to have eternal life. He doesn't want us or them to live in darkness. He forgives 'them' unconditionally. He loves 'them' unconditionally.

Our sins are history. Instantly. On demand. Immediate gratification if you will. Even our future sins are forgiven. He already knows what our sins will be and He has forgiven them. This is a tremendous blessing. You don't know what you are going to do, and whatever that is God has already made provisions for our forgiveness.

This scripture and the one that follows are similar to the Beatitudes, Matthew 5:3-12. These scriptures offer reaffirmation of His promises and His blessings, and of course, His love. As all scripture does, they inspire us to continue our mission in our ministries. They offer you comfort and peace. There is no greater news than the good news of our sins being covered.

Lord, thank You for covering my sins. Remove my desire to sin.

MAY 23

⁸Blessed is the man whose sin the Lord will never count against him.

Romans 4:8

This implies that the Lord will count sins against someone but we don't know who that is yet.

The important fact to remember is that we don't have to be the man whose sins will be counted against him. God promises forgiveness for all of us, for each of our sins without condition. He casts our sins in the sea of forgetfulness – never to be mentioned again. Never is a long time – not ever, really. Relating to forever, never means it will not happen. We will be held blameless.

We need to remember to not take advantage of such a blessing but to remind ourselves that God does not have to bestow that type of blessing on us. He could keep the same scorecard we've developed. He could remember our wrongs and hold those indiscretions against us and allow them to prohibit us from success. He could keep a tally of the number of bad thoughts and wrongdoings so that when we meet Him, He could remind us of each of our sins.

He could but doesn't. He does quite the opposite. He forgives us of our sins, our wrongdoings, our indiscretions, our misgivings – all of them. He forgets them all, too. When we meet Him in Heaven, I think that He will hug us and remind us that He loves us. He'll remind us that He forgave us so that very occasion could occur.

Being Christ-like includes not counting others' sins against them but we don't do this consistently. We often count others' sins against them and we spend quality time properly categorizing their sins, archiving them and filing them alphabetically. That seems like an exaggeration but we remember most of the wrong someone has done to us.

While doing your self-examination consider the following:

1) What do I remember?
2) Why do I remember?
3) What was my reaction to that event?
4) How have my feelings changed about the person(s) involved in the event?
5) Have I shared my feeling with the person(s) involved?

The answers to these questions will help some healing to take place. It may also help us be more like God and stop counting and start forgetting.

Thank You for forgetting my sins, Lord.

On This Journey

MAY 24

>²¹Being fully persuaded that God had power to do what he had promised.
>
> *Romans 4:21*

God does exactly what He promises:

1) He created the world and all of its contents.
2) Sarah, Abraham's wife, finally had a baby, Isaac, even after they had made some bad decisions.
3) He allowed David to be king.
4) He saved the Israelites from Pharaoh. He led them out of Egypt through Moses. He parted the Red Sea for their safe escape.
5) He promises to be our refuge and our strength.
6) He restored Job with abundantly more than he originally possessed.
7) He turned Saul into Paul. (The promise of forgiveness.)
8) Jesus was born to a virgin.
9) Elizabeth birthed John the Baptist.
10) Jesus lived sin free on earth for 33 years.
11) Jesus saved us from death through His own death.
12) Jesus rose and joined God in heaven.

Certainly, He has the power to do all that He's promised. He has done more than this but these are some popular acts. He also promises to forgive us, to provide for us, to hear our prayers, to fulfill our needs, to offer us peace, to give us the desires of our hearts, to offer us an escape from sin and to provide us a home in heaven.

He promised to love us and He has done and will continue to do so. His power is incredible and only benefits us. He is God. He defined Himself and everything is a derivative of Him and His awesome plan and power. He has awesome plans for our lives with promises He has yet to fulfill but the power to do it all. All we have to do is wait and eventually we will see His entire plan unfold before our eyes.

I respect and love You because of Your power.

Daily Devotional for Young People

MAY 25

⁵And hope does not disappoint us because God has poured out his love into our hearts by the Holy Spirit, whom he has given us.

Romans 5:5

'God has poured out His love into our hearts.'

His own love is found inside our hearts. It's in there. He put it there Himself. Even when we are mean, His love is still there. And when we tell the truth in order to hurt another person, His love is still there. His love shapes us and who we are is shaped by this generous outpouring of love from Him.

God defines love in 1 Corinthians 13. His definition is based on our characteristics. In order for us to be the definition of the love He has poured into heart, we are called to be patient, kind, long suffering, not envious, not arrogant, not boastful, selfless, not easily provoked, rejoice in truth, and not keep a count of wrongs. So by sheer definition, we have to be and do each of these things all of the time in order to be fully and completely demonstrating love.

Otherwise, if we miss one characteristic, then we are outside the definition of love. God expects us to love within His large boundaries and specific definitions.

With all these, we still find it difficult to love each other unconditionally. I have examined several of my own conditions. I have discovered that I can release my conditions if I decide to let them go.

My conditions of love are:

1) if you don't take advantage of my love;
2) if you love me back the way I want to be loved;
3) if you don't hurt me;
4) if I don't change my mind and stop loving you; and
5) if I can forgive you for hurting me.

The fact that I have conditions on my love and the type of conditions are not biblically correct. I pray diligently that I can let my conditions go because my conditions prohibit me from fully experiencing God's love. And when He is pouring out love, we can't afford to miss a drop.

Thank You, Lord for Your generous outpouring of love.

MAY 26

⁸But God demonstrates his own love for us in this: While we were still sinners, Christ died for us.

Romans 5:8

Extreme love! Would you die for someone else – a person whom you don't know? Would you die for someone whom you don't know and they didn't love you?

You've probably answered no to both questions. Now, I have a third question: would you die for someone you love? You've probably answered with several conditions, which included the person you would die for and under which circumstances you would die.

New dimension: would you die for hundreds of thousands of individuals who had done all sorts of wrong, some who loved your Father and others who don't, all who keep on sinning, without any condition?

Your answer is probably still no. We are not going to voluntarily die for others. Aside from the differing circumstances, i.e. the time, God's promise of resurrection, and Jesus' unselfishness, we are not inclined to follow Jesus' lead.

We don't love each other that much. God loved us so much He gave His only son for the repayment of our sins. Jesus died unselfishly by accepting God's will for His life.

Gary Chapman authored The 5 Love Languages in which he defines love languages and prescribes the best way to fill our love tank and keep it full. How loved we are is directly related to our level of happiness and the realization of joy. He suggests that when we learn our language, we are better able to receive love and give love as we should.

Our love tanks are important. When the tank is empty, feeling very little love, we experience unhappiness, among other things, and disables our ability to do more for God. A full tank promotes joy and a fulfilled spirit. While a full tank may not entice you to die for another, it could engage you in a loving relationship with those around including God. I have found that our tanks can be full and even overflowing if we just receive it.

Lord, thank You for Your love – unconditional and abundant.

MAY 27

²³For the wages of sin is death, but the gift of God is eternal life in Christ Jesus our Lord.

Romans 6:23

For every act there is a cost and consequence. This is life's repeated lesson. It's the most bitter lesson we learn. For every situation, there's a circumstance. For each problem, there's a solution. For every action, there's an equal and opposite reaction. Although it's a more popular physics law, life follows the same law.

> Theft = jail   Love = marriage
> Murder = death   Hardwork = success
> Adultery = divorce

There are dozens of scenarios where there is an action and then a consequence results. If we think of the consequence before we take action often we wouldn't take those actions nor make those mistakes caused by poor judgment.

The consequence of sin is death. He could stop your breath for a simple indiscretion just one – no matter how large or small the sin. Death is the consequence of wrongdoing as judged by God. Sin could cause a physical death but we want to discuss the spiritual death. Sin impacts your spiritual well-being.

"My spiritual well-being and wellness. What is that?" Your spiritual well-being is the health of your spirit. The health of your spirit means you fill and feed your spirit with love and nurture, God's word and knowledge of the trinity. Just the study of His word alone will enhance your spirit. "How do I know when to feed my spirit or when my spirit will need a lift?" Your emotions and your spirit operate as one. When your emotions are high strung, not calm, and you are hyper-sensitive, then it is likely that you need to feed your spirit.

Your spirit is a part of you, which seeks God and thrives on that relationship. I need to feed my spirit often because I don't like a slump in our relationship. My favorite way to lift my spirit is worship. Fellowship follows second. Worship is the full release and relinquishment of my "stuff" to Him who knows all and solves all.

There are consequences to our actions. I know that when I am full of the Holy Spirit then my actions won't prompt negative consequences. I avoid sin when I have a well-nurtured spirit.

Thank You for Your gift.

On This Journey

MAY 28

¹⁷As it is, it is no longer I myself who do it, but it is sin living in me.

Romans 7:17

Sin is strong. Sin promoters are quite persuasive. Keep in mind the sins and the persuasive conversation, which will be presented to you in order to entice you to sin.

Sin	Persuasive Argument	Old Response	New Response
Drugs	It won't hurt to try it once. You can't become addicted if you try it once.	Yes. I'll try it too.	No. I don't want to try anything that will interrupt the Holy Spirit's occupancy within me.
Sex	If you love me, prove it. You can't get pregnant the first time.	Okay, but only if I can't get pregnant.	If you love me, prove it and don't ask. The last time that someone proved His love to me, He opened His arms out and died. Are you willing?
Skipping School	We won't get caught. We'll go back to my house or to the mall.	Okay, I'll go but only this once.	Well no, I can't because Jesus will know I am there and that matters to me the most.

Those are just three examples of the situations, which will be presented to you. You have to be determined and steadfast about your Christianity and your position for Christ.

We have to stand up against the sin within so that it knows that we are weak but Christ is strongest. He is strongest over sin. He solves all sin issues. He is the resolution to all sin and its persuasive measures.

The responses may sound 'corny,' but consider the results: They serve as a call to action to the other person to either understand who you are and to respect you. The second is one of accountability for the other person, especially if they too are Christian.

Even if the sin lives in me, it doesn't have to be on display through me.

Lord, help me to overcome the sin which lives within me.

MAY 29

¹⁸I know that nothing good lives in me, that is, in my sinful nature. For I have the desire to do what is good, but I cannot carry it out.

Romans 7:18

'Even when I want to do right, I do wrong.' Especially when I try really hard to do right.

Recall one time when you had plans to do the right thing. Maybe you were going to clean your room or do your chores without being reminded but you started talking on the telephone and watching television. Your mother was on errands and you were going to do it before she got home. Before you know it, she was back home and you hadn't even started.

Maybe you really wanted the best grade on the test and you had your study planned. You spread your books all over your room. You are prepared to study. You start to read. You plan to stay up all night. You read more. You continue to read until your mother pats you on the shoulder because it's time to go to school to take the test. You didn't study like you planned so you cheat. You sit next to the smartest person in school so the answer source is acquired. You cheat on the entire exam as planned. As you hand in your exam, your teacher marks your paper with an F before your very eyes.

In these situations we have every intention to do the right thing but are unable to achieve our desired results. So how do we accomplish the right thing, thus the desired results?

There are 5 steps to do the right things:

1) Know what the right thing is. If we know what is right then we are better able to achieve the right thing.
2) Decide to do the right thing. This is where we need support; the next three steps are critical.
3) Study continually. Refresh yourself on the word of God regularly so as to do the right thing.
4) Pray continually. God is available for us to meet our needs, answer our questions and provide us with His mercy, grace and love. This piece is critical because it is dual communication and purposed for us to hear His voice and us to tell Him everything.
5) Yield to God and reject your selfish desires. If we consider the consequences of our actions, then that would stop some of our problems. Further, if we realize that God knows how our actions impact the rest of our lives, then we need to use that to reinforce rejecting our own desires, but we don't.

We won't always succeed but we always need to make the effort. Just consider that the consequences to cheating could be failing the course, getting put out of that school and not getting into the college of your choice, all of which is worse than failing one test. Doing your chores could have offered you several fun opportunities but you won't be able to partake.

Lord, I have an intense desire to do the right thing. Can You please help me succeed?

On This Journey

MAY 30

¹⁹For what I do is not the good I want to do; no, the evil I do not want to do – this I keep on doing.

Romans 7:19

Think about the thing you do but know it is wrong and you want to stop but can't. For me, it's speeding. I drive above the allotted limit. I have been ticketed and that doesn't completely curtail my behavior. My sister has been victim of 2 major car accidents and that hasn't curtailed my behavior, either. But the thought which comes to mind when I speed is how do I explain this to my daughter. Speeding has numerous consequences, including revocation of your license, accidents, money lost, injuries, and/or death.

In the interest of time, we'll just consider death because I was speeding to get somewhere. How important is it for me to be on time? If it's that important, then I should leave earlier for my destination. But if I speed then I die, who will raise my child? I will miss all of her life-changing events all because I was speeding. Speeding is selfish of me. So I consider, how much do I gain by speeding versus what I risk losing by speeding. The benefits of not speeding outweigh the risks of speeding.

So as you consider your 'thing,' consider the following questions:

1) Do I do this 'thing' to feel better about myself? Do I do this because my friends do it?
2) Does this affect my health negatively?
3) Does this impact my family negatively?
4) Does my family know that I engage in this activity?
5) Are there monetary consequences (i.e. increased car insurance rates)?
6) Am I engaging in illegal activity (i.e. drugs)?
7) Do I do something illegal to engage in further illegal activity (i.e. stealing to get drugs)?
8) Does God approve of my behavior?
9) Am I ashamed of myself for this behavior?
10) Would I do it if my parents and Jesus could stand at my side?

If you answered any of the questions 1, 2, 3, 5, 6, 7, and 9 in the affirmative, then you need to stop doing that 'thing.' Further if you answered 4, 8, and 10 in the negative, then simply stop. Those answers (if it was one or all) indicate that you are on a destructive path, which will only lead to bad results for everyone involved.

Besides, everything you do should have a benefit for you. As you answer those questions, you add whether there is a benefit to you. If not, stop. Simply stop doing it. Good things have benefits. Bad things have consequences.

Lord, intervene on my evil activity. Do everything in Your power to stop me from participating in evil.

MAY 31

[20]Now if I do what I do not want to do, it is no longer I who do it, but it is sin living in me that does it.

Romans 7:20

The power of positive thinking overwhelms a non-believer. Living in the affirmative enables you to live a more positive and productive life. What is this power and how do I overcome the negative, thus the sin which lives within me? God will help you to achieve the greatness you can conceive but you have to believe.

1) "I can do all things through Christ who strengthens me." Philippians 4:13 NIV
2) "And we know that in all things God works together for the good of those who love him, who have been called according to His purpose." Romans 8:28 NIV
3) "Consider it all joy my brothers when you face trials of any kind." James 1:2 NIV
4) "You of little faith." Matthew 8:26a NIV
5) "I will never leave you nor forsake you." Joshua 1:5 NIV
6) "For God so loved the world that He gave His only begotten Son that whosoever believes in Him should not perish but have everlasting life." John 3:16 NIV

God affirms us and lifts us. He never intended for us to be sinners nor deprived so He provides for us to overcome those obstacles. He truly wants us to have the desires of our hearts and be a successful Christian. We are stronger when we survive these obstacles. Not to mention our testimony has more impact after such events.

My mother reminds me as often as appropriate that I told the doctor that I wouldn't be taking any more medicine because I wasn't going to be sick any more. I was diagnosed with allergies and asthma. I am not recommending this but I am pointing out at an early age, I decided I would overcome this illness and all its side effects, I simply decided that I wouldn't be sick. I experienced my last attack at 11, if I remember correctly. I decided that nothing of that magnitude would ever overtake me again.

In everything that happens, I decide that I will accept or reject it. If I accept it, then I will believe in its success and put my energy and efforts into that success. If I reject it, then I don't allow it to become a part of me. It is easy because it is a decision I make and I am focused on that decision.

Great things result from positive thinking. I believe that in us there is more greatness than there is sin, but we give more credit and substance to sin rather than the greatness. Let's focus on the greatness and eventually stop sin and sin will take its rightful place as last and least important.

Lord, I want to depart from this sin which lives in me.

On This Journey

JUNE 1

[1]Therefore, there is now no condemnation for those who are in Christ Jesus.

Romans 8:1

If there is no condemnation, there is no guilt. If there is no guilt, there is high self-esteem. If there is high self-esteem, there is no sin. If there is no sin, then there is an enhanced relationship with God.

If there is an enhanced relationship with God, then all things are possible.

In my own words, condemnation means I put myself down because I have done wrong (sinned) and I haven't forgiven myself for my sins when clearly Christ has forgiven me. Condemnation is a sin. Jesus died and sacrificed to end condemnation. As we continue to condemn ourselves, we reintroduce that sin.

God's message for condemnation is clear: DON'T DO IT!! He demands we don't condemn ourselves because it is the opposite of His provision of forgiveness. Our condemnation prevents God's work within us. Our condemnation causes us to second-guess God's blessings and plans for us. Our condemnation prevents us from experiencing His full glory. Condemnation and guilt creates a barrier between us and God. Our communication suffers as well. With all this, we have given condemnation too much power.

Why do we permit condemnation any power? We have a forgiveness issue. We have a hard time forgiving ourselves.

My solution would be to forgive ourselves, accept God's forgiveness and reject the devil's tactics to interrupt our relationship with God. This has worked so far. When I know that I have to forgive myself, I count the consequences more carefully.

Further, we are far harder on ourselves than anyone else. It is reasonable for us to have goals and ambitions. It is unreasonable for us to never celebrate our successes. It is equally unreasonable to expect that we will not make some mistakes. It is reasonable that we define a mistake as a mistake and not a failure. Even if we do fail, we need to remember it's not permanent. Only death is permanent and Jesus has something to say about that, too.

Forgive me for me condemning myself, Lord.

JUNE 2

⁵Those who live according to the sinful nature have their minds set on what that nature desires; but those who live in accordance with the Spirit have their mind set on what the Spirit desires.

Romans 8:5

What does the Spirit desire?
- to commune with God and Christ
- to have unwavering faith in God and His plan
- to be committed to God's will for us
- to be in constant communication with God
- to do what is pleasing in His sight
- to love Him through obedience
- to accept His forgiveness readily
- to reverence Him
- to not sin
- to love others and help others as God prospers and leads us
- to fellowship with other believers
- to worship and study regularly
- to pray without ceasing
- to intercede (pray) for others
- to confess our sins freely and willingly
- to obey the commandments
- to share our faith
- to forgive others
- to reject sin
- to depend solely on God
- to use our gifts from Him to build His kingdom
- to govern ourselves according to the fruits of the Spirit
- to act Christ-like in all situations
- to remember that He is our provider and protector
- to remember that He will avenge those who do us harm
- to be still and know that He is God.

There are people who will always live against the will of God. We can't do anything about their behavior. Once we witness to them, then we've done our part. Some Christians who grieve and obsess over their loved ones who don't believe nor intend to live according to God's word. This behavior is not Christ-like either. He says for us to do our part and that's it. Some preacher-teachers parallel our evangelical duties as planting a flower. One person plants the seed. Another person comes along to water it. The next person sees the growth of the flower. If we all do our parts at the appointed time, He then will do the rest.

Lord, I want desperately to live with the Spirit's desires.

On This Journey

JUNE 3

[8] Those controlled by the sinful nature cannot please God.

Romans 8:8

Lord,

    I pray daily for forgiveness for the things I do wrong against You and those You created. Father God, I don't mean to do wrong and I want to stop. I know that You know all that I do – both right and wrong. I know that You love me because in spite of all that I do wrong, You forgive me. You also comfort me when I feel guilty.

    Lord, thank You for hearing my prayers even though Your word says that if I continue to do evil, You will turn Your ear from me. Lord, I don't deserve Your mercy nor grace. Lord, You are so generous with Your mercy, grace and love.

    Lord, help me turn away from my sinful nature. I don't want to have a sinful nature. I don't want to be a sinner but I just can't help myself. Also, I don't want to be weak when I am presented with sinful situations. But I know that You are my refuge and strength when I am weak. Lord, I submit unto You that I want to depend totally on You. I submit my whole self unto You. I am waiting on Your directions for what move to make next. Father God, thank You for forgiving me, even before I ask. Thank You for loving me in spite of my sinful nature. Thank You for the plans You have for me. Lord, I want to please You. When You think of me, I want You to be able to smile and be proud of me. I know that I disappoint You when I sin and disobey You. Father, please remove the sinful nature from me. I don't want anything unclean or unpure to live within me. You didn't create me to live in sin, but I do. I apologize for my sins. I really want to please You. I don't want You to grieve because of me.

    Lord, thank You for Your love. Thank You for comforting me when I am hard on myself because I've done wrong. Thank You for providing an escape for me not to sin. Father, thank You for creating me.

Thank You, Lord for being You.

JUNE 4

¹⁰But if Christ is in you, your body is dead because of sin, yet your spirit is alive because of righteousness.

Romans 8:10

When I think of the awesomeness of God, I get excited. Consider that the Holy Spirit lives within us. Even though that's the case, we still sin. Even though we sin, God still loves us. And He forgives us. God knows we will sin, how and when we will sin and He forgives us anyway, even before we sin. He forgives us before we forgive ourselves. That is awesome. When we are holding a grudge against ourselves, He has forgotten all about it.

The Spirit empowers us to stand for Christ and His righteousness. This means that we are to do the right thing because Christ lives in us. We still sin and He lives within us. That means we know our real accountability partner is ever-present. For me, I know I have to confess my sins faster and forgive myself more readily. And forget about them. But remember not to do it again.

Righteousness is not optional. It is required. Christians are required to do the right thing, all of the time especially when we don't want to or when it's really hard to do the right thing. Doing the right thing makes you feel great about who you are. It is hard to do but we have to do it.

I have often wanted to ask, but never dared to ask God, "Why do I have to be the one who does the right thing?" When I think this question, I quickly correct myself. I remind myself, "Why not me?" God will not put more on me than I can bear. God will provide an escape for me when wrong presents itself. Lastly, God will not let me fail His tests. God has promised to help me to do the right thing. "Why not me?" I can be trusted to do the right thing. He trusts us to do the right thing. He helps us to do the right thing.

He trusts us to be honest and for the right. We are alive because of this righteousness, honesty and forthrightness. It's okay for our bodies to be dead because sin cannot penetrate our spirit. Christ lives there.

Christ, thank You for living within me.

JUNE 5

[26]In the same way, the Spirit helps us in our weaknesses. We do not know what we ought to pray for, but the Spirit himself intercedes for us with groans that words cannot express.

Romans 8:26

How often have you said, "I don't know what to pray for"? I know I have said it quite a few times. I asked a church elder how did she know what to pray for. She responded that she didn't always know what to pray for either, but what she did was just tell God what was on her heart. Anytime she couldn't quite put her words together, she realized that God still answered her prayers and addressed her needs. She knew that the Spirit interceded for us but only then did she realize that the Spirit submitted her prayer because she couldn't put her own words together.

The best part of the Spirit praying for us is that we often will forget to pray for certain things. Further, we also know there are situations when we don't know how to approach God because we can't think of the words or we are too embarrassed or we don't understand the situation. The Spirit knows all and It can translate our 'stuff' and 'confusion' into words.

How does God understand the Spirit's groans? This understanding is all based on their relationship. God and the Spirit have an all-knowing relationship. God created the Spirit as an avenue for communication for us and for the Spirit to reside within us.

The Spirit also comforts us against our fears and relieves us of any anxiety we may be experiencing. It also comforts us against those who hurt us. The Spirit also bridges the gap between what our love tank is and where it needs to be. The Spirit holds us accountable for our thoughts, feelings and actions. The Spirit is our advocate and pleads with God on our behalf. It is compassionate and understanding and empathetic. The Spirit hears our cries and our pleas. It provides us a place for our storms and our situations. The Spirit lives within us and knows all of our needs and desires and wants. There are times when I forget that the Spirit dwells within me and I revert to dwelling on my issues when I need to realize that I need to spend my time communing and becoming more intimate with Him and the Spirit.

It takes God's infinite wisdom to appoint the Holy Spirit to do all that for me. And it is awesome that He thought through my issues in order to decide that I would need the Spirit for all of that.

Holy Spirit, thank You for interceding on my behalf.

JUNE 6

^{28}And we know that in all things God works for the good of those who love him, who have been called according to his purpose.

Romans 8:28

As a high school senior, I took pre-calculus. I was having a mediocre performance. There was a point when my average was a C. The teacher told me that I didn't need to continue in the class. She didn't think I could perform the work. I knew I could do the work, though. I told my mother and she wrote the teacher a letter. In this letter, my mother addressed my desire to remain in the class, my ability to do the work and asked her to have confidence in my abilities. I stayed in the class and earned a B. This helped me as I progressed to college calculus.

I found that letter recently. I read it differently now versus then. Now, I read it with renewed zeal for what I need to do.

This makes an excellent example of all things working together because I was able to realize how great my mom was and that she was on my team cheering me on through all my triumphs and challenges. The difference was made when I did my part. Only then could she support me. She wouldn't have been able to write that letter if I hadn't committed to doing well.

God views us no differently. God has a plan for us. God has a calling for our lives. Each of us has a unique purpose. We have to live according to our purpose and within God's plan.

Now when we sin, we are operating outside of God's will and His plan. We then make it hard on God to execute His plan without making some adjustments. There are times when we will falter but be assured that nothing deters God from executing His plan.

His plan does require our full participation. We have to do our part. God helps those who help themselves. There are people who have said that if God wants me to have something, He will send it right to me. At that point, they are on their couch or somewhere else the outside world can't access them. I don't believe this theory. I believe that in order to make an A, you have to study. To get a job, you have to apply. To get into college, you have to qualify and complete the required steps, starting with an application. To be picked for the team, you have to practice and play.

No matter what we do, we cannot modify the plan. God's plan will come to fruition and He will prevail. No matter how bad it seems, even the negative things that happen work together for our good, when we love Him and are called according to His purpose.

Lord, I love You. I want things to work together for me and I don't want to miss my purpose.

On This Journey

JUNE 7

^{31}What, then, shall we say in response to this? If God is for us, who can be against us?

Romans 8:31

A word of encouragement for those of us who are easily able to identify our enemies. There are persons who don't love us, don't believe in us, do not respect us, will lie on us, will cause trouble for us and don't have our best interest in mind. Those persons will not prosper. God does not offer them His favor. Rather, God protects His children. As a side note, when you are both His children, He supports the child who is right.

People are against Christians because of Christianity, rather than us independently. I wonder why people have to be against us. It is their job to be against us. When they are against us, the trials presented increase our testimony. These trials force us to depend on God, closing the gap on our intimacy with God.

Because of your relationship with God, many events and circumstances will occur. How we handle them makes the difference between us Christians and others. People who cause us to have difficulties also experience life-changing events of their own. They eventually realize that their efforts were in vain. They realize this with our confirmed commitment to God. Often these same "enemies" will ask you how did you endure or they will ask how can they have the same disposition. Your answer is simple: give your life to Christ. When we are active members of the body of Christ, then we experience peace in all situations, circumstances and events, positive or negative.

For this lifetime, people will be against us. When we are doing our best is when the most people will be on the enemy roster. I was once anxious about my enemy roster. I didn't want an enemy roster. "Why don't they like me?" I would ask. My answer came clearly one day in the heel of a white patent leather shoe on my back from someone who I thought liked me. While there are many surface reasons, like envy, the real root is your behavior. If you don't have any enemies and if everyone likes you, then you are doing God a disservice and are not being a true Christian. Christians have enemies. You cannot do both: be Christian and be liked by everyone.

Find peace in knowing that God is for us and nothing else matters.

Final word: my mother always said that people don't have to love me. She constantly reminded me that the world wasn't going to treat me the same as I was treated at home. The challenge was remembering that fact coupled with the fact that I can't take this behavior personal—it's not about me. It's hard to digest that the world won't love us but it's not supposed to—we're not a part of them.

Thank You for being for me.

JUNE 8

⁹That if you confess with your mouth, "Jesus is Lord," and believe in your heart that God raised him from the dead, you will be saved.

Romans 10:9

This scripture is the basis of Christianity. This scripture defines salvation and how it is achieved. Your salvation is a gift and neither your deeds, contributions nor behavior impact your gift. The most important fact about your salvation: you cannot do anything to lose your salvation. Keep this at the forefront of your memory. You'll need it later.

This is also the answer to the question of 'how do you know if you are saved,' normally posed by non-believers and new believers. Do you believe Jesus is Lord? Do you believe that Jesus is Lord over all and above all? An affirmative answer indicates you have submitted your life to God totally. You have affirmed that Jesus is Lord. To us as Christians, it seems really easy and simple. Some of us have never questioned this fact but there are others who cannot accept Jesus as Lord.

Do you believe in your heart that God raised Him from the dead? I am moved in a different manner each time I read how Jesus died for me and my sins. He suffered so that I might have life and have it more abundantly. He lived for 33 years without one sin—a totally sin-free life—so that I may experience life. I am forgiven because He hung, bled and died. He lay there for two days and on the third day, God resurrected Jesus and was placed on the throne of God's right hand. Jesus is in the highest possible place possible, ever.

I am saved. I am saved by His love, His mercy, and His sacrifice. I am saved because He loves me more than I can ever know. He proved His immeasurable love for me by dying for me. No one else will prove their love for me in that manner. "Romeo and Juliet" is a fictitious account of a family war which results in death. Nothing great came from those deaths. All greatness comes from His death.

His life was planned since the conception of the universe. God completes all of His plans without modification.

According to His plan, we are saved.

Lord, thank You for Your gift of salvation.

JUNE 9

Do not conform any longer to the pattern of this world, but be transformed by the renewing of your mind. Then you will be able to test and approve what God's will is--his good, pleasing and perfect will.

Romans 12:2

"And be ye not conformed to this world" Romans 12:2a KJV. It is simple to say but hardest to do. In a short time, we will cover harsh topics. In our life, we are presented with obstacles and tests. These tests are designed to strengthen, provide us a testimony, and a dependence on God.

DO NOT be persuaded by anyone to sin. Say no to suggestions of sex, drugs, theft, malice, mischief and disobedience. This world and its membership seek new members daily. They are persuasive and manipulative. They are focused on converting you to be one of them. This sounds radical or unreal, but it's true.

Sex happens because someone talks about it. There is enough conversation to peak your curiosity. Next thing you know, someone asks you to have sex and you agree. This life-changing event cannot be reversed so do your best to avoid sex. Sex is designed and reserved for marriage. Sex introduces intimacy at a level many are not mature enough to handle well. Sex does not mean the same thing to each person. Sex impacts your self-esteem. There are additional consequences to pre-marital sex, not limited to but including unwanted and often unexpected pregnancies and diseases. Interestingly enough, the world doesn't share those possibilities when they share the pseudo-glamour of sex.

The world's members will do anything to align you with them, including give you drugs for free, lie to you about the consequences of your actions, try to discredit God and His work and anything else to move you away from God.

News flash for them and reassurance for us: there is nowhere we can go that God cannot reach us, especially in the world. He created it and us, so He can call His children back to Him at anytime.

The best news is that you can renew your mind at any and every occurrence when evil lurks at your heart or mind. When we renew our minds, we pour more of God's good news into us so that there's no spare room for nonsense and worldly stuff.

This is your permission slip to say no with ultimate confidence that God will see you through your decision to walk away from the world's invitation to defy God and His will.

Lord, I want to more closely align myself with You daily.

JUNE 10

⁹Love must be sincere. Hate what is evil; cling to what is good.

Romans 12:9

The scripture is profoundly direct. Love is at best described as an action. Love is similar to bank deposits. You have a love bank and people make deposits and withdrawals. You thrive on these deposits. You depend on them for life and inspiration and motivation. Just like a bank account, in order not to incur problems, the deposits must be greater than the withdrawals. This is critical for your emotional health.

Everyone needs to know beyond a shadow of a doubt that we are loved especially by the people who we love and respect.

Be careful of people who say they love you whom you don't know well. It is often difficult to separate what is actual and what we want to feel. Love is hard to come by. Sincere love is of God.

If it is not sincere then it's not love anyway. You must rely on the guidance of the Holy Spirit to lead you when there is a question whether or not someone has your best interest in mind. People who love you want the best for you. Always.

Avoid evil at all costs. Hate what is evil because it is not of God. Cling to the godly. There are things that are ungodly around you. Guard your spirit against ungodly and evil people and events.

Allow God to protect your spirit and your heart. Sincere love will come.

Lord, thank You for Your love.

JUNE 11

[14]Bless those who persecute you; bless and do not curse.

Romans 12:14

It is hard to bless those who persecute you, but it's godly. In our Christian walk, it is our goal to be godly. When I have difficulties with people, I have to remember that my interaction with others is determined by me. Further, I once felt that there was some difficulties that I shouldn't have to endure. This was a mistake on my part because I'm not above persecution by the enemy – those who curse me. They persecuted Jesus first and more brutally so.

Remember that this just a test. When persons persecute you, your test begins. I increase my prayer time. I increase my faith. I increase my observation of my surroundings. I start to look for the lessons. I pay close attention to my intuition and instincts and spirit. I also fast during these times. All of this provides me with a clear and cleansed spirit to prepare to address this persecution.

I also realize that my persecutors will not succeed. Secondly, I learned through circumstances that my trials make me a stronger Christian. My behavior during such situations either elevates God or alienates God. I govern myself accordingly. As I stated earlier, it is never easy but it is required to bless them. Christ wants to know that you can bless your enemies. It is easy to pray for people you love, so that's already obedience. Our challenge is to become obedient in those areas where we are weak.

Lastly, and most importantly, these very experiences offer you additional testimony.

Lord, Your example of life is priceless to me.

JUNE 12

¹⁵Rejoice with those who rejoice; mourn with those who mourn.

Romans 12:15

Rejoicing when others rejoice requires compassion for others and a certain amount of self-esteem. When others are rejoicing and full of excitement and we are not happy with our situation, then it could prove difficult for us to rejoice with others. Yet it is that rejoicing that could prove beneficial to your broken spirit. It could provide inspiration to your lukewarm motivation. Also, your excitement may provide additional confidence and support for another. Often we have to consider that each person is not at the same level. You just may be the person Christ aligns with another individual to assist in moving to the next level of confidence and comfortability.

Mourning when others mourn demands empathy and compassion. I have found that sad situations bring people closer than they were before due to the fact that a bridge is being built when you reach for someone during their time of need. I often seek to see the depth of a person's pain when they grieve or shed tears. They are more apt to welcome you in because they need the comfort you offer. Normally, we wear a mask to hide ourselves. In these situations, the mask isn't active. Further, inconsequential issues diminish in importance, they are able to see more clearly and prioritizing the important items is easier.

Lastly, remember one day you will rejoice and you will mourn and you will want some companionship when it's your turn.

Thank You, Father God for instilling within the spirit of compassion and empathy.

JUNE 13

[1]Everyone must submit himself to the governing authorities, for there is no authority except that which God has established. The authorities that exist have been established by God.

Romans 13:1

No matter how wrong you think they are, they are the authority and should be respected as such. Your parents are one such authority. They have been given authority over you and responsibility for you by God. They answer to God for all instruction they render to you. They are responsible for your overall success or failure. They love you before your birth and they want the very best for you. They will teach you responsible budgeting through allowance, but could teach you poor budgeting by giving you any amount of money at any time you ask. They will teach responsibility by having you pay your own car insurance, but may not teach you the value of independence by paying all of your car expenses.

There are instances where you are wrong and must be punished. You must respond with humility. They are doing their job as described by God. "Spare the rod, spoil the child." Your parents owe you as many lessons in consequences as you need to correct those wrongs you commit. You deserve discipline when you disobey their instructions. Keep in mind – they discipline you because they love you. The police will not discipline you with love.

Your teachers, pastor, neighbors and other special adults have authority over your well-being. Be respectful of that position. Also keep in mind that one day, it will be your time. What you sow, so shall you reap.

God could not place you here and have plans for your life without adequate instructors, like parents, grandparents, teachers, pastors, church members, neighbors and family friends.

Lord, I owe it to You to obey the authorities that You have place before me, including my parents, my teachers, my supervisors.

JUNE 14

¹³Therefore let us stop passing judgment on one another. Instead, make up your mind not to put any stumbling block or obstacle in your brother's way.

Romans 14:13

What makes us place obstacles in each other's way? What makes us not help one another without regard for what we will receive in return?

It is easy to blame society for the woes and wrong-doing but God gives us His Spirit through Christ and the Holy Spirit. God fills us with His spirit so that we may love others like He loves us (John 3:16). He made us in His image; His likeness. This likeness is not easy, for He is perfect in every way.

He will judge us as we judge others. I often have to ask myself what would I do if God felt this way about me? Is this fair of me to place judgment and obstacles in the way of others when I go before God daily with pleas of forgiveness, petitions for healing and material goods, and an appeal for spiritual wealth?

No, it is not. Not to mention that my prayers fall on deaf ear. Be assured that when I cause others to stumble, I will be caused to stumble in that same manner. I conclude that God's love is bountiful and abundant enough for each of us.

What we as believers must do is examine our relationship with God. I have questions for thought:

1) do you want God to love you in His way or as a reflection of the way you love others?
2) do you deserve God's love?
3) do the people who you provide obstacles for deserve those setbacks?

We demonstrate our love for God through our love for others.

Lord, let me help others as You have helped me.

JUNE 15

⁵So that your faith might not rest on man's wisdom, but on God's power.

1 Corinthians 2:5

Paul shares with the Corinthians how God's power works. We as humans often doubt what we can't see or touch. According to the teachings of our society, we are taught if it cannot be touched, if it's not tangible and if there exists no scientific evidence to support the existence, then it doesn't exist.

The question that we must ask ourselves is why do we believe man over God. The answer is because we can touch them. But the reasoning is backwards when you consider God created us. God created everything so His wisdom is divine. His wisdom is certain. His power is profound. He supersedes all of us.

The key to that sentence is faith, your faith. It takes great faith to believe all the time in all the words, deeds and actions of God. Although there is daily evidence that proves He is worthy of your trust and faith, often we act with reservation. Without faith our relationship with God is not genuine. A relationship with God requires faith. Also required is a total dependence of Him.

Humans, us, don't have enough wisdom, even though He has blessed us with some, to compete with God's power or His wisdom.

The wisest action we can take is to have faith and trust in God.

Lord, thank You for Your power where my faith rests.

JUNE 16

⁹However, as it is written: "No eye has seen, no ear had heard, no mind has conceived what God had prepared for those who love Him."

1 Corinthians 2:9

"What God has for me it is for me."
My prayer partner says this phrase regularly and I always breathe deeply. This statement reminds me that I don't need to do anything to compete, worry, struggle, plan, or complain to receive God's gift or reap God's plan.

God has prepared events and items for me which are uniquely suited for me. He does this because He loves me. On top of which it's a surprise because "no eye has seen, no ear has heard, no mind has conceived." That's good news. That simply proves that God loves me like He said He does. Our love for Him is as important as His love for us. He is so flattered by our love for Him and loves us so much, that much like a earthly parent, He just needs to know that His plans will not return void.

He also plans for those who yet believe. Persons who have yet to accept Him as Lord and Savior still are subject to God's plans, including when He will call them to Him. He watches over each of us and takes care of us because we are His children.

This scripture reminds me that although I have excellent ideas about what I aspire to do or be, nothing will happen if it's not God's will, and further, none of my plans exceed God's plans for me. Also, when I see great things, I realize that God can always do better.

Remember that God has plans for you better than those you can conceive, see or hear on your own. When I think of an idea, I always pray and ask God for guidance. Remember that God is a jealous God and you are not to put anything before Him.

Thank You God for the gifts You have for me.

JUNE 17

^{10}But God has revealed it to us by His spirit. The Spirit searches all things, even the deep things of God.

1 Corinthians 2:10

The Holy Spirit, the third part of the Trinity, is an essential part of our lives. The Spirit leads and guides and offers us help for troubled times. It also soothes in tragedy. But mostly It speaks to us and assures us when we've followed the order of God. The Spirit knows what God wants and what His plans are and It helps understand how to follow His plan. Initially, you may wonder how you will know. I know I did. Later, I found out that I knew all along. It starts with doing the right thing in all situations. Your uprightness will bring you closer to God and the Holy Spirit.

The Spirit knows everything about us. It knows all the things that we don't tell or show anyone else. It searches us for the truth and loves us anyway. What I love most about the Holy Spirit is that It bridges any gaps between me and God. It speaks on my behalf in prayer to Christ when I don't know what to say. It translates my moans and groans to Christ then He too understands what I think, feel and need or want.

It has proven Itself to me on several occasions. When I couldn't exactly confess my indiscretions, I was still forgiven because the Spirit knew I wanted to be forgiven and that I needed to be forgiven.

When I learned to listen to the Spirit, life was much easier. I had no more questions about what to do, or whether to do it.

There is a popular and antique cliché: always follow your first mind. When your mind is of Christ then following your first mind is where the Spirit intervenes. When you are in tune to the Spirit, this will be easy.

Becoming one with the Spirit is a process that progresses to different levels of intimacy as you get closer to It. Become one with the Spirit.

Holy Spirit, thank You for revealing to me the things I need.

JUNE 18

¹⁶Don't you know that you yourselves are God's temple and that God's Spirit lives in you? ¹⁷If anyone destroys God's temple, God will destroy him; for God's temple is sacred, and you are that temple.

1 Corinthians 3:16-17

Throughout the Bible, the holiest historic events take place in a temple. The temple of the past and the church of today are very similar. Worship, prayer, teaching are all temple-church occurrences. And although that's the case, you are the temple God deems most important.

Develop a philosophy about your life and to protect your temple. I'll share mine with you. Here are the rules on how to keep my temple pure and sacred:

1) Drink plenty of water. It is a thirst quencher and a cleanser. I prefer Ozarka. Sometimes tap with a lemon.
2) Get some sleep. Sleep deprivation leads to illness.
3) Eat healthy, full balanced meals. Burgers and fries are not a balanced meal. Vegetables are required.
4) Exercise regularly. Exercise strengthens you and relieves stress and tension.
5) Have fun. Laughter is a medicine. Fun produces laughter.
6) Don't worry. Worry shortens your life. Put your burdens in God's hands and leave them there.
7) Don't over indulge in alcohol. Alcohol is a dehydrating substance. Alcohol is also addictive.
8) Don't do drugs at all. Why try something with a proven addictive results? I will never do drugs because my future is too important for that foolishness.
9) Have regular physical check-ups. Have anything unusual checked out. Take your health seriously. None of your body parts are replaceable; organ donorship is not guaranteed.
10) Don't have premarital sex. Stop having premarital sex. I wished that I never had premarital sex. It's something that you can never regain.
11) Developing this philosophy may not be easy, but use mine if you need to.

Thank You, Lord for making me a temple and honoring me.

JUNE 19

⁵Therefore judge nothing before the appointed time; wait till the Lord comes. He will bring to light what is hidden in darkness and will expose the motives of men's hearts. At that time each will receive his praise from God.

1 Corinthians 4:5

We as humans have the tendency to judge others, criticize others, and scrutinize others. But we are wrong for doing so. Judgment, criticism, and scrutiny gives the impression that we are above others and nothing we do will ever be subject to judgment. "Anyone who is without sin, cast the first stone." "Those who live in glass homes should not throw stones." "Judge and be judged." These statements and clichés speak to not being judgmental and of the consequences of judging. That is God's job and His alone. He doesn't need any help. He doesn't miss any details. Further, He has a way of letting each of us know that our sins didn't go unnoticed. Understanding not to judge is how we earn His praise.

The motive of our hearts is important. "God gives to those whose motives are pure." How do we keep our motives pure? How do we correct our motives when they are less than admirable? Why do our motives become unpure? He will expose what is unpure about our hearts. "Blessed are the pure in heart for they shall see God." Matthew 5:8. While keeping our motives pure can prove challenging, it is worthwhile. Our motives are what God uses by which to judge us.

Lord, remove the temptation to judge others. Let me not be judged by others.

JUNE 20

⁷For who makes you different from anyone else? What do you have that you did not receive? And if you did receive it, why do you boast as though you did not?

1 Corinthians 4:7

Paul writes the Corinthians because they need help. Their ministry is relatively young and they need leadership. This scripture, although without complete context, is applicable. Paul asks three questions to them. Let's address the questions.

He implies in the first question that we are excused from obedience to God. Even as Christians we may think that we can "color outside of the lines." Paul's question reminds us that we are not different than other Christians who sacrifice and obey. We must remain obedient and continue to witness to others through our behavior.

The second question affirms that God has met and continues to meet our needs. Further, He offers us the desires of our hearts. The thought that immediately comes to mind was even though He blesses us bountifully, we still manage to complain and are unappreciative.

Lastly, Paul further pronounces his disappointment by implying that the credit which God deserves He has yet to receive. Why is it that the Gift-giver gets no praise? It is similar to those people who believe they got here alone – with no Creator.

As it relates to us daily, Paul gives us direction in the rest of the Corinthian letter about our obedience to Christ, our neglect of Christ and our recognition of Christ. This scripture addresses these issues directly as well. We need to take heed to Paul's leadership.

Thank You, Father for making me Your child, different from others; yet committed to You.

JUNE 21

[10]We are fools for Christ, but you are so wise in Christ! We are weak, but you are strong! You are honored, we are dishonored!

1 Corinthians 4:10

This scripture speaks to apostles and their lifestyle. The role of an apostle is often misunderstood and neglected and underutilized. Being an apostle involves immense sacrifice. The role and the person in it exemplifies the scripture, "take up your cross and follow me." An apostle is "one sent with a special commission." This individual is trusted to teach the gospel of Jesus, which is Christianity.

This particular scripture speaks to the neglect of the apostle as a servant, which deserves honor and praise but receives little, if any at all. You might consider that we could regard that person who travels and teaches the word of God would be celebrated and well taken care of, but most times were not. Not only were they not helped, they were often persecuted. Paul was jailed on a mission. It doesn't sound rewarding so it raises the question why did he continue? By definition, Jesus was an apostle, the originator of apostles and the model by which we define all apostles. Why did He do it?

Jesus said if you lose your life to follow Him, you gain eternal life. Paul lived by that motto and the example of Christ. This led him to teach thousands in several communities.

Apostleship is a calling on your life, just like a preacher, teacher, disciple or any secular career. It is a serious responsibility due the evangelical nature of the role. The reward will be low at the onset because of the criticism, but steady because of those led to Christianity and greatest when one sits at His feet.

All callings require focus and dedication and fortitude. Examine your life to find your "apostleship" your calling and commit to work on that area.

Lord, remind me to honor those who sacrifice to honor You.

JUNE 22

¹²We work hard with our own hands. When we are cursed, we bless; when we are persecuted, we endure it.

1 Corinthians 4:12

Paul is writing to Corinthians and pleads with them for compassion. He attempts to explain the role of an apostle. Although the office of apostle has been vacant for quite awhile, I do contend the behavior and attitude of an apostle should still be followed.

Much like a disciple, an apostle is committed to completing the duties of the Lord. This walk is not easy nor is it respected as it should, however it comes with great rewards.

Paul implies the work and the rewards. I contend that we should take this literally and do just what he details: hard work with our own hands, be cursed and persecuted for the Lord. The rewards, blessings and endurance are abundant. God fulfills His promises through the rewards. The rewards we all pray for.

I know that hard work brings great rewards. I also know that rewards from Christ are not dependent on works. Further, some work may never be rewarded. I caution believers against believing that works always amount to rewards. Christ saved us purposely not based on works so that we don't attach the two and become disillusioned about our relationship and our salvation.

This scripture reminds me that hard work is inevitable. Rewards come as God desires. The hard work is worthwhile and required. These facts encourage me to remain faithful to God and my calling to Him.

God, thank You for the strength and courage for being able to stand no matter what comes my way.

JUNE 23

¹³"Food for the stomach and the stomach for food" – but God will destroy them both. The body is not meant for sexual immorality, but for the Lord, and the Lord for the body.

1 Corinthians 6:13

The oneness that we are designed to have with Christ presents itself in every aspect of our being and existence. Paul describes that oneness well for the role of the body. This scripture explains the role of the body in the most direct language possible.

The body is meant for the Lord not for sexual immorality which means sex outside of marriage. No sex before marriage. The Lord has plans for our bodies that are distracted because of sexual immorality.

The two things you need to know about sex:

1) When you have unprotected sex it is the equivalent of having sex with all of the people your partner has had sex with, which at best is dangerous. And,
2) You become emotionally attached to persons with whom you have sex. This is a spiritual exchange designed to occur when you have sex. This is misplaced if it is not your spouse.

As a Christian, we must commit to saving what belongs to God for Him. The spiritual oneness that we need to seek with God is crucial to our Christian growth.

I ask Christ often to increase my yearning for Him and His word. God is a selfish God and rightfully so. He created us and just like our parents want love and loyalty and respect, so does God.

Lord, Almighty, I commit my body, soul and spirit to You. I won't give away what belongs to You.

JUNE 24

[19] Do you not know that your body is a temple of the Holy Spirit, who is in you, whom you have received from God? You are not your own; [20] You were bought at a price. Therefore honor God with your body.

1 Corinthians 6:19-20

Why is sexual abstinence hard for us? Why is smoking unavoidable? Why do people try drugs? Why do we consume food and alcohol in proportions which our bodies cannot handle? Anything that I do with my body that is not ordained by God is a dishonor to Him. It is also disrespectful of His sacrifice for my life.

Believe me it took years and Christian wisdom and maturity to live this fact.

In late December 1998, I decided that I would surrender to God in obedience my body. In February 1999, I took a public vow of celibacy with 25 youth and 3 other adults. The 29 of us embarked on a journey that has tremendously changed our lives. "True love waits" has turned into a cliché phrase that hundreds of thousands of us have taken to heart. More importantly, into a commitment with Christ.

When I ask for God to draw me closer to Him, I had no idea that He would call me to stop having sex. Then He called me to stop over indulging in alcohol. Then He asked me to stop over eating. Finally, He made me stop spending money the way I had before.

For awhile I was overwhelmed. But one Sunday morning, a realization washed over me. I was sitting in the pew about to take communion and I was in prayer. God responded saying this is how communion is supposed to be. The sweet communion of the Holy Spirit feels like this.

"This" was the purity I had experienced since my surrender. The oneness we shared – the elevated intimacy that I was sharing with Christ and the Father and the Spirit at that moment had transcended all intimacy I had ever experienced. It felt better than anything I had ever experienced. It felt better than the "high" that sex, drugs, alcohol or whatever else promised. In addition, it lasts longer – forever is quite a time.

I was able to hold up my head and my heart to God about areas that had previously separated me from Him.

It was so sweet to commune with the Spirit this way.

Christ, I owe You a pure body for all that You have sacrificed for me to have this body.

On This Journey

JUNE 25

^{25}Now about virgins: I have no command from the Lord, but I give a judgment as one who by the Lord's mercy is trustworthy.

1 Corinthians 7:25

As a virgin, you a have a duty to God to serve Him and be concerned about His agenda. When you are married, you are concerned with the needs of your family.

The first thing however is to remain a virgin. Just say no hasn't really been effective. In 1998, I committed to the Lord that I wouldn't have sex again until I got married. This commitment was hard initially but the reward was fabulous. I learned that most females' self-esteem and self-worth were based on how other's felt about her rather than how she feels about herself. Lots of guys asked me out during that period of time. When I told them that I wasn't having sex, often I never had to speak to them again. There was no mystery to it. They wanted sex and since it wasn't happening, they no longer wanted to know me. They never wanted to get to know me. They were never interested in the things I was good at. They only wanted sex.

Sex is for marriage. The reward for me was that I learned where my real value was: the Lord loves me! Then I could love me. After I realized that I was whole again because of that commitment, the Lord sent my husband. I was only able to accept him as a pure servant. I had to be pure before God before I could be given the gift of a husband.

Virgin refers to the purity within each of us. We need to maintain that purity to remain close to the Lord. Any disruption of our purity disrupts that relationship until forgiveness of God is sought.

Purity is important. We should seek to remain pure at all times by any means necessary. Don't forget God will help us remain pure.

Thank You for all who are committed to a virgin life.

JUNE 26

[34] And his interests are divided. An unmarried woman or virgin is concerned about the Lord's affairs: Her aim is to be devoted to the Lord in both body and spirit. But a married woman is concerned about the affairs of this world – how she can please her husband.

1 Corinthians 7:34

Timing is everything. I wish that I had spent my time as a single person differently, more wisely. As a single person the only person you owe time to, who deserves your time and you best benefit from the time spent is with God in study and prayer. I love the gift of my marriage but I have to negotiate my time to accommodate both my husband and God. Marriage doesn't exempt me from study, but rather requires me to spend more time because I desire a continuously healthy marriage. God honors us when we honor Him. He honors the time we spend with Him.

Malachi 3:10 tells us that a tenth of your resources are to be returned to the source, God. Most often we refer to this tenth only in regard to money but this includes a tenth of your time. Two hours and 24 minutes is a tenth of 24 hours. This time is owed to God. We all, either of single or married, need to give the time God deserves to Him. We need to dedicate that time to Him so He can speak to us, and we commune with Him.

It doesn't have to be all at once. Sometime throughout the different parts of your day is sufficient. The same way you spend time with your friends or doing your favorite thing – you have to make time to spend time with God. That's the only way you will get to know Him.

Thank You for healthy marriages. They are gifts. Thank You for our time together.

JUNE 27

¹³No temptation has seized you except what is common to man. And God is faithful; He will not let you be tempted beyond what you can bear. But when you are tempted, He will also provide a way out so that you can stand up under it.

1 Corinthians 10:13

How great is thy faithfulness!

Often we think that temptation is just about sex but it includes being enticed to steal, cheat, and lie. Anything that is outside of the will of God is temptation. My rule of thumb is if you have to ask if it's right then it is probably not.

My mother's theory has always been "if you lie then you'll steal; if you steal then you cheat." What she meant was that doing any one of these things makes you suspect to do either of the others.

Now what that means of course is to avoid temptation at all costs. You are thinking how hard that is. And you are correct. However, the best way to avoid temptation is not to be there. You must be on guard not to fall to temptation. If your friends are about to rob a convenience store, then your best option would be to avoid being there.

Although this instance seems far-fetched, it has happened to some. You have to make a choice that you will seek God's guidance when you find yourself in a situation where you will be compromised.

Remember that when something happens in your life, that it isn't the first time this has happened to anyone else. "There's nothing new under the sun."

Avoiding temptation is important. It speaks to your faith in God's deliverance. He will deliver an escape and you need look for that route so that you can avoid that temptation.

Father, thank You for allowing me to escape from sin and temptation.

JUNE 28

²³"Everything is permissible" – but not everything is beneficial. "Everything is permissible" – but not everything is constructive.

1 Corinthians 10:23

The scripture speaks clearly to our decisions and its consequences. The opposite of beneficial is harmful or detrimental. Some things, which are permissible, are harmful and detrimental. Detrimental seems harsh however, to use another term would prove less than effective for the severity of some issues. Detrimental is related to deadly when I consider it. Consider things people do which are detrimental, which I consider deadly, without thought about the actual consequence. I made a list of those: sex, drugs, smoking, alcohol and driving illegally.

Driving illegally includes without a license, under the influence of drugs and/or alcohol, over the speed limit, recklessly, and without permission. All of these can kill you and/or others. Permissible but detrimental. Smoking is linked with lung cancer and emphysema, both of which can lead to death. Drugs are addictive and mind altering, which are both dangerous. You could die or worse, become an addict. The worst would be to harm or kill someone else while you are on drugs. Alcohol is similar in its effects and consequences but seems to take effect at a slower rate. The addiction takes longer. The effects on the body are different. Alcohol effects the esophagus, liver and kidneys. Drugs effect the bloodstream where the drug can be passed on to an unborn child by either parent; father during conception, mother, at conception and throughout the pregnancy. Drugs also effect the heart, which could cause a number of issues to occur such as stroke, heart attack, heart disease and clots. The brain is affected by both as they kill brain cells in large increments with small doses. All permissible, yet highly detrimental. Sex, unprotected premarital, is deadly. Sex without your spouse and/or unprotected is dangerous and costly. It could lead to any number of diseases, including those incurable, syphilis and herpes, and deadly, AIDS. Don't forget that unwanted pregnancy could result. Permissible, yet detrimental.

The opposite of constructive is destructive. To construct is to build. To destruct means to destroy, tear down, demolish.

Why would you do that knowing the consequences? The best reason not to is His love. Jesus Christ lives in each of us Christians. Does Jesus want us to smoke, drink alcohol, do drugs, have sex or drive recklessly? The answer is no. But we do it because it's cool or our friends persuaded us to. Can you make a commitment to avoid the destructive and detrimental?

Lord, help me avoid what's not beneficial or constructive.

JUNE 29

²⁴Nobody should seek his own good, but the good of others.

1 Corinthians 10:24

Putting others before yourself is Christ-like. Consider the unselfishness of both God and Christ when you take actions. Your behavior is what differentiates you from Christ. It is not at all appropriate to want to be like Christ yet don't want to give of yourself to others.

Consider what you have that may benefit others, then give it to them. Those who need it and would appreciate your gift. Whatever it is. Your material things. Your help. Your knowledge. Your love. Your testimony. Your food. Your money. Whatever you have that will be instrumental to the good of another, give that for another. One thing is so true of God is He sends blessings to who He can send blessings through.

A story that comes to mind is one where there were several members of a village sitting around a pot of soup and each of them had a long spoon. They were each trying to feed themselves but each time they tried to bring the spoon to their mouths, the spoon was empty when it reached their mouths. After several failed attempts, one villager decided to feed his neighbor. The neighbor ate. As a result they all started to feed each other. They ate until they were full. They soon figured out that they needed each other to survive.

As it is with this world coupled with our responsibilities as a Christian, we are to put others before self just as Jesus. My faith assures me that Jesus will honor that.

Thank You for inspiring me to seek good for others. Father, this selflessness is by Your design.

JUNE 30

[32] Do not cause anyone to stumble, whether Jews, Greeks, or the church of God.

1 Corinthians 10:32

Gage's paraphrase, "Do not cause anyone to stumble, no matter who they are or for any reason." This is important because at all ages peer pressure is present. The younger we are, it is more openly exercised. The older we are, it's called "keeping up with the Jones'." It is all the same peer pressure – doing something because someone else is doing it. What makes that happen I don't really know. What I do know is that we can overcome this pressure.

The first way is that we have to make a decision that we will stand against peer pressure, which would lead us down a road of darkness. Teens often pressure each other into trying drugs, alcohol or sex. The mystery here to most adults is what could one teenager say to another to influence him to introduce illegal substances or potent mixes to your pure being. Why does one teen listen to another who doesn't know any more about anything than you do? This is the most perplexing thing to most adults.

A better question is that do we not recognize that some of these influences may cause us harm, cause us to stumble? The next question is whom would you let cause you to stumble? How do we make that decision? The first decision was to stumble. Why was that? Why would we decide to stumble?

Let us decide not to stumble and let's decide not to cause anyone else to stumble. You are responsible when you cause someone to stumble. That's not something we want to be responsible for.

Helping fellow men is the example the Lord set for us; not to stumble; not to fall; not to falter. Decide that you will stand against peer pressure that will cause you to stumble. It's hard, I know. But what's harder is recovering from the consequences of submitting to that pressure of who are disguised as peers. Peer means friend but is often used to represent your age group. If your friends are encouraging you to do wrong, then they are not your friends. Consider the joy of walking away from that influence.

Lord, allow me not to cause anyone to stumble.

On This Journey

JUNE 30.5

^{26}For whenever you eat this bread and drink this cup, you proclaim the Lord's death until He comes.

1 Corinthians 11:26

The Lord's Supper or communion is a declaration and demonstration that you believe that Jesus Christ will return for us. Further, communion exhibits a relationship between you and God. This relationship is built on trust and faith, love and sacrifice. This is His last dinner before He dies to save us from our sins. He starts the relationship with His love and sacrifice. We maintain the relationship through our faith and trust. This relationship requires work, which includes guidance, obedience, communication, perseverance, and most importantly commitment.

This scripture is important because part of it requires your commitment to His return. This public exhibit means that you believe in Him, His death, His resurrection and His return.

Communion is entirely personal. I love that time with God. "Do this in remembrance if Me." You really shouldn't consume communion until you take the commitment steps involved. One of those is baptism which follows you accepting God as your savior. I really received maximum blessings of the experience when I have truly repented for my sins. The best communions ever for me were when I was first baptized and after I committed to True Love Waits.

Jesus will return for us. His love is powerful and overwhelming. Further, His promises are true. I treat communion very seriously. Communion is fellowship with God.

Father, thank You for returning for me.

Daily Devotional for Young People

MY VIEW ON THINGS

By Shannon Carroll

Through the years that I have been in my Christian walk, I have found that there are many different ways to find the answers to your problems. Now, knowing that all of the paths I have chosen to take have not always been the right ones, I found that if you just listen to what God is telling you to do you will be able to make the right decisions. Small situations like dealing with friends and teachers at school I always thought that I could handle but one day I decided to let God help me out and I found it to be a lot easier.

I know that I am only 15 years old but I have found that wherever you go God will come with you. I have had many different opportunities in my life to experience God's works. About 6 years ago my family and I moved to Virginia, which was a whole different setting for us. My family and I found that even though it seemed that everything was changing quickly it was for a good reason and it was all in His plan for our lives. Three years after we had been in Virginia He moved us back to Texas where we were comfortable.

God has blessed my family and I with so many things that I am very grateful for. He has blessed me with a loving father, mother, and sister. He has placed me in a good environment for me to learn new things and deal with different people and it helps me to grow in Him. Lately I have been growing closer to God and it makes me feel better inside and on the outside. People have noticed the change in my attitude and the way I present myself. Having God in your life really makes a difference because although I have been going to church since I can remember I can see changes in everyone.

My father and mother are pastors and we have a church called Abundant Love. At first it was a bit different to have a church of my own that my dad pastors and leads but I really enjoy being very active in the church and seeing all my family and friends coming and participating. In the service, I have a part where I get to go up to the stage say a youth affirmation. This is when I have all the young people and youth stand for us to recite the scriptures. The scriptures we recite come from Romans 12:2 and Jeremiah 29:11. I love these scriptures because in Romans it talks about how you should not follow what the world does but lead an example by God's word. That scripture helps me to keep a leveled head and remember that I do not have to do what everyone else does. In addition, one of my other favorite scriptures is Deuteronomy 28:13, this scripture says you shall only be at the top and never the bottom and above and never beneath. This encourages me and lets me know that as long as I have God I can get through anything.

JULY 1

[1]The body is a unit, though it is made up of many parts; and though all its parts are many, they form one body. So it is with Christ.

1 Corinthians 12:12

We are all important to Christ. We all work together for Christ and His purpose. We cannot achieve His purpose alone. It takes all of us. You know how it feels when one of your body parts is not functioning properly. You know what happens when your nose is running. Now with that in mind, think of how God feels when one of us is not cooperating with one another or disobedient to Him. How do you think He feels when this happens?

I think my disobedience saddens God. I believe my lack of trust and faith hurts God. I know He grieves when I blatantly disrespect Him and His commands.

I know that I feel miserable when my nose is stopped up. My nose effects my head. It effects my speech. It effects my hearing. It effects my breathing. It effects my energy. It effects my attitude. It effects my ability to sleep. All of this because of my nose. I quickly take medicine to cure me of this ailment. I don't like to feel that way.

Keep in mind, neither does God. He wants that "weakened" body part to get better and regain strength. He also expects us to seek Him for strength when we start to weaken.

We need to work really hard to maintain our stability for the body of Christ.

God, thank You for making us as a church function as one to achieve Your will.

JULY 2

²²On the contrary, those parts of the body that seem to be weaker are indispensable, ²³and the parts that we think are less honorable we treat with special honor. And the parts that are unpresentable are treated with special modesty, ²⁴while our presentable parts need no special treatment. But God has combined the members of the body and has given greater honor to the parts that lacked it, ²⁵so that there should be no division in the body, but that its parts should have equal concern for each other.

1 Corinthians 12:22-25

There are times when we ask why are we here. We wonder what our purpose is and what we need to do to complete that purpose. Most of the time we regret the fact that us being ourselves means a lot to those we love.

Family is the whole unit. You are a part of that whole. Two scenarios: one where you don't meet an obligation that impacts the entire family. The second one is when you do meet that obligation. You will have responsibility in that unit. You have certain duties to that unit. You may have to do housework or babysit a younger sibling. These things are your contribution to the success of the family unit.

The same holds true for the body of Christ. Each of us has a role. It is important that we each do our part but we must first seek that role. There are many things that we need to be obedient about – our commitment to Christ is at the top of that list.

One thing that you will realize as a Christian is that other people will start to depend on you. They will consider you an example and also start to draw strength from you. These people look to you and expect to see you at church for services and other times of fellowship. It will seem somewhat weird but as your spirit transforms as a maturing Christian, people will see that.

Often we don't acknowledge that as a gift and a responsibility but it is. As God reveals your gifts to you, it is important that we are obedient to church attendance, the study of His word and to any commitments we make to the church.

God will reveal to each of us as we are ready the plans that He has for us. Your importance and link to the rest of us will be clear.

Father, thank You for showing me how important each part of the body is to the whole.

On This Journey

JULY 3

²⁶If one part suffers, every part suffers with it; if one part is honored, every part rejoices with it.

1 Corinthians 12:26

When I heard the term "one bad apple spoils the whole bunch," I was discouraged and never realized that it came from the Bible. It's not exact but the sentiment is similar.

I am reminded of a family. It is rare when this is not true of a family. When one hurts, they all hurt. When one rejoices, they all rejoice. God has designed it that way. This is the love He designed. This is the love He wants us to share.

Consider this: the parts make up the whole. The parts are us; the whole is God. If we loved like He does then this is not unreasonable. He is this verse.

I consider this one of the ultimate experiences. As humans, we typically lack compassion and trust and overall love so to give that much of ourselves to another human being seems far-fetched at best. Some marriages don't even have this principle as a focal point. Imagine that the person who you have promised to spend the rest of your life with is less than compassionate about your feelings.

As I wrote this I considered how I could achieve this in my own life. I decided that I needed to pray for genuine spirits in the hearts of my friends and myself. Then I decided that I needed to openly show more compassion to others, especially those I love. I realized that I have to communicate more deeply and more frequently. I have to share more with those whom I love and who love me.

Most importantly I know that I have to be in tune with God so my judgment on these decisions will be accurately focused and delivered. If I am in tune with Him, I can then be in tune with others. Then I can really suffer when one suffers and I can really rejoice when one rejoices.

Lord, I come humbly to You thanking You for sharing with me how important we each are to You.

JULY 4

1 Corinthians 13

I attended a conference several years ago where some things had not happened the way I would have preferred. I walked past my mentor and she noticed my anger. She quickly sat me down and explained to me that my anger was misplaced. She instructed me to open my sword—my Bible—to 1 Corinthians 13. She asked me to read aloud the scriptures and replace love with my name.

I have placed the scriptures below with the appropriate blanks where your name is placed.

¹If _____ speak in the tongues of men and of angels, but have not love, _____ am only a resounding gong or clanging cymbal. ²If ____ have the gift of prophecy and can fathom all mysteries and all knowledge, and if _____ have a faith that can move mountains, but have not love, ____ am nothing. ³If _____ give all _____ possess to the poor and surrender my body to the flames, but have not love, ____ gain nothing. ⁴_____ is patient, _____ is kind. _____ does not envy, _____ does not boast, _____ is not proud. ⁵_____ is not rude, ____ is not self-seeking, _____ is not easily angered, ____ keeps no record of wrongs. ⁶ _____ does not delight in evil, but rejoices with the truth. ⁷ _____ always protects, always trusts, always hopes, always perseveres. ⁸ _____ never fails. But where there are prophecies, they will cease; where there are tongues, they will be stilled; where there is knowledge, it will pass away. ⁹For we know in part and we prophesy in part, ¹⁰but when perfection comes, the imperfect disappears. ¹¹When I was a child, I talked like a child, I thought like a child, I reasoned like a child. When I became a man, I put childish ways behind me. ¹²Now we see but a poor reflection as in a mirror; then we shall see face to face. Now I know in part; then I shall know fully, even as I am fully known. ¹³And now these three remain: faith, hope and love. But the greatest of these is love.

By the fifth verse, I was in tears. I then saw so clearly the error in my ways. Not just that day but in days past, too. I also decided to take action on the days to come. I heard me say that I was an exhibit of love. That made all the difference.

Lord, thank You for proving Your LOVE to me and shining Your love through me.

JULY 5

⁵For God is not a God of disorder but of peace.

I Corinthians 14:33

Imagine God's daily schedule. All of us ask, demand, whine, plead, talk, and thank Him on a daily basis all day long. Just consider that He hears all of us, saves us from harm, present us with gifts, wakes us up on time, puts us to sleep on time, calls saints to be with Him, calls us to salvation, reprimands us when we disobey, and loves us conditionally.

He does this each day for us. He orders His day according to His plans. He has priorities and makes decisions based on what His plans are. Nothing we can do distracts Him from His daily agenda. After God orders our steps and even when we deviate from His plan, He anticipates that and still moves us back to the plan.

God defined peace. He is peace. He is responsible for our peace. It feels great to experience His peace. In order to do this, you need to recognize disorder. Disorder normally has chaos or/and confusion attached to it. There is very little truth associated with it. Disorder inhibits progress. Often quite trivial disorder is clearly not godly and distracts you from God and His will. Any distraction from His will needs to be removed. You may have heard adults pray for God to remove anything that separates them from Him. That is a powerful request because you are operating on faith and God's omnipotent wisdom to make decisions about your life. He honors that but the results may be hard on you – but necessary.

The only way to experience His peace, which exceeds all understanding, is to dismiss all disorder. Even if it seems small or insignificant. Parallel 'little disorder or chaos' with a pebble in your sock. As small as that stone is, it causes great discomfort as you walk. You stop as soon as you notice it, to remove it. Once you remove it, you can walk in much more comfort and ease and you regain focus on you destination. If that rock was disorder, then you would enter His peace. You want that peace. I do.

God, remove from me what is disorderly for it is not of You.

JULY 6

[33] Do not be misled. "Bad company corrupts good character."

I Corinthians 15:33

The old cliché says "if you lay down with dogs, you get up with fleas." My mother said that to me for a long time in an effort to shield me from improper influences and such. I don't know how old the cliché is, but it'll always be true. It is a human misconception that we hang out with persons who do questionable or illegal things, but won't be associated with them or be accused of similar activity. This is not true. Bad company usually influences good character negatively not the other way around.

The motives are not pure of bad company. We know this and still believe that changing others is possible especially when they are doing wrong.

Now, don't get me wrong I don't want you to think that they can never change but let's talk about how that change can occur. Bad company can change. People who do bad things and influence others to do likewise can change. Our best Biblical example is Paul, originally Saul. Paul is the Christian leader of most communities in the New Testament. Saul was a warrior who was evil and often was at the mercy of God through David in the Old Testament. Lesson: God changes people using others. But that's at God's orders, not our unplanned adventures, not at our naïve desires.

The rules haven't changed, including this one. I learned by watching others to avoid certain things. Lastly, I found out when I was older that some things never happened to me because those around me had the impression that I would say no. When I found this out I was relieved. I know what I had avoided and I was glad. All we have are our word and our reputation. I had succeeded in my quest to maintain both. It's hard to say no but it's worth it every day.

Lord, please warn me against bad character.

JULY 7

³Praise be to the God and Father of our Lord Jesus Christ, the Father of compassion and the God of all comfort, ⁴who comforts us in all our troubles, so that we can comfort those in any trouble with the comfort we ourselves have received from God.

2 Corinthians 1:3-4

My father died in 1998. Although he was ill, I was still devastated. There is no way to prepare for the death of anyone close to you. But I will tell you beyond a shadow of doubt that God, the Father of compassion, is at your side the entire process. Healing from events such as death is a process, because there was no preparation for the loss.

The God of all comfort is truly His name and description in one. He dried my tears. Day by day, He made it easier to think about my dad and not cry. I don't miss him any less – as a matter of fact I miss him more because of successes I experienced which I cannot share. But I don't cry, not like I did initially. God showed me the reasons why my father passed. One of which was my maturity – I was equipped to handle his passing and didn't know it.

I prayed through that season and sought God's comfort. He delivered that comfort. Now I can help comfort others. Ironically but probably by God's own design, during his hospitalization, I played Kirk Franklin's "He'll Take The Pain Away." Little did I know how true those words, which I grew to love, would come true and carry me through my storm. The song also enabled me to minister to my mother. Once I shared the song with her, it seemed that her thoughts too became transformed. Soon she didn't cry as much. She comments on how he would respond to situations from time to time.

He is the Father of Compassion and the God of all comfort but you have to want Him to comfort you. You have to ask Him, then be willing to be healed and comforted.

Thank You for Your comfort and compassion.

JULY 8

¹⁶Therefore we do not lose heart. Though outwardly we are wasting away, yet inwardly we are being renewed day by day.

2 Corinthians 4:16

Using a figurative approach, "wasting away" may include sadness, disappointment or anything that would cause someone to ask you what's wrong. Outwardly "wasting away" – is that a good idea to show others when we are down trodden? There are two sides to this argument. One discussion would be yes, it is a good idea. Your outward distress may offer them an understanding that even Christians have issues and problems. There however is a responsibility you have to share with them what God is doing in your life during this time to bring you closer to Him and God uses this instance to further define your testimony.

The other discussion is no; don't wear your feelings on your sleeves. While those that argue for this position may have a point when they say that their outward wasting away will turn others from Christ because of one pristine image of Christianity, I don't exactly agree with these points unless you are ready to do two things:

1) tell the truth about what is going on in your life – good, bad and indifferent; and
2) be able to answer the question; "Why are you always so happy? You seem to never have any problems.

That question and statement requires us to speak to God's goodness. Keep in mind that I said that I don't exactly agree with the people who argue this point. I don't agree because those same people don't share the truth about what they've endured or enduring, nor do they share God's goodness. They simply wear the mask of happiness. This mask prevents them from actually being joyful because you cannot be joyful without sharing joy or hiding the truth when we are charged to share the truth.

Do not lose heart is synonymous with be encouraged. The Lord renews our strength daily. He gives us a new supply of strength and bread daily so we can continue to do His work. Your trials aid in the development of your testimony. You share your testimony with others so they are encouraged and so on.

No matter what we endure, God refuels us daily. He takes care of us and our soul and heart and spirit. Do not lose heart.

Lord, remind me of my duty to share with others how You lift my spirit.

On This Journey

JULY 9

¹⁸So we fix our eyes not on what is seen, but on what is unseen. For what is seen is temporary, but what is unseen is eternal.

2 Corinthians 4:18

Temporary defined: now you see, now you don't. Not quite Webster's but befitting to explain that temporary will disappear. In fact, everything and everyone is temporary. God created man from dust. From dust we came and to dust we will return.

The tangible definition of temporary: bikes break, problems get solved, TV tubes blow out, clothes wear out, cars break down, and people die. So what do we do to avoid focusing on the temporary? First, we need to recognize that issues are temporary and material things are also temporary. Second, we need to realize that we need to appreciate people because they are not promised to us everyday. Thirdly, we need to recognize that God created all things, including both the eternal and the temporary.

The scripture defines the eternal very well. It is the unseen. This may be a little hard to understand at first, but consider God. He is eternal and unseen. He created this world and He created each of us. He will still be God when nothing else exists.

So the focus must be on Him. He is a jealous God. He wants His unconditional love returned by obedience, forgiveness of others, exhibiting the fruits of the spirit (Galatians 5:22-23), avoiding sexual immorality, debauchery and other sins, and genuine love for His Son.

Study of His word and prayer also focuses on the eternal. Knowing God's word is a way of saying to God you love Him and know His truths are important to you.

In my Christian growth, I assessed my knowledge of His word and determined that I know more secular music and various information than I knew of His word. I dedicated myself to learning more scripture, applying and sharing that scripture, and knowing more songs, which are traditional. I focused on the eternal. When I spend time of Him, I am so fulfilled.

Lord, help me keep focused on the eternal.

JULY 10

¹⁴Do not be yoked together with unbelievers. For what do the righteousness and wickedness have in common? Or what fellowship can light have with darkness?

2 Corinthians 6:14

This scripture instructs us on friend and mate selection. The instructions are clear:

1) don't hang out with unbelievers,
2) righteous avoid wickedness,
3) you are strengthened by other believers,
4) don't seek common factors with those who are unbelievers, unrighteous and dark; and,
5) don't believe that you can transform unbelievers, change the wicked to the righteous or move darkness to light without God.

We are charged to pray for an unbeliever's salvation, but we are foolish to believe that we can change them by keeping company with them. "Metal sharpens metal" exemplifies the theory that we fellowship with others like ourselves in order to strengthen and grow.

There is too great a risk we take when we expose ourselves to unbelievers and wicked and dark. If we aren't able to withstand their challenges, then we fall prey to their lifestyle. As Christians, we often feel that we are invincible and while that is true, we are called to pray and minister to the unsaved rather than "hang out" with them.

Lastly, suppose you see a circle of people smoking marijuana or some other illegal substance. Isn't it natural to assume that everyone in that circle was participating? But what if that person who wasn't participating was you? Your explanation would somehow relate to your trying to discourage such behavior and how you were explaining that you needed to be their example. In the midst of your explanation no one believes you. But if you hadn't been there, you wouldn't be expected to explain why you were there; or your behavior or your lack of participation.

Lord, thank You for Your wisdom on friend and mate selection.

On This Journey

JULY 11

⁶Remember this: whoever sows sparingly will also reap sparingly and whoever sows generously will also reap generously.

2 Corinthians 9:6

Why do persons generally speaking want the most for the least? Is this the American way? Are we taught to be stingy or is it something we are born with? Is it selective stinginess? How do we decide who we are generous too?

This scripture also asks us to examine our motives when we give. Why do you give? To whom do we give? What do we give them? When do we give to them? How do we give to them? Are our motives pure?

Our motives for giving to others must be pure. Otherwise, we have given expecting something in return. What if you don't get anything in return? Will you regret your gift?

What if God reciprocates our giving style? God is generous and He shows us how to be generous. He equips us to give such that we can give generously to others. God gives to people whom He can send blessings through. He gives to us so we can give to others. Everything we have in our possession is not ours for the long term. Some of those possessions are specifically designed for others – not for ourselves. We don't recognize this always, but that's our selfishness and our stinginess. Sharing what we own is not common. We barely share with those we know and "love," much less people we've never seen or know. However, as Christians, we are charged to share.

Again God's example of sharing is monumental – He gave His only Son to save our very lives. Nothing we can do will ever amount to the value of His gift, so the least we can do is share generously what we have.

You get what you give, but when you give you shouldn't expect anything in return.

Lord, open our hearts to be generous.

Daily Devotional for Young People

JULY 12

³For though we live in the world, we do not wage war as the world does.

2 Corinthians 10:3

When God created this world, He had certain intentions. He didn't want the evil, but it exists anyway. It does serve His purpose though; it continues to prove that He is real and alive.

He has given real instructions about how we are to behave in this world. We are not to think the way the world thinks. We should not see things in the same manner as the world does. We are to be the light of this world no matter the circumstance. As Christians, we are to be leaders of this world giving righteous examples to the rest of the world.

Among our instructions, God gives specific instructions about how battles are won and fought. First, we wage war through God, not through the military. Secondly, we pray for our enemies. He prepares a table for us in the presence of our enemies. We will spend some time on this when we address this scripture. Thirdly, God said that vengeance belongs to Him, not us.

During what's considered to be a short lifetime, I have witnessed three wars in this modern era thus far. These wars negatively impact the national and international economy. Further, wars fail to accomplish the initial goal. Rather war usually results because someone or country didn't "win" the bet, the argument, the dispute or the debate. In addition, wars start when an agreement is breached, such as trade or treaty or commerce.

Is war the only answer between disagreeing or opposing countries? Certainly not, but seems the most popular approach of retaliation. Hopefully, you won't witness another war in your lifetime but remember God's word if you do.

Finally, remember your own personal wars have no place either. We need to adjust our approach – one where God is the lead advisor in settling the dispute. Of course, be reminded that to be Christ-like is to choose what He would choose and war is certainly at the bottom of His list if it was on the list at all.

Lord, forgive us for wanting to wage our own wars.

JULY 13

⁹But he said to me, "My grace is sufficient for you, for my power is made perfect in weakness." Therefore I will boast all the more gladly about my weaknesses, so that Christ's power may rest on me.

2 Corinthians 12:9

Paul's words again reach to educate us on how God operates. Paul's usual approach: first he reminds us of God's words, then secondly, he explains how it applies to him, and then lastly, how we may apply it to our situation.

No one wants to be or to appear weak. It's just not cool, right? Everyone wants to appear strong and confident and cool. But in all that "strength," can we see God? Is God getting the credit for that "strength" or does something else, like clothes or your social status get the credit for who you are? Our "coolness" distracts people from the opportunity to witness about God. Sometimes we are distracted by our own "stuff" and forget to give God His just glory.

But in our weakness, we seek God for more strength, for an improvement in that area. However, God gets His due glory when others watch your weaknesses develop into strengths. They are waiting to ask how did you overcome the "weakness." And when you give God the appropriate glory, their lives are transformed and you are blessed. They then know that "strength" is possible in their own lives. They witnessed you trust God and that's just what they needed to be reminded to trust Him.

Your weakness presents a transparency of yourself. None of us wants to be transparent where others can see our "stuff." We assume they will judge our stuff, but typically they are seeking a way to solve their own "stuff" without disclosing the issue.

We are made weak so that God gets what He truly deserves – glory.

Father, thank You for Your grace and my weaknesses.

JULY 14

[19]The acts of the sinful nature are obvious: sexual immorality, impurity and debauchery; [20]idolatry and witchcraft; hatred, discord, jealousy, fits of rage, selfish ambition, dissensions, factions, [21]and envy; drunkenness, orgies and the like. I warn you, as I did before, that those who live like this will not inherit the kingdom of God.

Galatians 5:19-21

It is hard to avoid sin, some harder than others, because the opportunity to sin is frequent – every minute of every day we have the opportunity to sin. Sin happens to all humans in some fashion or another. While it may not be one of the ones listed above, it could still be a sin.

God addresses sin in several contexts. One is that God will offer you a way of escape from the sinful situation before it occurs (1 Corinthians 10:13). Two, God has forgiven you of your sins – all you need to do is ask for His forgiveness (Micah 7:18). Thirdly, God loves us unconditionally so He sent His son to die for payment of our sins (John 3:16). Fourth, God demands we turn away from our sins when we accept Christ as our Lord and Savior (James 5:19, 20).

When Paul says that sinners will not inherit the kingdom of God, he only reiterates what God has already spoken. Further, it means that sinners who have not turned away from such behavior, nor accepted Jesus as Lord and Savior, and haven't sought God's forgiveness. I don't expect that Christians would do some of these things but I realize that two are quite common and recognizable: envy and jealousy. While a similar sin, there is one distinctive difference; envy involves an intense desire for another's possessions where action to gain possession of the item usually takes place. In plain English, she wants her _____ so badly, she tries to take it from her. There is a lust for the item involved.

As Christians, I would hope we wouldn't fall into that trap. However if we should, along with any other sins, we simply need to turn away from sin and ask for God's forgiveness.

Lord, help me to avoid all sins daily.

JULY 15

²²But the fruit of the Spirit is love, joy, peace, patience, kindness, goodness, faithfulness, ²³gentleness, and self-control. Against such things there is no law.

Galatians 5:22-23

The Fruits of the Spirit. This is the opposite of Galatians 5:19-21. There are six more sins listed there, than are "fruit" listed here. Why are there seemingly more sins than "fruits"? This could be my imagination but it just seems to be evidence to affirm my suspicion.

No matter though, there are things which falls under no law. Those are things we should try to master. From these things come such fulfillment, fulfillment you can be proud of.

The nine fruits please God. Love: Do we know how to love and do we know how to receive love? Do we question true love? Why? Joy: What does this mean? How do we accomplish this intangible inner-peace? Peace: This inner reaction to any outward upheaval is outstanding. How do we achieve this strength? Patience: This is easy once we have the first 3. This is my opinion based on observation of others who possess all four. Kindness: Kindness requires no special talent. Kindness is pure and comes from the heart. Kindness cannot be disguised or faked. Goodness: Genuine character is goodness. Faithfulness: Again, no talent required, just focus on your decision to be faithful. Gentleness: Related to meekness, in the way that we handle others in all situations. Self-control: This requires discipline and focus on the decision to be controlled. Self-control requires an understanding of the boundaries of self but of course first knowing that there are boundaries which exist.

The Fruit of the Spirit are essential for a Christ-centered, spirit-filled life. Some fruit is harder to fulfill than others. A few may last longer than the others, but all are pleasing to God.

Lord, may we possess the fruit of Spirit.

JULY 16

¹⁰Therefore, as we have opportunity, let us do good to all people, especially to those who belong to the family of believers.

Galatians 6:10

In my Christian walk, I have witnessed some phenomenal events which have disappointed me. Seeing some of the harsh words and deeds exchanged by Christians, I have questioned my walk with Christ. I realized though that's why we walk with Christ. He can fix the behaviors and attitudes of all of us to match His will.

We are here to help each other as Christ would do. Often I feel we forget that part of our commitment. We are to serve others in each area of our lives. Our service to others allows them to experience Christ in a personal experience. We serve others because of our obedience to Christ.

Consider that we each want to meet Christ but how will we treat Him based on how we treat those He sends to us to help? Doing good for others is a blessing and sometimes we miss our opportunity.

There is a story of a woman who knew that Jesus was coming to see her. She prepared all day for His arrival, so when she heard a knock at the door she thought it was Him. The person stood there and asked for a meal. She turned him away saying that she was busy waiting for Jesus. The second knock excited her because she thought surely this must be Him. The person then asked for clothing. She insisted that she positively did not have time to help him because she was expecting an important guest. He departed. The third knock was a person needing shelter. She told him that he would find help elsewhere. She rushed back to prepare for her guest. The last knock of her day was Jesus and she opened the door. She exclaimed that she had waited for Him to arrive all day. He responded that He had showed up several times and she wouldn't help Him. She responded that she didn't know what He was talking about. He said that people came to see you and you were too busy to help them. He went on to tell her that serving them meant you served Me. She was so ashamed and hung her head.

When we serve others, we serve Him.

Lord, help me serve them.

On This Journey

JULY 17

⁴But because of his great love for us, God, who is rich in mercy, ⁵made us alive with Christ even when we were dead in transgressions – it is by grace you have been saved.

Ephesians 2:4-5

Grace is bigger than your conception and the little box we would normally define most things. Grace is bigger than the tallest mountain and wider than the widest sea and deeper than the deepest ocean, and poetically I could continue but you are gathering that grace is huge – bigger than your finite imagination. Grace was in place before you were born and will be available when you have great-great-great-great-grandchildren and when they have great-great-great-great-grandchildren. Although we don't know when this is, until the end of time, God will respond in grace.

His grace is comparable to His love. His love created His grace, which is why neither will ever fall short. His awesomeness rests on His desire to keep us alive when we have done the absolutely unthinkable, unbelievable, and the unreasonable – the sins, the transgressions. Unlike God when someone commits a transgression toward us, we are ready to disown, disavow, disassociate, and anything else that removes us from the transgressor. We hold a grudge and we ignore the transgressor. We don't talk to them anymore.

God, however, knows that we are going to sin before we do so, is prepared to forgive us before we ask, forgives us before we can say please, and forgets the incident before we can say amen. If for no other reason, that is why He is God and I am not. He is able to do for us what we are not able to do for others. When I considered what the consequences are of not forgiving others, I soon stopped holding grudges.

His gift is immeasurable: He saved us, He made us alive even though we still sin daily and He loves us unconditionally.

Thank You for Your grace.

JULY 18

⁸For it is by grace you are saved, through faith – and this not from yourselves, it is the gift of God – ⁹not by works, so that no one can boast.

Ephesians 2:8-9

God's math is awesome. His grace + your faith = your salvation. Doesn't that seem simple, yet phenomenal? Salvation doesn't have anything to do with you, nothing you can do to receive or avoid it. God makes the decision and He gives you salvation as a gift. When I realize what He has done, I get overwhelmed. I usually cry and repent and He speaks to me to comfort me.

Salvation cannot be achieved by the bootstrap mentality. It can only be achieved by a gift from God. This is the dreamed level playing field. Who and what you are have nothing to do with this gift. The gift is for you individually. The best benefit of His gift is that you can never lose it or give it away nor can it be taken away.

Often times we do "things," we sin, and we feel that the sin is so big or so horrible that we feel that our salvation is in jeopardy. This is simply not true. God does not take His gifts back. No matter what we do. We should not abuse the gift but He will not take it back. We have to remember and dedicate ourselves to serving Him and asking for His forgiveness for the sins we commit. We need to recognize God for His wisdom and His grace. He has immeasurable forgiveness and mercy for us because of His love for us.

Not by works = not by what you do, not by what you are, not by what you have. Your status doesn't matter. You can't boast about how you received it because God gave it to you and the gift itself is enough to not want to tarnish it by not giving God His due glory. Boasting ruins the luster of the gift. It ruins the value and quality of the gift. It depreciates the gift. The gift is to be cherished and valued and spoken of with honor to the giver: God.

Thank You for Your gift of grace.

On This Journey

JULY 19

[20]Now to him who is able to do immeasurably more than all we ask or imagine, according to his power that is at work within us.

Ephesians 3:20

His power that is at work within us is our focus today. His power is at work within us. He is working within me. He works within me. His works are in me. His power is in me. He is in me.

HE IS IN ME!!! Now my attention is arrested. Why you may ask? Well, I represent God and Jesus and the Holy Spirit. He is in me. He resides in me amongst my junk, my stuff and my ugliness. He walks around amidst my fear, my hate and my disobedience. He breathes in the dusty, dirty, unkept facility where He cleanses and conditions daily. He is God and He fixes all that mess. You may ask are we that dirty and messed up? In so many ways, the answer is yes. We are not pure unless He is the leader of our lives. Each time we mess up, He cleanses us and He conditions us. His power is at work within us. This power is beyond our imaginations.

The reason that He is able to do immeasurably more than all we ask or imagine is that His power is greater than me. Let's consider what we can imagine:

- a new car at 16
- a full scholarship to the school of choice
- great grades
- loving parents
- a comfortable home

Those are things I wished for as a teen. God granted me some of what I asked for – a loving mother, my grades and my home. I received a partial scholarship. I didn't get a car until I was 23 years old. I bought it myself and it was used. He gave me what I needed and what I could afford. I certainly couldn't afford a car note. Everything He gave me was by His design – not mine. The blessings He gave me in the time He gave them and in the fashion He gave them to me was so that He could be glorified not so that I could be satisfied.

What He does for us is directly related to what He needs us to do to balance His purposes and to bring Him glory. His power is at work within us to assist in achieving His mission and objectives.

Thank You for Your power working within me.

JULY 20

[23]Church, to be made new in the attitude of your minds.

Ephesians 4:23

Simply put, you have to accept your newness in Christ with your own attitude. Easy? Not really.

First, there is the newness which comes with Christ and your acceptance of Him. Once we accept God's gift of salvation, we can never lose it so we have to consciously work to realize that fact. Sometimes we feel that we have done things that will revoke our salvation but there is nothing we can do to have our salvation revoked. The hardest thing to do after we commit a sin that we feel is so horrible, is to forgive ourselves, ask for God's forgiveness, accept the forgiveness, then move forward using the experience as a testimony of God's grace.

Second, accepting ourselves unconditionally; loving ourselves unconditionally. We don't do this well, but we will, eventually. Accepting and loving means regardless of the past and in spite of the "issues." "Let go and let God" is crucial for survival. Without it we would continue to hold ourselves accountable for sins we committed long ago which God forgave us for longer ago. Love anew is forgiven and free. Forgiven and free is a new attitude for your heart and mind, which you owe yourself.

Thirdly and lastly, we need to match our thoughts of ourselves to that of Jesus. He thinks of us better than we view ourselves. The evidence for this is how we love. He loves us in spite of ourselves. We don't love ourselves because of ourselves. He love us unconditionally. We love ourselves with stipulations and conditions. He knows we are capable of excellence. We strive for the mediocre. He wants the best for us. We cheat and deprive ourselves of excellence by taking short cuts and exercising impatience.

In Christ, we are new creatures – new beings. We need to accept our newness in the attitudes of our minds. Let us not be our own stumbling block.

Lord, prepare my mind for the greatness of my newness.

JULY 21

>²⁴And to put on the new self, created to be like God in true righteousness and holiness.
>
> ***Ephesians 4:24***

A profound realization is He created me to be like Him, in His image.

How can we live up to this awesome and phenomenal image in this world that doesn't care anything about us nor God?

1) Study God's word daily
2) Pray without ceasing
3) Share God with others
4) Invite people to go to church and church related functions (retreats, lock-ins, Vacation Bible School)
5) Keep focused on Him and His calling of you
6) Be reminded that once we announce to others we are Christians then our responsibilities increase and their expectations of us increase and most importantly as a Christian, you cannot have a "bad day" or "slip" or "make a mistake."

The last statement is important because our walk with Christ leads others to walk with Him. Without a clear understanding of our role, we will certainly miss various and numerous opportunities to win others to Christ.

Your new self is what people see as a transition from what they once saw. They need positive reinforcement that the new self is real and related to Christ's presence in your life. They depend on knowing this for themselves through their regular interaction with you.

We must protect their perception of us and our Christian lifestyle. As they mature, the perception will change slightly but we need to guard against their fall.

Our new self needs to be everything God expects of us. We need to recognize the areas where the new self is most required – those areas where Christ is not most exemplified. And as we continue to mature, these changes are easier to recognize and easier to execute. We starve for that holiness and righteousness.

Thank You for my new self, God.

JULY 22

[26]"In your anger, do not sin." Do not let the sun go down while you are angry, [27]and do not give the devil a foothold.

Ephesians 4:26-27

This by far is one of my favorite scriptures. It was given to me at a critical time of my youth as a Christian young person.

It spoke directly to me and my circumstances. While it is okay to be angry; Jesus was angry, do not sin.

Step 1: Okay to be angry; not okay to sin because of anger. This means no retaliation, no revenge, no sin – not even one. No matter what. It happens all the time. We return evil for evil, wrong with wrong. But two wrongs don't make a right. The only place two negatives can be positive is in algebra and most of you would prefer life without algebra.

Step 2: Do not let the sun go down while you are angry. Tomorrow and no other amount of time is promised to us. We do not know the hour of our passing or the passing of others. Settling disputes as soon as possible is best. You'll feel better. You honor Christ in this manner. Best yet, you will know that if you never get to see and speak to this person again, you have made peace with that one with whom you were angry.

Step 3: Do not give the devil a foothold. Most circumstances get out of hand when we tell others and they spread that information along usually with a twist, spin or some extra information attached. Well, we all know where that gossip is going. So, don't share your anger with someone who is not Christ-centered. Your situation could escalate to levels you never expected.

Use this scripture to govern your head and heart when you deal with others. You'll want these same rules to apply when you are the recipient of such anger.

Thank You, God for controlling my anger and limiting my sin.

JULY 23

²⁹Do not let any unwholesome talk come out of your mouths but only what is helpful for building others up according to their needs, that it may benefit those who listen.

Ephesians 4:29

Is this hard to do? Are you challenged to lift up others? Are you challenged to meet the needs of others? Why is this? Have you ever considered why that is? Let's investigate the directives of the scripture.

First, "do not let any unwholesome talk come out of your mouths," which includes foul language and gossip – the two leaders in unwholesome talk. Neither builds anyone up – you nor the person which it includes. Contrary to opinions, cursing is not a sign of maturity but rather it usually happens when you don't have other words available. A fellow Christian shared that I could avoid foul language if I expanded my vocabulary. As a matter of fact, I tried it and realized that her rule was true.

Gossip is something to simply be avoided – at all costs. Gossip, whether true or not or not sure – hurts everyone. Gossip is anything where you share information about another person with a third party that is not positive. People also say that gossip is vague to discern. Clearly, if it does not uplift anyone, it's gossip. If it did not originate from the person being discussed ("the horse's mouth"), then it's gossip. If you cannot name the source or you don't want to be named as the source, then it's gossip.

The rule is if you don't want it said or done or repeated in conversation then it's gossip, so don't you do it. Stop others from doing it.

Christians are designed to act as Christ acts. We are to build each other up. Our enemy has the other job. We don't need to assist the enemy – he doesn't assist us. When you hear "stuff" about others, pray for them so that they survive these circumstances and times, whatever they may be. It's our job as a Christian.

Father, monitor the words of my mouth.

Daily Devotional for Young People

JULY 24

³⁰And do not grieve the Holy Spirit of God, with whom you were sealed for the day of redemption.

Ephesians 4:30

The focus is the first part of the scripture: "And do not grieve the Holy Spirit of God."

Most often I hear this during the invitation to Christ because when God calls them to Him during that time, some deny Him time after time. This denial of the call grieves Him.

But you say this doesn't apply to you but have you ever known that God was speaking to you and you heard Him but didn't follow His commands? Or have you knowingly disobeyed God and you know the consequences? Or have you avoided witnessing to someone when you know that you were supposed to? Or have you ever denied Christ, knowingly or unknowingly? Or have you ever done anything that would offer an observer the opportunity to question or doubt your commitment to Christ? Or have you ever broken a commandment? Do you have a regular study time? Do you have a regular prayer time?

Any of these grieves the Holy Spirit of God. When I do any of these things, I picture God holding down His head and shaking it in disappointment of my actions. I know almost immediately when I have grieved the Holy Spirit. The consequences don't come immediately because the fact that I know that I have grieved Him is sometimes consequence enough. Unfortunately we will grieve the Holy Spirit for most of our lives. The key is not to grieve Him about the same thing with any regularity.

The bigger key is to be sure to know when we have grieved Him and immediately request His forgiveness.

Lord, let me not grieve You.

JULY 25

³¹Get rid of all bitterness, rage, and anger, brawling and slander, along with every form of malice.

Ephesians 4:31

Ephesians is one of my favorite books because all rules of life are contained within those pages. This scripture being one such rule.

Why should we be without bitterness, rage, anger, brawling, slander and other forms of malice? Better question is why once these qualities are attained, why do some persons try to keep them active?

These traits require too much energy to maintain. It requires energy to do all those things, even one or two at a time. Not to mention what amount of memory it takes to remember with whom and why you are angry.

Who wants to be around brawling, slanderous and malicious people? I don't. These are people who are always associated with trouble. They never have "fun" without serious consequences.

These block your relationship with God because they are tools used by the enemy to distract us from God and His will. None of them exhibit the behavior of Christ. Often we fail to realize how disruptive these behaviors are to our relationship with others including Christ and our loved ones.

Finally, what does one stand to gain from behaviors opposite the fruits of the Spirit, especially those that reject the Spirit? Simply put, Ephesians does not allow us to have to imagine its meaning or interpret its message, yet it offers us the straightforward approach to God's rules on Godly living. With so much to understand in this life at least Ephesians attempts to make it easier.

So get rid of and avoid all forms of malice. Your quality of life depends on it.

Lord, remove all forms of malice from me.

JULY 26

^{32}Be kind and compassionate to one another, forgiving each other, just as in Christ God forgave you.

Ephesians 4:32

I memorized this scripture as a requirement in a Christian studies class for married couples. It has been a tool I have used each day since I first put it to memory.

In each aspect of your life, you will be presented with situations, which demand you to be kind and compassionate to others, to forgive them as Christ forgives you. Often you will do this without hesitation. However, there are those times when you will need to be reminded about what to do and how to treat others.

Treating some people kindly and compassionately is not always easy but turn the table around. Is forgiving me all that easy all the time? Does Christ ever have a hard time forgiving me? Does Christ ever regret dying so that my sins would be erased? Yes. No. No. But for us the answers would be: No; Yes; Yes.

This scripture serves as our reminder of what we are to do at all times, not only when it's easy but especially when it's hard.

It's worth it to do because God will know how we treat others and also how we want to be treated.

Our compassionate and kind behavior is our opportunity to be Christ-like. When we give those opportunities away, what then do we sacrifice? Remember that we lose when we are not kind, compassionate and forgiving – not the other person.

Lord, remind me at all to remain kind and compassionate.

On This Journey

JULY 27

¹⁰and find out what pleases the Lord.

Ephesians 5:10

We study everything else. We know the characters and their intimate details of our favorite television shows, books and games.

Do we know what pleases God? How do we find out? Well, prayer and reading His word are the short answers.

Let's examine the long answer:

- prayer
- obedience
- love for others
- behave in a Christ-like manner
- obey the commandments
- forgiveness
- faith
- fruits of the Spirit
- respect Him
- read and study His word
- avoid vengeance, malice, and adultery
- avoid sin
- seek His will for your life
- follow His will
- commit wholly to Him
- honesty with Him
- trust Him

The solution is to find out what pleases Him and do what pleases Him. Pleasing Him rewards you. Pleasing Him brings you peace. He created us to serve Him and to please Him. Our job is to know what pleases Him. Our goal is to please Him consistently and because it is what He commands, not for any other reason.

Sometimes we do what we think or know pleases God because we expect something in return or as a reward. Unpure motives – watch our motives. Watch and monitor why or when you are doing. We cannot expect Him to honor our obedience when our motives are not pure. He may honor it but He cannot be expected. Find out what pleases God. Do what pleases God. Seek always to please God. I have learned that I must please God even though I don't want to.

Lord, help me know what pleases You.

JULY 28

¹⁸Do not get drunk on wine, which leads to debauchery. Instead, be filled with the Spirit.

Ephesians 5:18

Wine is figurative for our discussion today, rather than literal. Wine can be substituted for anything in which we overindulge – food, gossip, drugs, wine; you complete the blank for yourself. Wine can be substituted for distractions which keep you from being filled with the Holy Spirit.

Time is precious. The time we spend on frivolous things takes time away from us spending time with God and being filled with the Holy Spirit. Time is not promised to any of us. I cannot give up time with the Spirit for destruction such as wine, gossip or other destruction.

When we are filled with the Holy Spirit, it is hard to do what distracts us from God and the Spirit. How do we become filled with the Spirit? I'm glad you asked. I am filled with the Holy Spirit when I am focused on the Spirit. Being focused means praise, study, and worship of the Lord and wait to hear what He has to say and what He wants for me and my life. Further, my total submission to Him also assists in filling me with Spirit.

I can't overemphasize the importance of the Spirit. It would be unreasonable for you to understand fully the Spirit role and importance but at the same time we need to seek the Spirit and develop an attitude of knowing the Spirit and learning Its role.

The Spirit speaks for us and intercedes on our behalf. It comforts and consoles us in our times of need. The Spirit is an integral part of our relationship with God and Christ and It needs to be treated as such. We neglect the Spirit because we don't know how to react or respond to the Holy Spirit but more study and growth will bridge that relationship.

Holy Spirit, please continue to fill me.

On This Journey

JULY 29

³⁰For we are members of his body.

Ephesians 5:30

In biology, we learn that there are several organs we can't live without: heart, liver, kidney, lungs, and brain.

The heart pumps blood to all of the body keeping it alive and functioning and with oxygen.

The liver and kidney are involved in cleaning and they cannot be subject to large and continuous amounts of carbonated or alcoholic beverages.

The lungs take care of our oxygen intake and uses that oxygen to fuel the brain.

The brain is source of our thoughts and learning and storage of knowledge and memories.

What piece of the body will you be? The life-giving part, the life-sustaining part or the negligible part?

The parts we could live without: appendix, digits, eyes, hair, limbs, and breasts. Do we want to? No. Life would be different without these parts of your body.

To Christ, we are all equally important. Our contribution to the body is important. When we don't think that it is, is probably when it matters most. We cannot take a break from our role in the body – not even for a nanosecond. Just as we rest for that split second, we could miss our opportunity to witness the growth of the seed that someone else planted and yet someone else still watered. And when it was time to feed it, the seed of someone, we were out on break. We stopped working in our role.

We are members of His body; important to accomplish His goals. Where would we be if some member of His body had been resting when it was our turn to be planted, watered, fed or some other stage of our growth? Where would we be?

And we are important to the body and I am grateful.

JULY 30

[1]Children, obey your parents in the Lord, for this is right.

Ephesians 6:1

Everyone is someone's child, so this applies to everyone. No exceptions.

Obedience is a command from God. We are to obey God, Jesus Christ and the Holy Spirit. We are to obey our leaders and authorities who are given charge over us which includes our pastors, teachers, other school administrators, government officials and others in authority.

You are to obey you parents because you are a gift to them. Our obedience makes their life easier and more rewarding. We should not be a burden due to disobedience which is a lack of respect for the role of a parent.

The role of the parent is to train us up in the way we should go so that we will not stray. In this context, "stray" means to not deviate from God's instruction. Also, the parent provides for the needs of the child because of Christ's blessings and provisions, which is because of the child.

The parents is ultimately responsible for the outcome of the child. The parent is held accountable for the child's knowledge of God; growth and maturity and overall outcome. Our success and failures are attributed to the efforts of our parents. We are held accountable for what we do with what we are given. We have to do our best with what we have rather than blame them for what we perceive we lack, financial or otherwise.

The Golden Rule should be given some critical scrutiny at this time. Behave as you want your child to behave. Remember how blessed you are to have parents. Some children would love to have a parent but they don't. But those of us who have parents often neglect that blessing. Those of us with both parents need to really remind ourselves of our blessings.

Disobedience comes at a cost. Do we really want to pay that price? Obedience is a minimal requirement but it seems so hard to conform. Obedience to our parents translates into obeying God.

Consider the trust God has given your parents to raise and groom you as enough trust for you to obey them. Challenge them with respect and in love.

Lord, remind me to be an obedient child.

JULY 31

[2]"Honor your father and mother" – which is the first commandment with a promise – [3]"that it may go well with you and that you may enjoy long life on the earth."

Ephesians 6:2-3

God doesn't have to promise us anything but in this commandment He does. Why? Well my answer is the amount of importance He places on the commandment. There are other commandments, which are equally as important, if not more important, but they are not attached to a promise, which God will keep.

God promises that it may go well with you. So if I honor my mother (my father disappeared years ago, my stepfather passed away a few years ago), then things will go well for me and my life. For me, that translates into success as a parent and God gives me the desires of my heart and meet my needs for daily bread.

So if I honor my mother, then I will enjoy a long life on the earth. I will have a pleasant and long earthly life. Maybe even with all the things I need and want and ask for. And with my children.

Birth and children are miracles, which only God can perform. We owe them honor just for merely being selected to be a parent. Even though it comes with a promise, we need to honor our parents for no other reason than they were given custody over our lives. Some people are never blessed with children – not natural nor adopted. Children are a gift, miracle and blessing.

What happens when you have a gift that you really don't care for or it breaks or it doesn't perform as you hoped it would? Naturally, you start to scrutinize the gift. You start to wish that the gift would start to act as a gift, with all the joys and rewards which gifts brings. Act like a gift. Or better yet the miracles we are.

Lord, thank You for giving me parents to honor.

AUGUST 1

⁴Fathers, do not exasperate your children; instead, bring them up in the training and instruction of the Lord.

Ephesians 6:4

Mothers are held to the standard of not provoking the child. So 'fathers' can be exchanged with mothers or substituted for parents.

The parent/child relationship is special and requires mutual respect.

Parents are more apt to treat and to view you as a gift and miracle and blessing if you behave as one.

We will cover how to act as a gift and how to avoid being provoked and provokable. Also, we will cover how to receive the training and instruction God has planned for each of us.

Being a gift is half knowing what a gift is and the other half is to understand the role of a gift. Doing those "gift-like" things leads to avoiding provocation. A gift is a blessing, mostly bringing joy, increasing maturity of the recipient and increasing the responsibility of the recipient because the recipient has exhibited they are worthy of such an increase. So as your parent's gift, you have to realize that they are trusted with you. You have to trust them with you. You act as a gift when you recognize God is responsible for your placement and the future He has in store for you. You act as a gift when you receive the discipline and the instruction they are charged to give. Finally, you act as a gift as you thank God for them and the plans God has for your life, which starts with them as your parents and guides. You honor God through these behaviors.

If you are in your role as a gift, then you can't be provoked or exasperated. This sounds simple and it is. You have a ton of rebuttals about what they do, etc. But remember what's important – we each answer for our own actions individually. God sees what you each do – not only what one party does. As a gift, you have the favor of God, but if you are outside of your role, then you can be provoked. Once someone knows they can provoke you, they provoke you at will. They then control you and your behavior. Not 'gift-like' behavior.

Your parents have knowledge to give you. Your reception of that information is critical to the success of your future, which God divinely orchestrates. Your genuine and respectful reception of their guidance makes you a true gift, unprovokable, protected by God, and just as your parents were rewarded.

Last note: how long do you pay attention to a 'gift' which does not operate in its role? Not long. Act as a gift. Take the instruction and leadership – it is designed for you. When you are provoked, turn to God for favor.

Lord, remind me to act gift-like at all times.

On This Journey

AUGUST 2

¹¹Put on the full armor of God so that you can take your stand against the devil's schemes.

Ephesians 6:11

When it's hot, you wear shorts and sunscreen. When it's cold, you bundle up in a coat, gloves, scarves, hats, earmuffs and anything else to help you ward off the cold.

What if I told you that God has an armor where by wearing it, you can fight off your enemy at any time and in any weather? It exists – such an armor, a package, exists. You never have to take it off. It never has to be cleaned.

The armor of God is a protective covering, which enables us to stand against the devil and his schemes. You owe it to yourself to put on God's armor fully. Often times, we put on part of the armor, like the breastplate or the helmet but we need all the pieces at the same time. The armor makes us more confident about daily living. It also assures we know we are equipped to stand against the enemy whether you recognize the enemy immediately or not.

When you live on Earth, you put on the full armor of God. It's as simple as that. Six elements make up this armor. They each work best with all the others, but can be effective alone as you mature to wear them all.

What the armor protects you from: false teachings, false prophets and teachers, contradictory teaching, and whatever attempts to draw you away for God.

The armor of God empowers you to embrace your love for God knowing that God will make sure that you have each item you need. A saying that you may have heard before is "better to have it and not need it than to need it and not have it."

I would rather have the armor than wish there was some armor to wear. God has provided protection for us. It is up to us to take responsibility for making sure we share in our part of this protection. In order to do this we have to study to know how we are accountable to have the promised protection.

We need this armor to stand against the devil's schemes.

God, thank You for protection against the devil's schemes.

Daily Devotional for Young People

AUGUST 3

¹³Therefore put on the full armor of God, so that when the day of evil comes, you may be able to stand your ground, and after you have done everything, to stand.

Ephesians 6:13

'Why does the full armor of God allow me to stand? Stand on what? Stand against whom or what? Stand for whom or what? What is the full armor of God?'

All the questions are questions we would ask when we read this scripture. And for good reason. We need to know what we can expect and what we are expected to do, especially in tough times. Not necessarily in order, we will answer each of those questions.

The full armor of God is the belt of truth, the breastplate of righteousness, feet fitted with readiness, the shield of faith, the helmet of salvation and the sword of the Spirit. All of these implements ensure the full armor, the full protection of God. These tools work best collectively. The enemy specializes in locating a weakness in the armor and working on that weakness until its penetrated or until its protection is reinforced. You can stand with the armor rather than without because of all of the tools – the equipment. His tools equip us to stand our ground when the enemy comes and stand confidently, rather than timidly or with uncertainty which indicates weakness. Standing for Christ at our most vulnerable times increases our strength.

His promises and protection come through this armor. The armor has more than ample strength for us to stand and be prepared for whatever comes our way.

We're standing on God's promises against the enemy because of our acceptance of Christ. Even though it's simply stated, it's fully true and completely awesome. We stand for and represent Christ. We are His disciples.

Thank You, Father, for equipping me to stand my ground.

AUGUST 4

¹⁴Stand firm then, with the belt of truth buckled around your waist, with the breastplate of righteousness in place, ¹⁵and with your feet fitted with the readiness that comes from the gospel of peace. ¹⁶In addition to all this, take up the shield of faith, with which you can extinguish all the flaming arrows of the evil one. ¹⁷Take the helmet of salvation and the sword of the Spirit, which is the word of God.

Ephesians 6:14-17

This is one awesome armor. In the times when armies were wearing armor for protection from the enemy, they were uncomfortable and they were not 100% protective proof, but it's the best they had. In this case, the full armor of God is 100% protective and active and without flaw.

The belt of truth involves you knowing the truth, acting in truth and believing the truth.

The breastplate of righteousness creates a mentality of just behavior and falls closely in line with the truth. Ready feet based on the gospel of peace are essential. It comes from being able to recognize God's peace and how to maintain that peace. When God speaks, we must move quickly in response. If we are not ready then we will miss something.

The shield of faith is your protection against false teachings, doubt, and disbelief. We can extinguish flaming arrows of the evil one, which translates into a well-informed fight against the devil where all that is required is your faith in God and His word. Just our strong faith alone scares the enemy. Your faith is your weapon, so your success against the enemy is based on your proficient use of your weapon.

The helmet of salvation is a one-time confession of your belief in Jesus and the agreement which we are sinners, is never taken away, lost or given back. Salvation is a gift by grace.

Last but not least, the sword of the Spirit, which is the word of God, pulls the armor together and provides the guidance and direction needed for us. This is your physical weapon when used properly (daily and deeply) has been the downfall of the enemy without fail.

When we are completely equipped with all of our armor in place, we then defeat the enemy in a timely fashion with confidence and assurance of the outcome, with the full approval and support of God.

Lord, with all this equipment surely I cannot fail nor falter.

AUGUST 5

¹⁸And pray in the Spirit on all occasions with all kinds of prayers and requests. With this in mind, be alert and always keep on praying for all the saints.

Ephesians 6:18

This is an excellent opportunity to define several terms and offer explanations. Often as Christians, we create a box of confinement, constraints and limitations and put God in it. Without His consent I might add. So we'll take this opportunity to "unbox" God and release our minds to His freedom.

Prayer is best described as ACTS. Adoration. Confession. Thanksgiving. Supplication. These are components of prayer which can be used together or independently.

All occasions: for every reason, each season, anytime, anyplace. We don't need a special reason to talk to God.

All requests: no matter what it is. Nothing is too small to share or request from God. We only burden God when we don't talk to Him. We need to tell Him what's on our heart and minds so He can truly bless us.

Alert: look. It's the first word most of us read. LOOK! Pay attention to your surroundings. Know what you are amidst.

Saints: those are dedicated Christians whose faith is secure and whose focus is steady and whose beliefs are firm. It is us. Saints are not created overnight. We as believers are also saints. So pray for one another.

The basis for our Christian growth is prayer and reading. God will answer us and grow us up. God will help us remove that box we've placed Him in. Eventually we will get beyond our mental limitations and allow His abundance to govern our thoughts and behaviors.

Pray.

Lord, I cherish my prayer time with You.

On This Journey

AUGUST 6

¹⁹Pray also for me, that whenever I open my mouth, words may be given me so that I will fearlessly make known the mystery of the gospel.

Ephesians 6:19

"Teach me how to love and adore You Master,
With my whole heart I will bless You Precious Lord.
There's no burden You can't see me through."

Paul speaks here of teaching and preaching and evangelizing the gospel. For us, it's simpler. For me, it means that my daily words and my daily actions reflect Christ and the gospel. My actions, behavior, and attitude will reveal the mystery of the gospel. We cannot wait for an opportunity better than daily to show others who Christ is in our lives.

To attempt to live each day according to His will and His example requires prayer. PRAYER. Nothing but prayer will help you overcome your obstacles.

Take a moment to think of what you do that disappoints God. Let's use disobedience of your parents as an example. A great prayer for that obstacle (you would agree that disobedience grieves God, wouldn't you?) would be: Dear Lord, help me overcome this rebellious spirit which interferes with my ability to obey my parent(s) and consequently, You. Lord, I don't want to be disobedient and disrespectful. I really want to be in Your will. Please help me, Father. In Your Son Jesus' name I pray. Amen.

Your sincerity speaks volumes to God. He will honor our sincere petitions and do just what we ask of Him. He does not want us out of His will, so He is prepared to help us be in His will if only we ask and are honest about being better. This submission to Him reveals the mystery of the gospel to our audience (our peers, our enemies, and complete strangers) through our actions.

Pray over your situation, whatever it is – God has seen it. He knows already but He will forgive you and fix it.

Thank You, God for the power and privilege of prayer.

AUGUST 7

[24]whatever I need. Paul addresses God and requests grace for all who love the Lord Jesus Christ with an undying love.

Ephesians 6:24

An undying love, a love we cannot extinguish no matter what, a love which nurtures and overwhelms you when you consider that you cannot love Him more than He loves you. This love we should have for Christ is exhibited through our obedience and our attentiveness to Christ. By attentiveness, I mean study the word, spending time in prayer, and sharing the word of God.

I thought I would take a moment to share with you why I love Christ and how I love Christ.

I love Christ because He loved me first. He created me in His image, which, means I am able to forgive and love unconditionally, to avoid sin, to live a life which exemplifies Christ and His example. I can also study His word so I can know how I can continue to be in His image. I love Him because He sent His only Son to save me and my ungrateful and sinful soul through His death and resurrection. I love Him because He has plans for me; He creates in me a passion for achievement. He inspires me to yearn for what He has for me.

Let's move to how I love Him because why I love could take several more days. I love Him by serving Him. I love Him by serving Him and by serving others. I study His word. I listen for His voice. I obey Him even when I disobey Him, I obey Him by asking for forgiveness for that sin, then I forgive myself. I forgive others because He forgives me – that's loving Him. I love Him through the stormy times as well as through the sunshine because He created them both. I love Him more when I know more by studying His word. I pray to Him about my thanksgiving and concerns. After I pray, I move out of His way to provide Him room to do His will.

Grace is His everything wrapped in your favorite wrappings and color just for you because of your love for Him. We have to love Him as unconditionally as He loves us. Of course, His love far outweighs ours but we need to try in our every effort to exhibit our undying love for Him.

Lord, sustain my love for You to an unconditional and undying level at all times and in all seasons.

AUGUST 8

[27]Whatever happens, conduct yourselves in a manner worthy of the gospel of Christ. Then, whether I come and see you or hear about you in my absence, I will know that you stand firm in one spirit, contending as one man for the faith of the gospel.

Philippians 1:27

Okay, I must admit that this is not always easy. 'Whatever happens' refers to everything that happens, including the good as well as the bad. Our response to the bad is to be worthy of the gospel of Christ. I realize that case doesn't always exist. We, as humans, are more likely to respond based on how we feel about our circumstances or situations.

Redirecting our energies and attitude in a positive manner proves more beneficial. The statement 'you may be the only Jesus that some non-believer may see' is most true when we choose to conduct ourselves in a manner worthy of the gospel of Christ or in a manner unworthy. It never fails that when we misrepresent our Christianity, we find ourselves wishing we had behaved better. Someone witnessed our behavior and now have a different impression of us, and consequentially Christ.

Our daily living and behavior impacts others more than we know, especially people who we are not aware are watching. How will we ever be able to explain to someone that that was a slip of the tongue or a mistake or an isolated event. That stranger only knows he saw us do something that was questionable, or worse, wrong. We cannot correct that, so at all times we have to conduct ourselves in a manner worthy of the gospel of Christ.

My mother taught me that if we behave as if Jesus was present, our actions would be impeccable. She reminded me that He is present within me and He is watching.

Savior, regulate my conduct so that it is worthy of the gospel of Christ.

AUGUST 9

²⁸Without being frightened in any way by those who oppose you. This is a sign to them that they will be destroyed, but that you will be saved – and that by God.

Philippians 1:28

In order to completely understand this scripture, you may want to read verse 27. In essence, verse 27 addresses conduct and taking a stand for Christian conduct.

Here we are encouraged to take that stand without being afraid of the reactions of others or what they may do. God wants us to stand firm on our Christian teachings and upbringing.

We often trade in our stand for God for popularity among our peers. Similar to Peter, we never believe we will deny Christ but we have. Our ability to mature and grow in Christ hinges on our willingness and our strength to stay true to God rather than to stand on the instability of ourselves and our peers. Your truest peers are those whom you don't have to prove anything to and they are equipped to hold you accountable to God's standards rather than the popularity contest we really have consented to enter.

Once I redefined my standards for real friendship, my real friends showed up. My best friend is my prayer partner. We pray over each other's lives with all of our concerns and triumphs and desires. We don't care about the material belongings. We certainly don't hold each other accountable to standards set by society.

We as Christians have to upgrade our standards to move closer to Christ's standards.

There will always be those who oppose us. This is because we are standing for Christ. This is when you know you are doing the right things when others oppose you.

Master, remind me that when I can take a stand for You that is the most popular response.

On This Journey

AUGUST 10

⁹Therefore God exalted him to the highest place and gave him the name that is above every name, ¹⁰that at the name of Jesus every knee should bow, in heaven and on earth and under the earth, ¹¹and every tongue confess that Jesus Christ is Lord, to the glory of God the Father.

Philippians 2:9-11

Jesus is awesome. He was born a human to a wonderful couple who were blessed and called by God to perform a wonderful feat: birth and parent Jesus. Mary and Joseph couldn't ask for a bigger calling on their lives. Jesus lived 33 years without one sin. I want to go without sin for 33 hours or 33 days. Don't you? Again, Jesus has accomplished what no one else ever will: be the one and only son of God, save the whole world from death because of our sins, act as the intercessor of all believers such that God will answer our prayers, and live an entire life without one sin.

Being that awesome, one might wonder would Jesus ever get haughty? Well no, He wouldn't. I know this because He remained meek and humble through all of His accomplishments and tasks. Two examples stand out. The first one was the water to wine miracle of His humbleness where He in fact told Mary that it was not time to perform miracles. The second one was the baptismal of Jesus by John at the Jordan, where John wondered why he was able to baptize Jesus.

He is to be exalted. We will bow on our knees and confess that Jesus is Lord. Whether you did know or not, eventually we all will bow and confess that Jesus is Lord.

I have an awful time imagining and understanding what anyone could worship over worshipping Jesus. Based on what He has done and continues to do, that's enough to worship Him and His love.

Lord, thank You for Your Son, the One above us all.

AUGUST 11

¹⁴Do everything without complaining or arguing.

Philippians 2:14

Why do we complain? I'm sure why we complain; complaining doesn't change anything. Either you do it or you don't. Why complain? It doesn't get easier.

Mostly, we complain about school and work. School is designed for you – not for the teacher. I remember once I complained about one of my teachers to my mother. My mother reminded me that I was the one in need of a diploma and a degree. The teacher already apparently earned both already. She wondered why I would not willingly accept the teacher's instructions. I had no response for anything she said and soon realized that she was right. I also realized that I had only short changed myself by not fully investing in my studies and tapping the instructors as the source they were designed. When I realized those facts, I had a much easier time being successful. I had never considered how much time it required preparing to teach class if it is quality education, but time outside the classroom is required for a successful classroom.

Arguing is simply a waste of time but for no other reason than a waste of time. What do we gain by arguing? Again, my wise mother advised me to never argue with a fool because a stranger won't know the difference. I didn't immediately understand, but as I matured I understood better.

That wise word means that if you don't engage in arguments, you are the wise one. Just imagine two people arguing. As a bystander, you don't know the facts or circumstances, all you think is "why are they arguing?" What could be so serious that they needed to argue? That thought process usually ends with you thinking that they used poor judgment by arguing at that time.

Neither complaining nor arguing propels us forward, so why invest the time or energy?

Lastly, arguing is usually the result of wanting to correct someone so that they are no longer wrong. One day a thought crossed my mind and it gets me away from arguing: why can't they just be wrong? Let them be wrong. It's okay for them to be wrong. They've survived this long being wrong, so why stop them now, especially if it involves an argument.

Father, remind me not to complain or argue.

AUGUST 12

⁶Do not be anxious about anything, but in everything, by prayer and petition, with thanksgiving, present your requests to God.

Philippians 4:6

This sounds hard because it is, however, it is essential to do. I asked God to be selected as a deacon. Then I got a call for the selection process to start. They gave me some information that they would be selecting within a week or two. When I didn't hear anything, I got anxious. Then I remembered this scripture. At the very moment the scripture came to my remembrance. I immediately asked for forgiveness for my anxiety. I had to remember that if God has designed that position for me, then it will happen. Likewise, if I'm not prepared or it's not best for me then I won't be selected. God is in control, so why should I be anxious if I say that I am faithful and believe that God will provide? I put it back in God's hands and quit being concerned about it.

Be anxious about nothing! Nothing means nothing! Don't be anxious about your grades, your parents, your success, your family's health or anything. Instead, submit your desires and concerns to God in prayer and petition, with thanksgiving. Give your concerns over to God and leave them with Him. He is in charge and since we don't control anything, why are we anxious? Because we feel that if we spend time on it, we will receive our desired results.

We have to realize that we cannot change the plans of God no matter how we operate outside the parameters of God's plan.

As a fact of human health, anxiety degrades your health. Anxiety can cause ulcers, high blood pressure, anxiety attacks, depression, and other issues. Why risk your health over something God already has answered. It just makes sense. I know it's hard to not be anxious but God promises to listen to your prayers.

Thank You, Lord for accepting my prayers and petitions to You.

AUGUST 13

[7] And the peace of God, which transcends all understanding, will guard your hearts and your minds in Christ Jesus.

Philippians 4:7

The peace of God is phenomenal and overwhelming. It takes some time to experience His peace in full but once you do, you'll never forget it and you'll want to experience it all the time. Typically, we don't experience His peace because we don't understand it, as stated in the scripture, or we are not still enough to experience His peace.

Being still is a feat alone, much less being still for a long period of time – long enough to experience His peace. Time alone is important. More specifically, quiet time alone in the presence of God is paramount. Notice I use the word "experience" versus saying that God has not offered you His peace. I use "experience" because you don't know when God gives you peace or what He guards our hearts from or our minds from. I know there are some definite situations when I experienced His peace. I know He protected my mind and/or heart from danger and harm.

Whether you know when it happens or not, God's peace guards our hearts and minds in Christ Jesus. He does this because He created each of us and He doesn't want any harm to come to us in any format. It grieves Christ for us to be hurt or harmed.

Understanding God's peace is difficult at best. "It transcends all understanding." By definition, transcends means that His peace goes beyond the limits of my understanding. Of course, experience is different from understanding. So experiencing His peace doesn't mean I understand it. Why we need to understand why someone who loves us gives us His peace also transcends my understanding. Do we really need to understand? I don't need to understand. It is because of His love and that's all I need to know because I do know that love influences us to do things for those we love that no one understands.

Thank You for Your peace, Lord.

On This Journey

AUGUST 14

⁸Finally, brothers, whatever is true, whatever is noble, whatever is right, whatever is pure, whatever is lovely, whatever is admirable – if anything is excellent or praiseworthy think about such things.

Philippians 4:8

There is no sin against what is good or thoughts about what is good. We seem to fear what is good and we fear that what is good will end. Often, our pessimism overrides our ability to enjoy what is good, including our blessings.

Also, I wonder why we are more drawn to 'bad' than to what's 'good.' 'Bad' seems so much better and so much more thrilling. 'Good' lacks thrill and excitement but is longer lasting. I made a list of 'good' which keeps me occupied, excited and sin-free.

- Reading
- Writing
- Bike-riding
- Music
- Manicure
- Pedicure
- Hair salon
- Massage
- Golf
- Cooking
- Walking

Among that list surely you could find some things that you will enjoy and find 'good' or you can develop a list of your own.

Get used to 'good' and blessings. Think of the noble and praiseworthy. So a man thinketh, so he is.

Master, there are things which are noble, true, right, pure, lovely, admirable, excellent and praiseworthy. Lord, help me to see them each regularly.

AUGUST 15

¹¹I am not saying this because I am in need, for I have learned to be content whatever the circumstances.

Philippians 4:11

Such a tall order for such a young Christian – I mean me. Contentment accompanies maturity. Contentment is learned and viewed as an asset. The only problem with contentment is the contrast it provides for the independent, driven, highly motivated, and success-thirsty young woman most of my peers and I are. We set our goals and develop desires which we grade our level of life success or accomplishment of achieving. As we achieve those goals, it puts us closer to our "level" of contentment. The only problem is that once we achieve some of list, we add more to the list. We never really complete the list, so we just keep climbing and climbing this proverbial ladder where our success is supposedly found and enjoyed. This never really happens. Instead of enjoying each achievement on its merit, we overlook the total significance of that achievement in order to reach the next item on the list.

Contentment is the ability to enjoy each moment for the blessing it is. Contentment is allowing yourself to not achieve anything in particular for any given period of time and still enjoying life for the value it holds. Contentment knows that life in the proverbial fast lane doesn't have to be fast to live a settled life.

Contentment is achieved, and learned but mostly appreciated for its value and worth. Contentment is maturity. I know that I've achieved maturity and contentment when I don't have to achieve anything and the success I once sought already existed because success isn't based on achievements.

Lord, mature me to contentment.

On This Journey

AUGUST 16

¹³I can do everything through him who gives me strength.

Philippians 4:13

God is our power source. He powers us to do all things. His power never runs out. We lose sight of the depth and breadth of His strength and power. Everything means everything. All means all. He gives me strength to do everything.

I can do everything includes:

> making good grades in school
> talking to my parents
> telling the truth regardless of the consequences
> only taking what belongs to me
> be true to myself
> keeping God's commandments
> obey my parents and teachers
> praying to God
> attending church regularly
> intercede for others as God calls me
> maintain activity in a ministry at church
> respect those persons older than myself
> respect my parents
> accomplish the goals I desire
> obeying God
> abstaining from sex
> avoiding sin at all cost
> reading and studying God's word
> dealing with the death of a loved one

Everything you can imagine, you can do through Christ because of His strength. Sometimes my prayer partner and I laugh at one another because one of us will remind the other that they must not know the magnitude of the God I serve. At which point, we laugh because God can do all, which always exceeds our imaginations and certainly our expectations.

Don't put God in a box by saying what can't be done. Unlike humans, when God says everything, all or always, He really means everything, all and always.

God, with You, nothing is impossible.

AUGUST 17

¹⁴Yet it was good of you to share in my troubles.

Philippians 4:14

Sharing our troubles is against all societal teachings. We are taught to keep our woes to ourselves. Does this mean that we are not supposed to have difficulties? No, really it means, you stop others from learning from our errors. Is that good for the growth of the Christian family? No, it's not.

Our troubles come to provide us strength. "What doesn't kill you, strengthens you." Have you ever heard that phrase? Trouble is designed to drive you closer to God. After this trouble reaches resolution, then the results becomes your testimony. A testimony, which once shared, provides encouragement to others.

My husband was involved in a destructive relationship when we met. Through his storm, he grew. When it was all over and we moved our friendship to marriage, he shares his testimony with others who have had his similar circumstances. Those individuals have experienced better relationships because of his willingness to share his 'troubles.'

I share often the type of relationships I endured before I met my soulmate, including the relationships where sin was present in the form of premarital sex. I don't know how much longer I would've had to wait on my husband had I not submitted to the will of God by not having premarital sex.

Both testimonies move people to understand their own actions and use what happened to us to understand a fraction of what God does.

Various people shared in our troubles, triumphs and testimonies. So for every one that we experience, there is a small group of people who support us through each of our troubles, triumphs and testimonies.

Lord, thank You those in my circle who are compassionate when I share my troubles.

On This Journey

AUGUST 18

¹⁶For by him all things were created: things in heaven and on earth, visible and invisible, whether thrones or powers or rulers or authorities; all things were created by him and for him.

Colossians 1:16

Imagine a birthday party where you invited all the guests, created all the invitations, all the plates, napkins, cups, all the food, all the decorations and party favors. All the guests come to see you. They are attentive to you and your desires and your wishes and commands. This is how we should respect God. He created us to do His will, follow His word and obey His commands. Why shouldn't He expect us to do these things? Better yet why don't we do it? After all, He created us and all of the gadgets, which distract us from Him.

What would happen if He revoked all of us and our gadgets? Although we don't like it, He would be well within His rights if He did. How can few ocus on the One who created us? I made the following list, but you feel free to add to this list.

- Spend 2 hours and 24 minutes with Him daily
- Pray daily
- Study His word daily
- Meditate on His message daily
- Share Him with others
- Attend church and bible study regularly
- Use your spiritual gifts for the growth of the church
- Follow His commandments

Just these eight things will enhance your relationship with Christ. He seeks an intimate relationship with each of us, all we need to do is submit and participate. The reward for the intimacy is greater than what appears to be the sacrifice.

Lord, remind me when I forget why You created me.

AUGUST 19

²Set your minds on things above, not on earthly things.

Colossians 3:2

This is temporary. What is this? Everything. Earthly life is temporary. Stuff is temporary. Consider that cars can and will wreck. Money is spent. Houses can burn. Businesses can fail. Our loved ones pass away. So will we. All of these things are earthly. Earthly is temporary and the Earth is made of dust.

Above is heavenly and God-focused. Above is permanent. Above is the destination. Above is the focus. Our minds set on things above means focusing on God first, the focusing on what it means to please and communicate with God. It also entails knowing what it takes to reach above. The process to the above destination involves, rather requires intimacy with God.

It takes work to set our minds on things above. I knew someone once that said in 20 years, will it matter. I modified that to say in 20 minutes will this matter. In most cases, it won't. Is this really worth getting upset or excited about? What is this going to cost me? And of course, in 20 minutes, who will care? These are the earthly things that we usually focus on but shouldn't. Most importantly, when we focus on earthly and temporary things, we can't focus on those above. Our biggest life errors happen during this time. Our decision making abilities become skewed because we start basing our decisions on these earthly things. When these things fail us, instead of realizing why – they are earthly and temporary – we are devastated. We can't believe 'that' was such a disaster. But when we refocus and dismiss the earthly, we can allow the Lord to speak to us and make decisions based on what He desires. Usually tunnel vision would cause problems, but when the tunnel is focused on the above things, you don't have to worry about the surrounding factors.

Lord, I want to keep my focus on You.

On This Journey

AUGUST 20

⁵Put to death, therefore, whatever belongs to your earthly nature: sexual immorality, impurity, lust, evil desires and greed, which is idolatry.

Colossians 3:5

We won't need a detailed explanation of each of these things, or do we?

Sexual immorality: simply said; any sexual activity outside of your marriage is immorality. No sex until married and only to whom you are married.

Impurity: lies, deceit, less than honorable intentions, sins, to name a few, are included in this category. Impurity is not exact and hard to achieve consistently but needs consistent effort.

Lust: If your desire overcomes you, then you have lusted. Your heart's intentions define lust. Avoid lust at whatever expense. Lust is a powerful distraction from God and His will. We are to lust after no one and nothing.

Evil desires: This includes anything you desire to do against someone that is unjust or unrighteous. Also, evil desires encompass the desire to sin in various ways.

Greed: Hoarding and storing and having too much are all considered greedy. Greed means not sharing, too. Not giving to those who need when you have it and have enough to share is truly selfish and greedy.

Those five activities are idolatry and part of our human nature, all of which we need to put to death. We cannot do this alone. My prayer partner prays that our flesh be on the decrease and the Holy Spirit be on the increase. This prayer makes me immediately reflect on times when my flesh has taken over a situation and led me away from God's will.

We have to commit to God that it is permissible for Him to override our flesh. Then we have to obey His will, which is to avoid idolatry.

Master, I need help with the death of my earthly nature.

AUGUST 21

¹⁰And have put on the new self, which is being renewed in knowledge in the image of its Creator.
Colossians 3:10

The new self is exciting! The new me yearns for the Lord. It thirsts for His love and His attentiveness. His image is super imposed on the new me, so that I can be like my Creator.

The new me, the new self is being renewed in knowledge in the image of my Creator. When He renews me, I am full until past overflowing.

Why does He create a new me, a new self? He created the first me which was perfect and flawless then I sinned, He forgave me, then He created a new self which is closer to Him, renewed in knowledge of Him. All because He loves me and cares for me. He wants me to know of Him and His wonder and His strength and to have faith in His desire and ability to save me, even from myself.

The new self is great because it reminds me that He often thinks of ways He can improve our relationship, even though that's my responsibility. His loving kindness overwhelms me. He avails Himself to me and I wish that I was always able to detect when He needs my immediate attention.

The best way to thank Him for the new self is to share the new self with others. I wonder when He does this – what was I doing? Did I know immediately that my knowledge had increased? Did I respond like He wanted me to? Another way to thank Him is for me to acknowledge the new knowledge, act on this knowledge, sharing it with others and being responsible for that knowledge through my actions. In other words, I must act like I know that I have a new self and work harder on my intimacy with Him.

Thank You for my new self and my increased knowledge.

AUGUST 22

¹²Therefore, as God's chosen people, holy and dearly loved, clothed yourselves with compassion, kindness, humility, gentleness and patience.

Colossians 3:12

Paul authors Colossians and he offers substantial advice and information and wisdom. This passage speaks volumes about God and us. First, God chose us. He then made us His chosen people. Such a responsibility, but a gift indeed.

Secondly, we are to be dressed in compassion, kindness, humility, gentleness and patience. We are holy and dearly loved, according to His word, which He continues to prove.

Humility is based on humbleness and meekness. Humility opposes pride and haughtiness and boastful behavior. Of the five characteristics, I wanted to address this because it is hard to come by. Humility is difficult to understand and then hard to adopt as behavior. But it is most important to master. Before pride masters us.

These five characteristics are just basics for living a Christian lifestyle. Having them in our hearts should not be difficult, but sometimes are. For me, humility was the hardest one to possess. I thought I had reason to be proud, when I really don't. As a matter of fact, I thought because I was a Christian that I was allowed an abundance of pride when in reality I'm allowed exactly the opposite – no pride, only humility and the other four characteristics. Clothing ourselves in those five is the best we have to offer for the huge work in which we are engaged. Most importantly, whose we are.

Thank You for choosing me.

AUGUST 23

¹³Bear with each other and forgive whatever grievances you may have against one another. Forgive as the Lord forgave you.

Colossians 3:13

Forgiving others is a huge issue for some people. Their tolerance and patience for others and their mistakes or shortcomings come at a great expense to both parties involved. 'Bear' is synonymous with patience. Patience is a virtue. Virtues and acting with virtuous values are Christ-like. Think of who shortens your patience with them for whatever reason. Why do they shorten your patience? Why do you find it difficult to 'bear' with them? Now, consider someone who extends your patience or someone who finds favor with you. Why do they find favor with you? Why are you patient with them?

Your answers will vary but as we mature the variance changes significantly. Forgiveness will also come hard to that person for whom you have no patience. Why do we feel justified in holding a grudge rather than forgiving? The Golden Rule holds significance here: "Do unto others as you would God do unto you." Does Onedia's version of the Golden Rule change how you forgive, love, etc., to others? It will. Maturity in Christ will bridge that gap for you when you don't think you can. You will forgive someone for a trespass that you thought unconquerable. You said you never would but you do. Almost instantaneously you forgive that action and you embrace that person as if it never happened.

The phrase 'God hates the sin, not the sinner' amplifies one difference between Jesus and us which separates us by the realms in which we both reside. In other words, that is why we live on Earth and His home is in heaven. When we want to hold a grudge, we do. We feel that forgiveness is selective and optional. But most paramount, we disengage from the person who we can't forgive versus simply holding them accountable for their actions then forgiving that action. It is how Christ treats us and quite fairly I might add.

Father, allow us to better bear and forgive one another.

On This Journey

AUGUST 24

[14]And over all these virtues put on love, which binds them all together in perfect unity.

Colossians 3:14

Love is healthy for the soul. Love provides the nourishment, which leads to growth of all souls. Love provides the foundation for all things, which flourish. Love is an action, rather than words. Christ defines love as obedience. Christ exhibits love by sacrifice.

Love heals. Love is not afraid, yet bold. Love disciplines. Love hopes. Love is painless. Love is important. Love breeds life and love creates more love. Love is best without conditions or strings or attachments. 1 Corinthians 13 best explains. God best defines love. Christ best exhibits love.

But how can we be exhibitors of the love virtue? Do we know whom we love? Why we love them? How much or to what degree do we love? Do we ever stop loving anyone? What's the difference between loving people and things? Those answers can be found in God's word. I do however want to point out that God doesn't stop loving us. Love is active rather than passive.

Abraham and Isaac provide the perfect example of love and its sacrifice and its rewards. God told Abraham to take his son, Isaac, to a mountain and present him as a sacrifice. Abraham loved God and loved his son. He, his son, a servant and a donkey go to the mountain. Abraham and Isaac go to the top of the mountain. As they ascend, Isaac asks what are we sacrificing. Abraham responded that the Lord will provide. They continued on their way. When they arrived, Abraham started to prepare to sacrifice his son, Isaac. To add to the importance if this story, I want to remind us that Isaac was born to his barren mother after a family fiasco when Abraham and Sarah's maidservant had a child together. Sarah and Abraham's marriage suffered. Now that you have a little background, we'll resume. Abraham had drawn the knife to sacrifice Isaac when he heard God call him. He diverted Abraham to the bush; there was a ram. God gave him a ram to replace his son.

Abraham loved the Lord more. Through his actions and willingness to sacrifice his own gift, Isaac, to do as God has asked, he demonstrated to God there is no greater love. God rewarded him because of his willingness.

Love is an action. Remind me, Lord to act in love.

AUGUST 25

[15]Let the peace of Christ rule in your hearts, since as members of one body you were called to peace. And be thankful.

Colossians 3:15

Peace seems hard to understand for some Christians, so naturally it's hard to experience and achieve for those same people.

The peace of Christ is awesome and when that peace rules your heart situations change. You handle them differently and you view the situation differently. Peace is often difficult to establish or recognize, however, it is sought and desired.

The most important part to understand about peace is the reward peace offers. Peace is a recognition of God's love for us and our love for others. Our peaceful response to 'issues' and 'situations' signifies to others, Christians and non-Christians alike, that we are true Christians who follow Christ's example and leadership. Our peaceful response could be exactly what someone else needs to see to follow Christ.

Peace is important to our growth as Christians. My mother tells me that if I am not quiet, then I cannot hear God speak. Similarly, if I am not peaceful, then I cannot experience His presence.

'Be thankful' is the second hardest thing to remember. Thankfulness is often missed because we take our blessings for granted. One of my prayer warriors asked his class to thank God for things they would have for tomorrow. As he recounted their responses which included cars, homes, and cash, he was most saddened because when he thanked God for breath of life, health and strength they seemed surprised. He explained that without those, there was really no need for the material things. 'Be thankful' – thank God and your parents for the daily blessings, which we often take for granted and wouldn't notice them until they were removed.

Be thankful:

God	Parents
Health	Food
Life	Shelter
Strength	Clothing
Breath	Protection
Parents	Education
Family	Transportation

Lord, let me be peaceful and thankful beyond measure.

AUGUST 26

¹⁶Let the word of Christ dwell in you richly as you teach and admonish one another with all wisdom, and as you sing psalms, hymns and spiritual songs with gratitude in your hearts to God.
Colossians 3:16

The word of Christ dwelling in us richly is an attitude and a lifestyle. There is a huge difference between having knowledge of His word and His word dwelling in us richly. It is the difference between what you know and what you do with what you know. Your actions are the best indicators an observer has of your relationship with Christ.

In order to teach and admonish others with wisdom, you have to embrace your deep knowledge of the word of God and be able to use that knowledge to govern yourself as the word is written. Easier said than done. When His word dwells in you richly, your behavior, and actions differ from others who don't know. It is easy to know what to do and harder to do it.

Teaching others is one duty that you have to do carefully. Teachers are held to a higher level of accountability than non-teachers. As a teacher, you need to possess the knowledge that your 'students' need and be able to answer questions that your 'students' may have and seek the resources required to help propel their growth. Admonish each other with all wisdom. Admonish is to chastise, to discipline. This may include criticism of others. All of which requires wisdom because you are not above criticism, admonishment or discipline. Remember the reap-sow rule. Wisdom reminds you to take other's feelings in mind, also, to approach the other person with the attitude and actions of Christ. As I sing songs with gratitude in my heart to God I pray this prayer regularly. I want my being to be full of gratitude – an attitude of thankfulness. A gracious attitude that again exhibits the behavior of Christ.

These are all attainable attributes but requires the focus of our Christianity and of course, full participation of God to accomplish any of it, much less all. I have to keep God at the forefront of my mind and heart every minute. I find the more I desire His intimacy, the harder I have to strive to overcome the obstacles that would like to prevent me from experiencing His intimacy.

Lord, I pray that Your word dwells in me richly daily with wisdom and sing with gratitude. Also, Lord, help me be the light You have called me to be.

AUGUST 27

¹⁷And whatever you do, whether in word or deed, do it in the name of the Lord Jesus, giving thanks to God the Father through him.

Colossians 3:17

Do it all in the name of the Lord Jesus. All means all. All is inclusive of:

Homework (participate honestly, don't cheat, don't lie)
Chores (dishes, cleaning your room, feeding the dog, cutting the grass, watering the plants, vacuuming the carpets, sweeping the floors, cleaning the toilets, etc.)
Obedience to your parents (inclusive of curfew, household rules, etc.)
Working (choosing to work means accepting the responsibility of what working entails which doesn't include your parents and developing a quality work ethic)
Social interaction (curfew, monitoring your activities such as avoiding sex, drugs, alcohol and smoking cigarettes, saying no to peer pressure against doing wrong, such as vandalism, etc.)

Do it all in the name of the Lord Jesus. With this in mind, I wish to pose a few questions.

1) Would you cheat on your test if Jesus was sitting next to you?
2) Would you clean as you were asked? Would you tell the truth if you knew Jesus was looking?
3) Would you make curfew if you knew Jesus was waiting at your door for you?
4) Would you want Jesus to walk up while you were speaking disrespectfully to your parents by questioning them?
5) Do you work as if you were working for Jesus or as if Jesus was watching?
6) Do you want Jesus to walk up while you or you and friends are smoking crack or sniffing cocaine?

These questions seem farfetched or do they? When we accepted Christ, we invited Jesus to dwell within us. We know that He is with us daily and we are also to treat our bodies as the temples they are because Jesus dwells there. We owe Jesus a clean, safe place to reside considering what He does and what He has done and what He has planned for us.

"What would Jesus do" became a catch phrase years ago. My question is: "are we willing to do what Jesus would do all the time?" Secondly, "are we willing to share with others that we are doing what Jesus would do?"

Jesus, thank You for reminding me to do all I do in Your name.

On This Journey

AUGUST 28

[20]Children, obey your parents in everything, for this pleases the Lord.

Colossians 3:20

I only want to make one person happy: God. I can say that boldly and proudly because if I do what pleases God, then He will provide for favor with everyone else and with everything else.

Considering what it takes to please God, other's needs should fall into place easily. If I obey God, then I will obey my parents.

Obeying your parents is a commandment. In my maturity as a child, I discovered a few things. My obedience made my mother's life easier. My parents divorced when I was 6 years old. I was a typical teenager in that I stayed on the phone longer than curfew and I was always on the phone and I had my own phone. I differed because I was an active Christian early in life and wasn't ashamed, I never tried drugs or smoking or drinking and I earned great grades. I didn't learn the power of obedience until later, but when I did I fixed my behavior and my attitude quickly. I learned that my compassion, not pity, for my mother helped her through her storms. My prayers and my Christianity led her to Christ again.

I also discovered that I owed it to her to be obedient. Most importantly, I owed God my obedience to my mother. I thought I could talk on the phone whenever I wanted and do my chores when I felt like it because of my grades.

I owed God because He said so. I agreed to His word and rules when I accepted His salvation. I owed my mother because God said and through her, He provided.

He provided her with me. Children are a gift to their parents and parenting should not be a burden because of our behavior. He provided her with a job. He provided her with a home – one we owned. He provided a relatively safe environment. He provided me with love through her. He provided her with enough motivation to ensure my success. These may seem like life's basics but when you consider that most children don't experience even the basics of life.

One day imagine cominh home and everything you were accustomed to was gone – no lights, no house, no food, no cars, etc? Hard to do. But understand that obedience makes it easier for parents to sacrifice for us to have what we want. When you want the extras, like video games and clothes, what do they give up? Maybe a book for themselves, their own new clothes, a new car, or manicure. But when they ask us to do our chores, do we roll our eyes or smack our lips or talk back? By the way, what do they give up when we leave lights on in rooms we are not in?

Obedience and honor to our parents represents our love for You. I want to love You with my whole heart, please help me, Lord.

AUGUST 29

[21]Fathers, do not embitter your children, or they will become discouraged.

Colossians 3:21

This a very tricky scripture. Not because of what it says, but what it doesn't say. Consider geometry, which is based on if-then statements. Consider that we as children, no matter how grown we are, are obedient to our parents (Colossians 3:20), then our parents should not provoke us. Or should they? There is a delicate balance as a parent between discipline and guidance and provocation and abuse. Use your 18 or 22 or 25 years that your parents offer you to guide you and motivate and influence you to learn – learn from their successes and their mistakes. They possess a certain amount of wisdom that if we use it properly we could avoid our own pitfalls and progress at a much faster rate.

Ask questions about their past that will help you better understand why they react the way they do. I do find that family history is hard to uncover sometimes but at least they know you care. Further, they know that you care about the lesson even if it comes without the actual history. Learn what you can without hurting them. They love us and want nothing more than to see us succeed and sometimes they may live vicariously through us or they may push their own dreams on us. But all of it is out of love. It will be hard to see initially, but the love is real. Let them be parents for as long as possible. It's important. Their success as parents depends on your success and the results of your life. Sometimes it's hard to believe that their life is graded by how you live.

Most often when we "mess up," the first thing people ask is 'where is his mother' – no matter how old. When we succeed, they still ask where the mother is; it's just not as vocal there.

Let's make them proud. Let's bless them with our success so that they may resume the life they started before we were born.

Lord, keep me encouraged.

On This Journey

AUGUST 30

[23] Whatever you do, work at it with all your heart, as working for the Lord, not for man.

Colossians 3:23

"I'd rather a handful of dedicated workers, than a hundred with lukewarm enthusiasm." This quote will vary as you hear it in your lifetime but the bottom line is the same – if it has no heart, it means nothing. Why some people do anything they don't have a passion for is beyond me.

"With my whole heart, I will bless You, Precious Lord." This is part of one of my favorite songs, which also supports the point that you cannot do anything you can be proud of without the participation of your whole heart. 'With all your heart' means indulge yourself fully into what you deem worthy. Totally invest in your beliefs and what drives you.

'Anything worth having is worth working for' is a statement that you will also learn to appreciate. It will come to your remembrance when you want to do something sloppy or half way.

The key to life and a sure indicator of our growth and maturity is deciding what influences our passion and what really matters and doing those things, and doing them well. Developing this passion and work ethic proves valuable for a successful lifestyle. The Lord honors our efforts when we put forth our whole heart. Why should God help you bridge the gap between your desire and your actual ability when you don't really want that – His efforts would be wasted. You don't really want it and you won't really appreciate it.

Work at it with all your heart, whatever you do. Also, consider that someone will be watching you to see how you do what you do. If you weren't concentrating with your whole heart, then what example have you left for them?

Thank You for showing me the depth of my heart.

AUGUST 31

[24b] Since you know that you will receive an inheritance from the Lord as a reward. It is the Lord Christ you are serving.

Colossians 3:24b

We often forget it is the Lord Christ we are serving. We were made to serve the Lord. It is our duty. It is our responsibility. We are designed and created to provide progress for Christ. We are not here to serve ourselves or others unless it serves Christ. How can we serve God and then how can we serve God better?

First, God has given each of us a talent. That talent is for the benefit of God. We are to use this talent to serve the Lord. This talent should reap benefits for God for the growth of the church. This talent glorifies God.

Secondly, we serve Him by serving others. For some, this is considered difficult. His word says that when we serve the least of beings then we've served Him. Service to the poor, the physically and emotionally challenged, the elderly, the sick, the shut in and children serves God. God sends blessings to whom He can send blessings through.

Lastly, in order to fully serve Christ, we have to pick up our cross and follow Him. Put down our earthly wealth, pick up our cross and follow Him.

Donnie McClurkin sings a song entitled "Beyond The Veil", in which he details that what he wishes for is to worship Jesus face to face. God didn't ask me what I wanted for my reward and inheritance but I know what He has is better than what I can imagine or ask for. I do agree with McClurkin; I wish to worship Him face to face. I look forward to my reward and inheritance.

Thank You for my inheritance. Serving You is important to me. I will do it better.

On This Journey

SEPTEMBER 1

²Devote yourselves to prayer, being watchful and thankful.

Colossians 4:2

One of the most important events in your Christian life and growth is your prayer life. Prayer is the gateway to your communication with Christ. The time you spend in prayer is critical for your growth and important for your witness as a Christian.

First, let's establish your time to pray. In the morning when you wake is a great time to thank God for what He has planned for the day. It doesn't take long for you to thank God for a great night's rest and today's blessings. At night, before you rest is a good time to thank Him for His grace and His blessings. You can spend a little extra time listening to His direction. So establishing your regular time with God is easy. You will meet some obstacles while you maintain your prayer time. Pray that God assists you in establishing and maintaining an interference-free prayer time with Him.

Secondly, share with your loved ones your prayer time. Two things happen:

1) you will have fewer interruptions because they will respect your time;
2) they will help you maintain your prayer time by holding you accountable for your prayer time.

Thirdly, submit to spontaneous prayer time. You will be blessed by this time with God. When you feel that you are supposed to be praying, you will experience God in a new way. Our most powerful conversations have occurred when I may simply be driving and start to pray. During the prayer, God moves in my life and on my heart. These prayer times have changed my life.

Lastly, engage your family in prayer. The family changes through prayer. Prayer glues, builds, firms a family and its foundation. It may not be easy initially, but God will also bridge that gap for you. When you finally see the result, don't forget to thank God for His blessings.

God, thank You for our time together.

SEPTEMBER 2

⁵(Be wise in the way you act toward outsiders; make the most of every opportunity). Let your conversation be always full of grace, seasoned with salt, so that you may know how to answer everyone.

Colossians 4:5

Your conversation is a portion of how your reputation is calculated. When your conversation is kind and honest, trusted and complimentary, others seek your conversation, which will include your advice, counsel and confidence. However, you know that you should avoid gossipers at all costs. You also avoid those who reject your ideas and cast a negative light on your desires and dreams. I know I do. As hard as it is to say, sometimes it is those closest to us that are our biggest critics, rather than our greatest fans and supporters. It seems opposite but sometimes it's true.

Your conversation should be warm, welcoming, meek, trustworthy, wonderful and powerful because you have a source from which all of these attributes come. You should encourage others to do what they desire and dream. You'll need that same encouragement one day.

Avoid negative talk and those who are negative. They will cast a negative shadow on your desires and dreams and will discourage you from pursuing what God has for you. Likewise, you don't want to cause anyone to miss their blessing because you were not encouraging.

Some definite rules of any conversation are:

1) think before you speak,
2) listen completely before speaking, and
3) seek to understand what the speaker wants from you before you respond.

Often we respond before we listen completely to what the other person needs for us to do. They may simply need a listening ear, but you started giving advice. They may need you to pray with them but no other feedback was wanted. So take care to inquire how they want you to respond.

Listen completely to what they have to say. Don't anticipate their statements. Try not to interrupt. Listen attentively.

Finally, think before you speak. Further, think of the Biblical solution through scripture rather than the society's solution. Anyone can say what the world would do, so be the Christian and share what Jesus said to do.

Lord, allow the words of my mouth to be full of grace and wisdom.

On This Journey

SEPTEMBER 3

¹¹Make it your ambition to lead a quiet life, to mind your business and to work with your hands, just as we told you.

1 Thessalonians 4:11

Leading a quiet life is the exact opposite of the societal direction we are given. The world says we should be the center of attention; on top of the heap of the pile; have it all; no guts, no glory, and on and on. However, who said that a quiet life didn't possess being all of those things.

Quiet life involves prayer, study, devotion, and focus on God. Remember, we are in the world, not of the world. We define our lives by different standards – ones where we measure our success as to whether or not it pleases God; not whether it excites or disappoints the world. Quiet also lends itself to meekness. "Blessed are the meek, for they shall inherit the Earth."(Matthew 5:5). God favors the meek in this manor because meekness lacks boastfulness, pride and encourages the quiet lifestyle.

My grandmother is meek and I have always prayed to be likewise. It takes time, because usually it's more about maturity in the word of God. Also, your quietness encourages people to choose you rather than having to volunteer or otherwise. This is significant about the quiet life. People will seek to understand you and your source of strength. All to glorify God.

Mind your own business is easier said than accomplished. In order to be effective, we need to reserve our comments until asked. Sometimes we will never be asked. As a young person, I thought it was best to be the picture of knowledge and let everyone know. As I grew older and observed this meek grandmother, I learned that everything I knew didn't need to be disclosed, whether at that time or at all.

Just as we do, others also have a right to their privacy. We need to respect that privacy. This privacy extends to and includes avoiding gossip, hear-say, and rumors, which all obviously not fact-based and not source-drive. What do you gain by sharing another's private information – no matter where it comes from? We don't. Wear that shoe on your foot. You will find that it doesn't feel the same as when it was the gossip about someone else. Now it's the truth about your parent or your grades, etc., that others are sharing.

Possess a skill – work with your hands. These assure you a steady financial lifestyle; then you won't have the time to mind other's business and not be quiet.

Lord, help me lead a quiet life, mind my business and provide me with more work with my hands.

SEPTEMBER 4

[12]So that your daily life may win the respect of outsiders and so that you will not be dependent on anybody.

1 Thessalonians 4:12

The respect of others is important because you then influence them in their walk with Christ. Sometimes we feel that it's not fair that all eyes rest on Christians, but it's true and it happens and it's important that you are respected because of your Christian lifestyle. Remember that we are often the only Jesus that some people see.

When outsiders witness us sin, they respond in ways we often don't care for and they feel that we may then be hypocritical but we need to understand that we are held to a higher level of accountability, fair or not. We need to learn to adapt to that level of expectation rather than lean on the excuse of humanity. We need to believe in the Trinity the way we speak of Him. Jesus can bring us out of whatever our issues and whatever our storms.

"So that your daily life….so that you will not be dependent on anybody." Independence is a trait well-respected by most everyone. This independence should bring honor to God, thus spotlighting your lifestyle. How we achieve this independence is equally as important as achieving the independence. How we achieve the independence is based on how we define independence.

I define independence with several perspectives: spiritual, emotional, financial and mental.
Spiritual independence: accepted Christ as Lord and Savior; study God's word without being told or coerced; winning others to Christ by sheer behavior; eagerly seeking a better understanding of God and His word.
Mental independence: not led into temptation; does not lead into temptation; mature thought process; seeks Godly counsel.
Emotional independence: relates well to others with the love of Christ; responds well when others don't relate well; draws others to them.
Financial independence: acting responsibly with God's resources including tithing, saving and living debt-free.

These seem steep in responsibility but they are Christ-centered and focused. Christ will help us achieve and maintain this independence.

Lord, help me influence the lives of others through respect and independence.

On This Journey

SEPTEMBER 5

[16] For the Lord Himself will come down from heaven, with a loud command, with the voice of the archangel and with the trumpet call of God, and the dead in Christ will rise first.

1 Thessalonians 4:16

He will return! Great news! The Lord will come for me! What will we be doing when He returns? Does that change your thought process about your behavior? If we choose to decide what to do based on whether the Lord would arrive while you were in that action, often our behavior would be quite different. So what will we be doing?

studying	eating	drinking
prayer	sleeping	drugs
at church	telephone	smoking
witnessing	school	pre-marital sex
singing	chores	gossiping
ministry work	shopping	partying
serving God's people	peer-tutoring	sports
peer-counseling	football game	browsing the Internet
musical/concert	sporting events	on the phone
	television	
	amusement park	

Right, wrong or indifferent behavior, He will come while we are engaged in some event. While that's important, remember that He is watching our every move and action and thought. Does this make a difference in our behavior? Often times it doesn't seem to matter. Why is that? Forgetfulness, disobedience, etc. are reasons but we are approaching life with negligence. Our approach needs to resemble respect and reverence for God and His ever-presence in our lives and around us.

When we accepted the gift of salvation, we invited Christ to dwell in our hearts. We need to be reminded that He has not moved, He has not been evicted, our salvation has not been reversed or returned, so He is still there.

What do we do daily?

What will we be doing when He arrives?

Thank You, Lord for coming to bring us to You as You promised.

SEPTEMBER 6

¹⁷After that, we who are still alive and are left will be caught up together with them in the clouds to meet the Lord in the air. And so we will be with the Lord forever.

1 Thessalonians 4:17

"Beyond the Veil," a song by Donnie McClurklin, speaks of his desire to see God face to face.

"Yet there is one thing my heart desires is to worship you each day without fail. This is my earnest prayer. This is my earnest plea bid me completely beyond the veil. Beyond the veil is where I see all your glory; seated on your throne in majesty and power; I lay prostrate before you."

As you know, I find quite a bit of inspiration from music and this is no exception. In this instance, the words to this song clearly express how I feel as well. I want to worship Him face to face.

The experience will overwhelm me, I'm certain but I will get over that eventually. Being overwhelmed doesn't outweigh the actual experience.

Just imagine that I am getting my nails manicured, or anything else, when He arrives and we meet Him in midair, similar to Peter's experience on the water. This will be the highpoint of our Christian experience and walk. An experience which will certainly turn life around and anew.

The veil of which Mr. McClurklin refers is the Holy place where God resides and if we are behind or beyond the veil, we are in His presence. Above all blessings, grace and miracles, beyond the veil is the ultimate in all of that. Being in His presence is what my heart desires. I can only imagine the impact of the experience.

But I count on Him holding true to His promises:

1) He will return for me/us.
2) He will meet us in midair.
3) We will be with Him forever.

Mr. McClurkin used music and poetry to express what Christians await to experience for their lifetime – to meet the King of Kings, the Lord of Lords and the Prince of Peace.

So we need to decide how we will be living and behaving and we need to live as if it were anyday – not reckless and crazy but forgiving, loving and compassionately.

Decide now because He will return.

In Your presence is where I desire to be Lord. I look forward to being granted that privilege.

SEPTEMBER 7

¹²Now we ask you, brothers, to respect those who work hard among you, who are over you in the Lord and who admonish you. ¹³Hold them in the highest regard in love because of their work. Live in peace with each other.

1 Thessalonians 5:12-13

How do you decide who works hard among you? Is this judgment on another or is this defined by God's word? While I believe it's much of both, I also believe that people decide how much they will or won't work. We have to be careful not to treat them differently based on our different working environments and work ethics. Notwithstanding, there are those among us who work hard and we need to certainly respect those persons. Along with respect we need to learn from them about their work and their drive to complete that work and pursue it diligently on every occasion.

"Who are over you in the Lord" I define as preachers, pastors, teachers, leaders and the elders among you. These persons care for us, pray for us, study to assist us with our growth and they are responsible for our spiritual growth and maturity. According to God's word, they are held to a higher level of accountability. There is respect that should be automatically attached to that.

We don't always respect them. In fact, sometimes we blatantly disrespect them. I remember as a child that we treated our Sunday School teacher and the Vacation Bible School staff terribly. I wish I could say we didn't know better but we knew disobedience was a sin, so anything else is an excuse. Why do Christians use the church environment to disobey the Lord? Just a question to ponder.

A word about respect; remember that one day you may be the teacher or pastor or leader or elder and you will expect that respect. Also, remember that our respect us not optional; it is a command. Now, if I may offer some words of wisdom. If you have a problem with giving respect to a particular person, you should go and talk to that person and share your feelings and request an explanation for your concerns. This conversation should then provide you with some clarity and closure allowing you to respect that individual. If you are still having difficulty with the respect, then you should seek God's guidance through prayer and study. It is worth the talk, I promise.

Lord, let me not forget to respect those who work to increase my knowledge of You. Remind me that when I'm the teacher to exercise humility.

SEPTEMBER 8

¹⁴And we urge you, brothers, warn those who are idle, encourage the timid, help the weak, be patient with everyone.

1 Thessalonians 5:14

A call of compassion that Paul has issued needs to be followed or adopted or adapted; added to our daily living. Compassion is defined as a feeling of deep sympathy and sorrow for another's suffering or misfortune, accompanied by a desire to alleviate the pain or remove its cause.

Compassion is exhibited in our actions so what do those say about how compassionate we actually are?

> Are we kind to others?
> Are we concerned about other's feelings?
> Are we patient with others?
> Do we think of others before ourselves?
> Do we do the right thing?
> Are we loving to others?
> Do we share Christ with others?
> Do we listen to them with our undivided attention?
> Do they know we care?
> Do we give them the information we know to help them?
> Do we encourage the timid?
> Do we help the weak?
> Do we comfort them when they worry?
> Are we welcoming to others?
> Do we contribute to the uplift of another's spirit?
> Do we give ourselves to others unselfishly?

Those should give you a great understanding for what compassionate behavior looks like. There are people who live by the 'every man for himself' rule. This would be okay if Christ had set the example. As we know we are to follow His example and not that social rule.

Lastly, have a test walk in those moccasins (shoes). Consider what it would feel like if you were the idle one or the weak one or the timid one or no one was ever patient with you. How would that feel and more than anything, how would you survive? Then on top of being mistreated or ignored or neglected, you discover that you are being ignored by Christians.

Those shoes are not comfortable and they don't fit, do they?

Lord, remind me to be kind and compassionate to those who need the kind and compassionate me.

On This Journey

SEPTEMBER 9

¹⁵Make sure that nobody pays back wrong for wrong, but always try to be kind to each other and to everyone else.

1 Thessalonians 5:15

An eye for an eye. A tooth for a tooth. If you hit me, I'll hit you back. Turnabout is fair play. Dog eat dog world. Every man for himself.

These are the rules and lifestyle of society. Vengeance belongs to the Lord. Not us. God has plans for our enemies including preparing a table for us in their presence. Revenge is a sin. Not our job. Make no mistake.

Christ calls for us to be kind to Christians as well as non-Christians. We don't really need to spend any time on why kindness is demanded.

We are focused on avoiding temptation of revenge, vengeance and acting out of anger and not doing wrong for wrong. First of all, two wrongs don't make anything right. Just because someone else has wronged you doesn't mean you are able to pay them back. It does mean that you treat them the same way and better than ever before. "Kill them with kindness." My question to myself is always why do I always have to be the better person? God's answers vary in degree of detail but the basis for His answer is "because I said so." I have decided that we have enemies so our dedication to God and our respect for His words and commands are being tested. He wants to know we do believe what He says. God says that He will prepare a table for us before our enemies.

For me that has meant that He has performed miracles in my life and blessed me abundantly, allow my enemies to witness those miracles and blessings and then allow them to question why I am worthy of such blessings and miracles. This has happened mostly at my work environment. In whatever your situation, when you are faced with trials and struggles with others, you are to seek God and His will; He will provide the rest.

David could've killed Saul three times but he didn't. David did leave evidence of the possibilities to Saul so that he would know it was possible but never took action.

It is hard not to "pay people back" for what they do but God has a plan and we need to trust.

Lord, I trust You to address those who wrong me and keep me kind to everyone.

SEPTEMBER 10

[16]Be joyful always.

1 Thessalonians 5:16

My brother exemplifies this scripture and I don't even know that he knows it. He is a minister and diligently studies God's word. I've never asked why he can be joyful always – I've never had to ask. There are some things that as a Christian come naturally. Joy is at the top of that list.

When I discovered this scripture, I thought of my brother and James 1:2 (NIV) which reads, "Consider it pure joy, my brothers whenever you face trials of any kinds."

Your joy defines your attitude and your joyous attitude will draw people to you. With that you will then be able to lead others to Christ.

Joy differentiates us from non-believers. Joy is what makes us smile when trouble us at its peak. Joy is what we have in spite of our trials and turmoil. Joy is excitement when someone meets Christ. Joy is hearing the Lord speak to you. Joy is understanding God's word and using it to mature as a Christian. Joy is inviting your friends to church and they accept the gift of salvation. Joy is love unconditional – as a giver or recipient. Joy is true love. Joy is pure and true and authentic; the result of a genuine relationship with Christ. Joy can not be replaced and there is no equitable substitute. Joy is not an emotion – it does not waiver based on feelings, but continues to increase based on your relationship with Christ.

Joy is the pinnacle of peace where your thirst for Christ is different – your peace experience becomes monumental.

Joy is important. Joy is noticed not by your smile yet by the depth of your smile, the content of your conversation and your behavior. Joy is a benefit of Christianity.

Even when it's hard, Lord, help me be joyful.

On This Journey

SEPTEMBER 11

[17]Pray continually.

1 Thessalonians 5:17

Pray without ceasing. Pray with no end. Pray continually. Prayer is communication with Christ and God and the Holy Spirit. This communication needs to be consistent and comprehensive. Is this difficult? Sometimes it is but what kind of effort do we give to pray continually?

Our communication with God is important. Prayer is half of the way we hear from God. Study and reading of His word is the other half. It is crucial we stay connected with Him.

The amount of communication is directly related to how we receive God's direction and how well we hear Him when He speaks. The importance of the communication is being able to hear Him when He speaks. The main complaint of Christians is that we want answers to our prayers but we are normally not quiet or still enough to hear God speak. With that having been said, we need to have a quiet place and a quiet time so that we may hear Him speak.

Pray about everything! Yes, that means that test and that paper and that teacher you can't seem to get along with. Of course it means praying for a better relationship with your parents; for some it may mean praying for having parents. Yes, it means praying about the monumental as well as the minute. Usually, we say that something is too small to share with God. This is where we fail. Prayer is about trust. We have to trust God at His word to leave our burdens with Him – all of your burdens. God has to trust that we will give everything to Him – not just what we define as "big enough for God."

Now the hardest part is praying continually. Yes, in between classes, in between your own thoughts and your own sentences. This is when the "prayer rules" may not actually apply. You may have to pray walking with your eyes open in a crowded room, rather than the traditional 'head bowed, eyes closed, on knees at night' prayer. While that has been traditionally defined as the most respectful, it prohibits us from praying continually. So we must seize the moment to pray and we must improvise on how we accomplish our prayer times. So if this means you are in class or the restroom or in church or at the mall, you can pray and you will pray. It is more important that you pray than where or how you pray.

Lord, thank You for our open line of communication.

SEPTEMBER 12

[18]Give thanks in all circumstances, for this is God's will for you in Christ Jesus.

1 Thessalonians 5:18

The four (4) components of prayer are explained in the acronym ACTS. A is for adoration, C is for confession, T is for thanksgiving, and S is for supplication.

My husband taught me a valuable lesson about prayer one evening during our dinner prayer. First, let me say that my husband's dinner prayer is not limited to blessing the food, rather it is an all-inclusive prayer. So much so that I wonder sometimes if he will ever get to blessing the food. We were in prayer and he thanked God for the rejection we received for a mortgage for which we had applied. When we got rejected, we were truly confused because we were just approved for a larger amount with another company. He thanked God boldly for the rejection. I almost questioned him but the Spirit said no, don't question it even though it's what you want to do.

In the meantime, we stopped and really paid attention to what God was showing us. To shorten the story, months later we saw the former secretary of the builder where we were rejected. She asked us how it was going and we explained that we were building on the property we already owned and it was going well. She then shared with us all the problems she had experienced while working there inclusive of the details of some problems some clients experienced while building their homes. One home was missing a structural beam – not a good thing. God obviously did not want us there. He showed us that that place was not for us. By the way, He didn't have to show us but He did and we are grateful for Him showing us and for our obedience in His will.

Thank Him for everything, especially when you don't understand what He is doing or why He has done it and what most of us ask – why is this happening to me?

Thank You, God for all of our circumstances.

On This Journey

SEPTEMBER 13

¹⁹Do not put out the Spirit's fire.

1 Thessalonians 5:19

The Holy Spirit possesses a fire – an inextinguishable flame. The Spirit's fire is ignited by God's charge and directive and His desires. God created the Holy Spirit as He did all of us. He has a path designed for each of us. The Holy Spirit's role is based on the flame, the fire.

What is this fire? It is a yearning to please God. This fire burns incessantly until we submit whole-heartedly to God's will. It is a desire to make God happy with our actions.

The most important attribute of the Holy Spirit for me is the intercession the Spirit does on my behalf. The Spirit speaks to Christ and God for me when I cannot gather my own words to say to God what I want. When I first learned of the event of the power of the Holy Spirit I didn't believe but I know that the Spirit intercedes on my behalf. Romans 8:26 reads "In the same way, the Spirit helps us in our weakness." We do not know what we ought to pray for, but the Spirit himself intercedes for us with groans that words cannot express.

Power and fire express characteristics of the Holy Spirit. Just the power of intercession ensures that I don't put out the Spirit's fire by any means or for any reason.

The Spirit's fire should ignite a fire in you. It does in me. Now you ask what does this fire do or why this fire? The fire within us keeps us motivated to serve the Lord. The fire keeps us sharing our faith with others and ministering to others. Further, that same fire stimulates our love and obedience for Christ. There are times when we find it difficult to be a Christian, but just at that moment when we are at the intersection of the cross roads, that fire sets in and takes over those thoughts. With the amount of love the Lord, Christ and the Spirit possess, they will not let us come this far to turn away from us. That's why the fire can't be put out.

God, I will help the Spirit's fire burn.

SEPTEMBER 14

[20]Do not treat prophecies with contempt.

1 Thessalonians 5:20

Let's define prophecy first. Prophecy is the view of the future. Prophecy was the scriptures, which described the coming of Christ. Prophecy is also the scriptures, which describe the return of Christ. Prophets are usually the ones who introduce the prophecies according to what God has told them.

Two things happen with prophecies.

1) Most time it is not believed; and ,
2) it is scrutinized because of the messenger.

These are things we must avoid because prophecies are from God and they will be fulfilled according to His will. When we disbelieve a prophecy, we are saying that we don't believe God. This is when the saying, "we walk by faith and not by site" becomes important and paramount. Often we have to stretch ourselves to simply accept God's promises and His love.

His prophecy is designed to increase the knowledge of Him and our faith. Keep in mind that the prophecy is true and it will come to pass. So when you believe what He says and then your faith allows you to believe so when it does come to pass, you are able to rejoice about the victory.

So don't treat prophecies with contempt. We will live to regret that contempt because when it comes to pass, we will have given false information to others, then we are foolish because we have to retrace our steps to recover that false information.

When in doubt about what to believe or the source of certain information, go to God in prayer and He will direct your path and provide you with clarity for you next steps. God will always provide direction in our times of uncertainty. He makes clear all misunderstanding and any doubt we may have.

Lord, help me to believe Your words of prophecy through that of Your designated prophets.

SEPTEMBER 15

[21]Test everything. Hold on to the good.

1 Thessalonians 5:21

"Test everything" is dangerous for some of us. As an inquisitive young person, I was always testing everything. That included my mother, my grandmother, my teachers, and anyone else who I could test. I first learned this word and the definition of inquisitive in third grade. So I can understand all stories about your curiosity and your inquisitive nature. I also encourage you testing everything. I do however want to encourage you not to test the laws as established by local, regional and national authorities.

Now, I do implore you to hold onto the good. Let's decide what is good. If you can answer yes to all the questions then it's good.

1) Does it enhance your spiritual life?
2) Does it increase your morale?
3) Does it enhance your physical well-being?
4) Are others able to grow from your experience?
5) Are you growing from your experience?
6) If Jesus is watching would you still do this?

These are just a sample of the questions which will allow you to examine the difference between what is good and what is not.

Interestingly, I have found that when people know you are only interested in what is good, they often respect your decision and avoid exposing you in what is not.

My college roommates were caught drinking and they were underage. They were sure to report that I wasn't a part of their drinking party. The resident advisor knew this to be true so she excused me from the incident. Also, they didn't persist when they offered me a drink; they offered to be polite.

People, especially people who know you and your beliefs, will respect your desire to do what is good. It is up to us to maintain that respect and positive image that others see us for.

Lord, thank You for establishing what is good and giving me the ability to distinguish the difference.

SEPTEMBER 16

[22] Avoid every kind of evil.

1 Thessalonians 5:22

"But I didn't know it was evil." A common statement by most of us but this is an excuse and not allowable. We as Christians know when evil exists. We are to avoid evil and sin at all costs. The benefit is awesome. Too awesome to submit to evil.

Since we know what is evil, why do we have a hard time avoiding it? Well, I'm glad you asked. Evil has a way of presenting itself as more fun, more exciting, more interesting, more popular, etc. Whereas good or neglecting evil could be boring, not fun, plain, etc. I have found that the worse we do, the more popular we become but as soon as we announce Christ as our Savior and stand for Him and His word, our popularity wanes. We must be strong enough to withstand our new deflating popularity because of our past life and embrace our new fellowship, because of our faith.

Avoid evil. A simple command with some difficult attachments sometimes.

Prayer aids in avoiding evil. Avoiding evil is impossible without prayer. Evil is conquered by prayer. We cannot overcome or avoid evil with simple will power or discipline or with desire. Evil and its administrator, the devil, knows what our weaknesses are and uses that information to present situations we would be unable to avoid. However, with prayer, all evil can be and will be avoided.

Learning to say no is important. It is how we avoid evil. No is essential to our vocabulary. We must know when and how to say no and stand your ground. The "Just Say No" anti-drug campaign is corny and had no significant measurable results but the statement is true. Saying no is hard because we want to be popular and we want to gain the approval of others. However, I decided long ago that I didn't want to be popular if it means interfering with my relationship with God. I decided early in life that I wouldn't do drugs nor smoke cigarettes. I decided at age 29 that I wouldn't have sex until I was married. These promises led me closer to Christ and I could hold on to what was good – me.

Lord, steer me away from and protect me from evil.

On This Journey

SEPTEMBER 17

[23]May God himself, the God of peace, sanctify you through and through. May your whole spirit, soul and body be kept blameless at the coming of our Lord Jesus Christ. [24]The one who calls you is faithful and he will do it.

1 Thessalonians 5:23-24

Sanctified and blameless in front of God is answered prayer; is proof that God heard my cry and my plea. He will do this because He promised us He would.

He is faithful to us without condition and without circumstance. He is faithful to us even without our consistent faith. His faith is better than mine because He doesn't forget to be faithful nor does He waver on His faith. I forget to be faithful when I doubt His power or when I ask with reservation or when I reduce my desires and expectations or when I try to fix my own problems even though I told God about them; I could go on and on about my unfaithfulness.

The truth is God is faithful to us at every moment but I select when I will be faithful and that's not fair to God.

He is faithful all the time. Examples of His faithfulness:

1) He woke us up.
2) He fed us. (This does not include junk food.)
3) He clothed us. (Even if it's not name brand.)
4) He saw that you passed that test. (Did we really study and participate in class?)
5) He is always there when we decide to pray. He is ready to receive our burdens. He gives us peace and rest.
6) He will never leave nor forsake us.
7) He loves us. (And He proved it. Jesus died for our sins.)
8) He has plans for each of us.
9) He has given each of us a gift or talent.
10) He has given us salvation as a gift. It has not to do with our works.

He is faithful and everything He has said has come to pass. Everything He says will come true, we can count on it to happen. His promises are true. We can count Him. He is faithful.

Thank You for Your great faithfulness.

SEPTEMBER 18

⁶God is just: He will pay back trouble to those who trouble you ⁷and give relief to you who are troubled, and to us as well.

2 Thessalonians 1:6-1:7a

I genuinely love people and I become angry when I have to stand up to someone. I dislike me most when I have to defend myself, so this was a comforting scripture for me. My best example of this being true was one year at work. I survived three different supervisors – none of which had my best interests in mind, certainly not at heart. I fasted once a week, prayed daily—all day—and wore black everyday because I felt mistreated. My first manager was promoted and I found out later it wasn't really her fault but my peer who later was transferred, was the saboteur. That peer has also experienced some severe career trouble. The second manager was transferred and demoted in a new city. She openly admitted to others that she was trying to get me fired.

The third manager is experiencing severe career trouble and eventually admitted that she never really tried to see my point of view.

My point is those people troubled me and consequently, God brought varying trouble to them. He also gave me relief.

I also think that during that time God tested my faith. God wanted to know whether I would trust Him to handle them or whether I would try to handle them myself. He wanted to know if I would fast and pray and leave my burdens to Him. He wanted me to prove my love to Him – obedient or disobedient. I chose obedience. He kept His promises.

Lastly, I never say anything about their troubles, not to them or to anyone. I don't gloat in someone's troubles. It's their time to learn who God is. They may even turn to me for that leadership. I have to be ready. Lord doesn't do that for us to then turn and make fun. I feel that He wouldn't show you their troubles if He thought you would turn and make fun or something as equally as immature.

Thank You for taking care of me and paying back those who give me trouble.

On This Journey

SEPTEMBER 19

¹⁰For even when we were with you, we gave you this rule: "If a man will not work, he shall not eat."

2 Thessalonians 3:10

Do you know anyone who never has a job and they don't seem to have any desire to work but are always asking for the belongings of someone else? Why do they think it's okay to do that? Why don't they work?

While I have no answers to those questions, I do know that this is a true statement. Speaking on work – an ideal arrangement is one where what you love to do and what you do well is one and the same and you earn more than enough to pay your bills. Again, ideal is what we all pray for, however, sometimes we have to do work that is less than ideal. If you work, then you eat.

I have witnessed conversations where people have said that they couldn't find work and they have several excuses as to why they can't. Further, I have heard one of those excuses that "God will provide" and He will. Keep in mind that God helps those who help themselves. You have to apply for a job to be considered for a job. So if you don't go look for work, work cannot find you on the couch at home.

Now let's talk about work which applies to you while you are at home with your parents. We will refer to chores as work. You need to work in your room. Keeping your room clean is the minimum. Details include: folding your clothes, hanging your clothes, dusting your room, including all furniture and light fixtures, and taking all dishes back to the kitchen. Washing your own clothes would be nice.

Keep in mind, the more you do, the better off you are. So volunteer to wash the dishes, clean the kitchen and whatever else your parents need.

Why do we work at home? Because our parents went to work to provide for us and we need to help them to keep neat what they have provided. Parents tend to be bitter when we are not cooperative with the work required to keep a home in order. I didn't always do everything I could to help my mother and I regret that. With all the things that parent(s) do and survive, anything and everything we can do helps them through whatever it takes to survive their work.

Think of it this way, if you work, it's easier to eat. Don't be burdensome by not working when you should.

Lord, thank You for blessing me with work.

SEPTEMBER 20

¹³And as for you, brothers, never tire of doing what is right.

2 Thessalonians 3:13

It is sometimes a thankless job, but somebody has to do what is right. It is expected of Christians. We are supposed to do the right thing. It is hard to always do the right thing, but we will manage to do it. Most times I find it easy to do the right thing, but there is one situation when I find it difficult. I find it hard when people wrong me. I have to concentrate on doing right and being obedient. I have to focus on my prayer life during this situation. It seems that I am also tested repeatedly in a short period of time. I usually ask aloud to no one in particular why do I have to do the right thing all the time.

The answer is yes, I have to do the right thing all the time, no matter what. The reason is because I am charged to do so. I do the right thing because I love God and my obedience translates into love for Him. Doing the right thing is what I pray to have everyone do, so if I want others to do the right thing then I have to do the right thing first.

Will you get tired of doing the right thing? Will you get tired of coming home on time? Will you get tired of saying no to drugs? Will you get tired of saying no to cigarettes? Will you get tired of saying no to alcohol? Will you tire of saying no to skipping school? Will you tire of saying no to sex? At some point or another, the answer to all those questions will be yes. But the reality is you have to continue to say no and do the right thing.

I find encouragement to do the right thing by knowing that God offers me grace and forgiveness and love, all unconditionally. All He asked me to do was be obedient, do the right thing and obey the commandments. And finally consider this: does God get tired of loving me, providing for me, listening to me, taking care of me? The answer is no. Knowing that, how can I get tired of doing the right thing?

Thank You for guiding my path and making it straight.

SEPTEMBER 21

[12]Fight the good fight of faith. Take hold of eternal life to which you were called when you made your good confession in the presence of many witnesses.

1 Timothy 6:12

Ephesians instructs us to put on the whole armor of God (Ephesians 6). This is what we need to fight the good fight of faith. Some have asked what is the good fight of faith. Some still ask. You have noticed that your Christian walk is subjected to challenges. Your faith hurdles you over those challenges. Your faith pushes you to face those challenges. Your faith forces you to depend on God and use all available Christian resources in order to advance past this challenge.

The fight sometimes is to keep your faith. Other times the fight is to share your faith. Then the fight could be to use your faith to overcome your challenges.

You will hear this statement throughout your life. Each time, though, it will mean something new and different. Each time you will learn something new about yourself and about your faith. You will experience a new level in your relationship with God. Each time you will grow and so will your faith. About that time, then you will be able to tell other Christians to fight as well. Likewise you will be able to tell them how to fight and why they should fight.

Pray. Fast. Read. Study. Call your prayer warriors. Fight the good fight of faith.

As you mature as a Christian, you will learn to take hold of the eternal life who called us. The eternal life, of course, is God. Embracing God exhibits your increasing faith and Christian maturity.

When you don't think you can finish your fight, just embrace God. He wrote the instructions – He's sure to have answers.

Help me fight, God. Keep me fighting the good fight.

SEPTEMBER 22

[7] For God did not give us a spirit of timidity, but a spirit of power, of love and of self-discipline.

2 Timothy 1:7

Where did we learn to be timid? When did we learn? How do we get rid of it? Why do we insist on holding on to timidity?

God permits us to act with confidence and boldness. So, why don't we? Do we know that we have His permission? Maybe, maybe not. One way I found to transition from timidity to confidence was to ask for help from the Holy Spirit then I found it easier to act with confidence, power, love and self-discipline. I do need a reminder every so often to do these things and fortunately I have one; a human one: my husband. My husband exhibits humility with the authority of Christ's power, love and self-discipline. His demeanor earns the respect of others at home, church and work. There are issues and people who intimidate me, but I realize that intimidation is a choice and whomever and whatever causes us to act timidly is our fault and choice.

When I learned this, I didn't act with arrogance but I reviewed and adjusted my behavior to act with confidence and power. I resolved in my spirit that I would act in every way according to God's word. This resolution translates into me acting with a spirit of power, love and self-discipline, without haughtiness or arrogance, with integrity and most of all without timidity.

Persons who are timid, which includes me some times, need to address why we are timid and how we can overcome that spirit, which is not of God. One thing that helped me was to realize that there is power in the truth. Then I know that it's never what you say but how you say it that matters.

Lastly, my husband always stands up for his values, views and nothing stops him from that. So I see and thus know now that people don't attempt to intimidate and I then stop making excuses for standing for my views and don't be afraid to tell the truth.

Timidity soon passes and becomes a distant memory.

Lord, thank You for Your power, love and the authority to act without timidity.

SEPTEMBER 23

²²Flee the evil desires of youth, and pursue righteousness, faith, love and peace, along with those who call on the Lord out of a pure heart.

2 Timothy 2:22

While I don't condone the excuses of what we do in our youth, I know there are things we have done and will do in our youth and because of our youthfulness and immaturity. Do realize though that most of the same information available to adults is available to young people especially the Bible and all the tools to understand His word? Lack of knowledge is usually not an acceptable excuse for the mistakes we make.

The great asset as a youth is that you have a choice not to repeat the mistakes of others. We have a choice to pursue righteousness, faith, love and peace and learn to call on the Lord out of a pure heart as a young person. My parents and grandparents and siblings are not perfect so I have a chance to see what they do and decide not to repeat their behavior. At the same time, the opposite is also true – I can decide to follow in their footsteps whether they are right, wrong or indifferent.

If I were the author of this scripture I would certainly offer this as advice because of my youthful experiences rather than not. As an experienced youth, I agree with the motive of the scripture. The author writes, 'flee the evil desires of youth' because those desires are not worth the consequences, which accompany those desires. Experience teaches us that, however, as a friend once said do you want to buy this lesson or do you want it for free. What she means is for no charge you can learn from someone or for a fee, you can experience it yourself. My mother used to tell me she was my leader down the yellow brick road of life and my job was to follow and she was going to show me the pitfalls and peaks. But she said that I wasn't a great follower and I tended to wander off. In essence, she wanted to share some of her experiences with me so I didn't repeat some of her mistakes but according to her standards I wasn't always an attentive pupil. She has never asked me what I learned from her but she observes my life as a young adult and knows that her parenting was valuable and valid.

It's always easier to react in hindsight (after the event has passed) but the author intends for us to benefit from his experience. I don't have to experience everything for myself in order to know that I don't want that experience. Drugs and smoking are two such examples. Observation teaches me that nothing good comes from either experience thus I can spend my money and time on something else.

Heed the author's advice as often as possible; you don't need to see everything for yourself. The cost could be more than you can afford – these lessons are not free.

Thank You, Father, for Your ability to pursue righteousness, faith, peace and love.

SEPTEMBER 24

[2]People will be lovers of themselves, lovers of money, boastful, proud, abusive, disobedient to their parents, ungrateful, unholy, [3]without love, unforgiving, slanderous, without self-control, brutal, not lovers of the good, [4]treacherous, rash, conceited, lovers of pleasure rather than lovers of God – [5]having a form of godliness but denying its power. Have nothing to do with them.

2 Timothy 3:2-5

These four scriptures are packed with teachings. People, in this text, refer to everyone, not just non-believers. Yes, there are Christians who fall into these categories. There are Christians who indeed profess to love God but do one, some or all of these things. The author warns us against such things so that we are not vulnerable to these things by being exposed to those people. Most people have just a few of these traits – not all of them at once, but the ones which concern me are 'disobedient to parents' and 'having a form of godliness but denying its power.'

Disobedience functions with a hefty price tag, especially to our parents. God outlines explicit details of the consequences of disobeying our parents (Proverbs). All young people think that once they are adult age that they no longer listen to, need or obey their parents. This is far from the truth. My mother deserves my full respect and obedience all the time. I am an adult and a wife and a mother. She is still my mother. And the Bible, the rulebook, did not change. So yes, even after 18, 21 and 30 and so on, obedience is still required. It is a different obedience but it is obedience.

Now, daily obedience includes your daily chores, your school commitments and general respect. Often we don't feel our parent(s) deserve our respect and obedience but consider that you may be the right example in your family so you need to do the right thing and you will see some changes in your home. We don't have the right to judge our parent(s). God made them too; He has a plan for them and they answer to Him too. Again, the same rules apply. Obey our parents.

Denying the power of godliness is dangerous. God's power is not to be denied. Denying God's power empowers the devil. Further, we give the impression that God's power is optional and can be escaped when neither is true. Why would we want to possess God's power but deny it? That is a self-defeating act. We might give the impression we are more powerful than God and that God is our cosmic bellhop; we ring Him when our power is insufficient. Yet our power has been insufficient all the while. I'm thankful that God is patient because in my desire to do my own thing, I am certain that I have angered God on numerous occasions. I disobey and He continues to protect me and lift my burdens and listen when I call.

Our behavior dictates to the world God's power. They are watching for how much we credit Him for the events in our lives. That credit is how His power is evaluated. We cannot afford to deny His power – we won't live without His power.

Thank You for Your godliness and Its power.

SEPTEMBER 25

^{16}All scripture is God-breathed and is useful for teaching, rebuking, correcting and training in righteousness, ^{17}so that the man of God may be thoroughly equipped for every good work.

2 Timothy 3:16-17

'In righteousness' provides parameters so that we don't misuse or misconstrue (twist) His word to fit our selfish needs. We often 'beat' people over the head with the Bible. We must be careful because it is how we must all live not just the unjust. We will all be judged by the same words. I started there because this does happen. Now, I once asked who wrote the Bible or something similar. This is a great question but it felt silly at the time. The best visual I can give is that God wrote it using the physical attributes of others. God is the author of every word in the Bible. He uses many different voices and personalities to present His word and this allows Him to show us by example of others, His power, love, faithfulness, mercy and grace. I consider that He could've written the whole Bible without examples such as the confrontations between Saul and David, Saul becoming Paul, the narratives of the disciples, the travels of Paul, and the coming of our Savior. God spoke and there was light. The Bible could've originated the same way. But God created it over time through individuals who give quality examples of His power in situations where we might find ourselves.

While I might not ever have an issue of blood, I have an outstanding example of faith and determination. While I may never walk on water, I do know that I can ask for the seemingly impossible and that God can do all things.

I was married and had Biblical examples of what my marriage should and should not be like. We don't know what we are supposed to do as a child but the Bible gives us the rules. It also shares what can happen when we leave home to see the world and we need to return home to our parents.

The Bible is a living breathing instruction book from God to us in order to equip us to do His work and follow His will.

Spend time with His word. It is an expression of His love and our love for Him. Just imagine how you feel when someone pays attention to your creation; that excites you. I knew my husband loved me when he read all of my poetry and knew it and had questions and comments.

God feels the same way when we study and submit in obedience to His word. Just imagine when we share His word.

Thank You for Your powerful word.

SEPTEMBER 26

⁶An elder must be blameless, the husband of but one wife, a man whose children believe and are not open to the charge of being wild and disobedient.

Titus 1:6

An elder is a distinguished position among the Christian community and the church. This is a well-respected position for his spiritual leadership, his moral standings, and the ability to lead his home. Elders are chosen by other elders.

What do you want to be in life? Do you want to be a public figure? Do you want to be the president of the United States? When did you decide that you wanted to be the President? My point is that you find out the qualifications of the position then you live the lifestyle that will produce the results of the Presidency. There are certainly things which will prevent you from becoming the president but your chances are slim if you violate the qualifications.

Don't forget just as with the qualifications of elders, the decision-makers lack forgiveness once a violation of those qualifications has occurred.

We discuss this to point out that our lifestyle determines our destination and distance. In this particular instance the elder has to be married, never divorced, maybe not even widowed, children must be taught and believe the word of God and be disciplined and obedient. All of this is because people respect people who speak from experience and the ability to show his success as a Christian, husband, father and spiritual leader. His example provides leadership and wisdom to those he counsels. The wisdom he imparts needs to be biblically based and morally sound. This wisdom only comes with successful experience in those areas. We choose, then we ask for the favor to be chosen. Then we lead a lifestyle worthy of being chosen. We want to respect our leadership so as leadership, we want to be respected as leadership. If we want that respect, we have to earn that respect. Lastly, if we live as to be selected as an elder, then we allow our parents to be available for elder selection..

Lord, allow me to be worthy to lead among Your people as elder.

On This Journey

SEPTEMBER 27

[8] Rather he must be hospitable, one who loves what is good, who is self-controlled, upright, holy and disciplined.

Titus 1:8

Words to live by – the Bible has several hundred thousand, but these by far are some we need to imbed in our hearts and exercise daily. These six traits, similar to the fruits of the spirit, are essential to upright living.

Hospitable alludes to courtesy; being courteous to all human beings. Why are we mean to others? Even if they are mean to us first. This also raises the question, which was the catch phrase of the late nineties, 'What Would Jesus Do?'

<u>Loves what is good:</u> yearns for the good to happen, seeks the good in others and is optimistic that the good will eventually prevail.

<u>Self-controlled:</u> discipline, obedience, and able to think before speaking or acting. Most importantly, seeking the guidance of God.

<u>Upright:</u> righteous, blameless, seeking righteousness, seeking the justice which is due, and sound thought process.

<u>Holy:</u> avoiding obvious disobedience and sins; upholding the covenants and ordinances as set forth by God and His word.

<u>Disciplined:</u> well-behaved, well-mannered, obedient, and Christ-like.

God is clear about what pleases Him. He charges us to obey but we have to obey. Nobody can please God for us.

Father, help me remain in Your favor by exhibiting these six behaviors and traits.

SEPTEMBER 28

⁶I pray that you may be active in sharing your faith, so that you will have a full understanding of every good thing we have in Christ.

Philemon 1:6

Would the word shy or embarrassed best describe how you feel when you think about sharing your faith? Or maybe neither – maybe you are a great sharer of your faith. But most of us are not. For those who are great, thank you. Because of you, the rest of us have faith. You invited someone to attend your church with you or maybe you talked about your experiences and they wanted to know more. The bottom line is that you were instrumental in leading someone to Christ. You were part of the process of planting the seed of Christ and He did the rest. Your obedience pleases God.

Now for those of us who hesitate when its time to share our faith, there are steps I'd like to share with you.

Pray: pray that God offers you the opportunity to share your faith with truth, boldness and courage.

Study: study to show thyself approved to witness to others. Your ability to have an effective witness is based on your knowledge of Christ through your experience and His word.

Active: your active participation with God through prayer, study, and church attendance will show in your life and lifestyle. More often than not our lifestyle leads others to Christ rather than simply our words.

May these words encourage us to witness and share our faith. Thankfully we have proof that God will equip us to share, but we must be ready to share. When He does offer the opportunity, we must not deny God by not sharing God's goodness. We must have faith that we will be able to respond to the questions and say what God has in store for us. Finally remember the very person who shared with you, may have been shy before they witnessed to you. Aren't you glad that they were obedient? So let's go and be obedient.

Savior, equip me to share my faith so others may know of Your love.

SEPTEMBER 29

⁷Your love has given me great joy and encouragement because you, brother, have refreshed the hearts of the saints.

Philemon 1:7

My prayer partner and I have lengthy discussions about love. We as humans will spend our lifetime searching for, discovering, experiencing, surviving what we grow to understand as love.

God invented and clearly defined love. But we use other definitions by which we experience love. Love comes in the format of Eros, Philos and Agape. We'll define that later. In the meantime, love is abundantly important to each of us no matter how we define it. We need love. Need is a strong word and should only be used in severe situations. We need love, each of us. We need love in each of its formats – hugs, talks, time, gifts, and encouraging words.

You may never know what your love may mean when you give it to someone else. But when we love others, we meet their needs – needs we don't know about. In this scripture, it is the rare occasion where the recipient actually tells the giver what it means to receive their love.

Love offers us life. We cannot survive without love. There are actually people who starve for love and they will not be successful because they need love but have no resource for it. My prayer partner and I discussed this in depth and pray about their survival regularly.

Dr. Gary Chapman authored The Five Love Languages in which he defines the love languages, describes the five love languages and offers an in depth analysis of love and how to achieve a loving relationship with others which is equally fulfilling for all persons involved. He also discusses your love tank where the tank is based on how much you have stored there.

This starvation exists because the love tank is near empty or completely empty. Loving others is important. God exhibits the best example of love. He created us, sent and sacrificed His Son and continues to grow us. Loving others is our charge, our duty. You never have any idea what your loving words and gestures may mean to another. We often neglect what we mean to others. We need to shift our thoughts to knowing that our presence in other's lives means something and we need not take it for granted.

Give your love.

Master, remind me to bless others with my love.

SEPTEMBER 30

¹³To which of the angels did God ever say, "Sit at my right hand until I make your enemies a footstool for your feet"?

Hebrews 1:13

Patience and favor are important here. He shows you favor when He makes your enemies a footstool. You exercise patience as you obey and wait while He works.

God recognize our enemies before we do. He protects you from them. Your personal maturity determines whether or not God exposes your enemies to you. When I learned that God's plan for my enemies didn't include my help, He made my enemies my footstool. Included in that lesson, was to give God the glory. I had a boss that was intentionally trying to fire me. I was told this after the ordeal was over. I did recognize the trouble when it arrived. My actions and attitude determined His actions. I fasted once weekly, gave more of my spare time to God on my drives to and from home, and started listening rather than speaking. Eventually my prayers for favor were answered. He revealed my enemy, her plan and then He removed her from the location. After the incident ended, I spoke only of my closeness with God. The outcome would be different if my actions and attitude had been different.

Saul could've died at David's hands on two or three occasions. David didn't kill Saul when he had a chance because God didn't design that plan. David, however, did leave a sign letting Saul know that Saul's death was possible. Saul realized that David was benevolent but his behavior didn't change. Saul still sought to kill David. God delivered Saul to David because of David's obedience.

"Vengeance is mine," said the Lord. The question I pose is will God ever say to us, "sit at my right hand until I make your enemies a footstool for your feet"?

Lord, keep me humble in the face of my enemies.

On This Journey

HOW TO SHARE YOUR FAITH

One of our Christian responsibilities is sharing our faith with others. We are supposed to tell others why God is Lord of our lives, how good God is to us, how He blesses us and all the good news about God. With all that God does for us, it seems it would be easy to tell others. If it is so easy, why don't we do it? Most Christians never tell non-believers about God, even if they know them. Few Christians ever even invite others, believers or not, to a church service, not even the holiday musical. I find myself guilty all the time. I think after a person has left my presence "I missed a great opportunity to share God and His word and His blessings with that person." When I considered who I needed to share God with, I decided that all people fit into one category: everyone. We need to share God with everyone, but let's pick a starting point. Let's start with our family, they may already know God so it's easy to share God with them.

Once we get past our initial fear, then we can progress to friends and then to strangers. When to share is totally Christ-directed. God will lead you to share at the right time. Be ready to share when your friends approach you with their issues or they confide in you their troubles or triumphs. God will provide you His peace and comfort when He prepares you to share. He will give the right words at the right time for His predetermined person.

Where, like when, is determined by God. It is all predetermined and will be appropriate. How will you share your faith, you ask. God provides the message He wants you to deliver through His word, prayer, and mediation. What will I say? What will I say to someone who has never met God? What will I say to a soul that needs comfort and is no longer a part of a church? What will I say to a homeless woman and her children? What will I say to a teen who wants to commit suicide? God will provide. You will start with your testimony, most likely. Your testimony is built around how you personally came to accept God as your Savior. Nothing outweighs your own experience with Christ. Scriptures you know will come clearly to your memory at precisely the time you need them. I know that this is not easy but it is our charge as a Christian. Your faith is more powerful than you realize. Your very testimony could save the life of another in more than one way. Be prepared and willing to share your faith.

OCTOBER 1

[25]Therefore He is able to save completely those who come to God through him, because he always lives to intercede for them.

Hebrews 7:25

Here, He is Jesus Christ. Jesus was human for 33 years. He performed miracles. He shared the gospel and the message of God everyday He lived on Earth. He came because God planned for our mistakes, our sins. God sent His only Son so that I might have life and have it more abundantly. "For God so loved the world that He gave His only begotten Son that whosoever believeth in Him should not perish but have everlasting life." John 3:16 (KJV).

Jesus graciously followed God's plan for His life and ours. He is able to save us because He was sacrificed for our lives. He loved me and He proved it to everyone because He died for me. His compassion for me and my life overwhelms me. He was born into sin. He lived sin free for His lifetime of 33 years. He suffered and died. All for me. Even after all of that, He's not bitter – He loves me even more. He pleads my needs, wants and requests to God. He covers me with His love and prays to His father, even when I don't deserve His intercession. The biggest exhibit of His love is His forgiveness of my sins and He continues to intercede for me.

I heard a tale about an angel who was opening Heaven's gate for a bus. As the bus got closer to the pearly gates, the angels got nervous and tried to close them back. They saw thieves, criminals, and other sinners and became frantic saying to God they were coming to Heaven. God told them to look at who was driving. Jesus was driving the bus. God reminded the angels that Jesus had saved them and He saved those on the bus and He would save more lives. Don't forget that Jesus is driving the bus.

Thank You for saving me and interceding for me.

On This Journey

OCTOBER 2

²²Let us draw near to God with a sincere heart in full assurance of faith, having our hearts sprinkled to cleanse us from a guilty conscience and having our bodies washed with pure water.

Hebrews 10:22

With your mind made up to be pure and real and true to God, then go to God knowing that you will never turn back. Not for anything.

> **Step 1:** submit to His call to you. You answer positively.
> **Step 2:** grow closer to God through study of His word, and intimate prayer time.
> **Step 3:** faith that never wavers.

These steps are those we take when we submit to God and Christianity.

The most important part of this scripture is the sincere heart. God knows our hearts. One thing is certain: I don't lie to God. He knows the truth. Omniscient means to know all. If I can't admit the truth to God during prayer out loud then I avoid the topic. He knows the truth and I feel that I would rather address the situation when I can admit my feelings than lie to God. He respects me more for that.

A sincere heart takes care of the assurance of faith. Also, a sincere heart is a pure and clean heart void of a guilty conscience. Then washed with pure water.

Deniece Williams sings a song entitled "Whiter Than Snow," in which she pleads to God to make her whiter than snow. She tells Him that she wants to be whiter, whiter than snow. I like the song for a number of reasons but mostly because she sings with sincerity and depth. The song is a publication of a private moment with God. She sings with faith of what He can and will do if we have a sincere heart.

Lord, draw me nearer to Thee.

OCTOBER 3

²⁴And let us consider how we may spur one another on toward love and good deeds.

Hebrews 10:24

Spur means to encourage, motivate and inspire. How can we inspire one another toward love and good deeds? I decided to make a list:

1) By example of love and good deeds.
2) Loving others.
3) Doing good deeds for others.
4) Inviting others to join us when you do good deeds for others.
5) Share scriptures with others about love.
6) Specifically, deeds which exhibit love and good deeds:
    - giving to and feeding those less fortunate than we
    - meeting the needs of others and never mentioning the action
    - hugging others and hug them until they let go
    - listening to their dreams, aspirations and desires
    - show others you believe in them
    - engage others in your life and your testimony
    - pray for others and with others

It takes a lot for some people to give to others, for any number of reasons. However, giving of yourself to others is required of Christians. Fellowship with others is a gift, and required. God gives blessings to who He can send through. Love and good deeds for others is a blessing to the recipients. He blesses us when He can trust us to share by blessing others. One more word on love. In order for us to love others and for God to love us, we have to love ourselves. Loving ourselves requires us to forgive ourselves, be honest with ourselves, courage to achieve our desires and love God more than anything or anyone.

We can love others without sacrifice no matter what you may have heard. Besides, we don't do anything for God to love us the way He does, so why should others do something for us to love them?

Lord, help me love others so that they may love others too.

On This Journey

OCTOBER 4

[26] If we deliberately keep on sinning after we received the knowledge of the truth; no sacrifice for sins is left, [27] but only a fearful expectation of judgment and of raging fire will consume the enemies of God.

Hebrews 10:26-27

When you do something for the first time and you find out that it is wrong, you are probably "excused" for your action(s). The next time you exhibit the same behavior then you can no longer be "excused" for your action(s). We cannot continue to do what is wrong and not expect just punishment, whatever that may be. Punishment from the Lord doesn't always come immediately, so often we think we have gotten away with something when in reality we have sinned twice: once, for the action and second for the non-confession.

His word says what is done in the dark shall come to the light. It is foolish to believe anything otherwise. My mother used to say this usually when I had just done something wrong or was about to. I found out later that she was waiting for me to tell her what I had done. This was my opportunity to confess, however I don't recall ever actually doing it. I am different with God, though, I usually can't wait to share with Him when I've sinned.

I remember one evening I wanted to see the guy I was dating. So I drove my mother's car without her permission to his house. She was out with some friends. I knew exactly how long I could be gone. So I visited him and returned home thinking all was well. She returned home later but did something I didn't expect. She touched the hood and checked the gas gauge. I was caught. I didn't replace the gas I had used and she knew exactly where she left it from earlier in the day. Would replacing the gas have saved me? Not necessarily. My situation could've been worse. I could've had a wreck, the car could've stalled, even at the gas station something could've happened or worse, a fatal car accident on my way there or on the way home.

The bottom line is I did something wrong. In addition, I ruined my mother's trust for me. Anything she did to me was less than I deserved, for which I am grateful of course, I never did that again.

Lord, give me the wisdom to stop deliberately sinning.

Daily Devotional for Young People

OCTOBER 5

[1]Now faith is being sure of what we hope for and certain of what we do not see.
Hebrews 11:1 (NIV)

[1]Now faith is the substance of things hoped for, the evidence of things not seen.
Hebrews 11:1 (KJV)

Faith is easy to explain but hard to consistently have. To best explain faith, we'll do two things; we'll look at what faith is not and some examples of faith in the Bible.

What faith is not:

- Faith is not second guessing God for what He is able to do.
- Faith is not asking God for the desires of your heart but not believing that you'll ever receive those desires.
- Faith is not saying that you believe in God then handling your problems yourself, or trying to anyway.
- Faith is not believing the miracles of Jesus Christ.
- Faith is not saying I'll believe it when I see it.
- Faith is not thanking God for the desires of your heart until you actually receive them instead of thanking Him when you ask Him for your desires.
- Faith is not luck, coincidence or happen stance.

Some examples of faith in the Bible:

- God asked Abraham to sacrifice his son and Abraham acted on faith. He traveled up the mountain with his son, who asked his father where the sacrifice was. Abraham replied, "The Lord will provide." Because of his faithfulness, the Lord provided a ram in the bush for the sacrifice.
- Job exhibited unwavering faith when he lost everything even his friends and his family and almost his wife. He lost his will to live. He remained faithful to God through the entire trial. Because of his faithfulness, God doubled his previous blessings.
- Peter called to Jesus, "if it's really you, then call me out to you." Jesus replied, "Come." Peter walked on the water to meet Jesus. After a few moments, Peter stopped focusing on Jesus and became scared because he started to sink. He yelled out, "Jesus save me. I'm sinking." Jesus saved him as He replied, "Oh ye of little faith."

We have to exercise our faith consistently, no matter what the circumstances. He promised to provide. He will. He hasn't failed us yet.

Thank You, God for increasing my faith.

On This Journey

OCTOBER 6

[1]Therefore, since we are surrounded by such a great cloud of witnesses, let us throw off everything that hinders and the sin that so easily entangles, and let us run with perseverance the race marked out for us.

Hebrews 12:1

We are taught that life is a race. Several clichés come to mind: "Only the strong survive." "The one who dies with the most toys wins." "This race is won by the swifter man and the one who thinks he can." "Every man for himself and God for us all."

I don't know where any of these came from but they support a material-consumption based lifestyle driven by money, the greed of money and the accumulation of goods which require money. If life is indeed a race, even a Christian lifestyle, let's examine "the race marked out for us." He has a plan for each of our lives. For some of us, that plan will not include lots of money. We cannot base our success on the level of our bank accounts. Our prosperity He promises comes in the fullness of life His plan provides for us. If His plan for you is an overseas missionary, He will then provide for you the necessary provisions and the fulfillment for that to be prosperous for you.

We often want our plans and God's plans to match when in fact they could be totally opposite. Our faith and Christian maturity requires us to submit to His will fully and completely. Our wants often exceed our consciousness to submit to God's total will.

This is when the sin that entangles us so easily distracts us from our course. Of course, we need to request help for this is when we need the perseverance.

Perseverance is the ability to maintain your course without wavering. Perseverance is God power meaning you are equipped to overcome anything at anytime.

Lastly, timing is important. We are a microwave society versus a conventional oven. We want instant results rather than slow and perfect. We are on God's time. He has a plan with His timeline. In His perfect timing, we will see results.

Thank You, Lord, for keeping from some of the sin that so easily entangles us and thank You for marking our course for us.

OCTOBER 7

[10] Our fathers disciplined us for a little while as they thought best; but God disciplines us for our good, that we may share in his holiness.

Hebrew 12:10

I always wanted to be the child at school who did anything and everything but never got into trouble. At least I thought that until I found that only those who are loved are disciplined. My revelation was both great and saddening. It was great that I was so loved. I did decide however that I didn't really want any attention in that format so I chose the positive side of the attention by behaving.

On the other hand, I was saddened because there were actual children who were unloved. Discipline comes with rules, meaning that in order to understand why your parents discipline you, you have to understand what it is. Discipline is directions, rules and obedience. Without regard for rules, avoiding following directions and disobedience can lead to discipline or punishment, as some of us know it. It is built around consequences. As a young person, we don't know that the consequences of "running" or going through a red light means a ticket, at best, or death(s), at worst, until we are told or taught or we experience it for ourselves. The same is true for other things. Our parents discipline us to show us that nothing happens without a cost or consequence. Now, the critical objective for most parents, which we find out much later in life, is for them to discipline us so that the police or similar authorities won't ever have to. Parents who are consistent disciplinarians are mostly satisfied and even proud of their children and do not regret the discipline they imparted on their children. Often , those parents whose children are in trouble with authorities have regretted not employing enough discipline. Other factors are present beyond love.

The fact remains that the children whom God loves, He disciplines, without excuse. As His child, we must be ready to accept that discipline when we sin and are disobedient.

Thank You Lord, for Your loving discipline and continual forgiveness.

OCTOBER 8

¹⁴Make every effort to live in peace with all men and to be holy; without holiness no one will see the Lord.

Hebrews 12:14

How many times must we forgive? Seventy times seven. What do we do when we have a disagreement with our fellow man? Take it to your brother. If he doesn't hear you then take it to the church elders. If that doesn't work then be done with him. What do we do when someone hurts us? Turn the other cheek. Jesus lived it daily for 33 years, without sin and these are His teachings, all found in the New Testament.

People approach you based on your behavior. Let me explain. My oldest brother is a very even tempered man. In order to know he's angry, you almost have to ask. He might say that I exaggerated but it's true. One of his co-workers said to me that his method of response is always the same. He tells you what you need to know and always tells you truth but tells you in such a way that you still have your dignity when you're done. Because of his behavior, people approach him differently than they do most people.

Most of us feel that peace comes at a price but it doesn't cost your respect or your salvation. It will cause you to be calmer and congenial towards others. Remember to live in peace is to live with Christ. Others may only see Jesus when they see you so you have to consider the impact of your actions on the Christian journey of someone else.

Sure my brother gets angry but his behavior is the difference in how others respond.

My staff saw me make a transition from always knowing how I felt to never knowing how I felt because that was not Christian behavior. I stopped showing my emotions and communicated strictly the information that I needed them to respond to and the emotional pendulum stopped swinging so widely and so frequently.

Peace is a progressive achievement. You will see different phases during this progress. You will also see others drawn to you because of that peace. At which point, you can involve them in achieving that same peace by way of God holiness.

Lord. thank You for Your peace.

OCTOBER 9

[1]Keep on loving each other as brothers.

Hebrews 13:1

Brotherly love is a commodity – one which we take for granted. We have a choice at our leisure to love another – at least that's what we believe. Tomorrow is soon enough to love others – that's when I have time to get around to it. That's our attitude. A poor attitude at best. Assuming tomorrow is promised. Some people think that tomorrow is just another day. Tomorrow is "one more day than we deserve." But our actions speak volumes in the opposite direction. We need to change our actions, consequently our attitudes.

Try this:

1) Tell your parents/guardians "I love you" for absolutely no reason at all. Don't rush. Don't hesitate. Just say it. Mean it. Do it.
2) Write your best friend a note talking about all of the wonderful memories you've shared. Share how you feel about her/him.
3) Make and keep a list of things you want to do or see before you were either ill or died. Start immediately on the list.
4) Invest in other's lives deeper than they are in yours.
5) Be honest. Be true. Love yourself.

Brotherly love starts with each of us.

"Each day we have is one more than we deserved."

Lord, grow in us a brotherly love that endures.

OCTOBER 10

⁵Keep your lives free from the love of money and be content with what you have, because God has said, "Never will I leave you; never will I forsake you."

Hebrews 13:5

Society dictates the material quest. We fall right into the trap. We put our faith in money. We put our trust in money. We base our success on the amount of money we earn, accumulate and access. But the truth of the matter is that money fades. That money will only provide for a few things. God provided that money. He is first. Always.

Nobody and nothing can make the promise He follows with though: "Never will I leave you; never will I forsake you."

Everyone in your life will leave you at one point or another. Likewise you will leave some people in your life. You will spend forever with no one, except Jesus and God. When I've found myself alone and was surprised, it was then I realized that He was true to His word. Nothing changed between Him and me.

Most importantly, for whatever reasons that they left me and I them, God will not use those reasons. He will not leave me in spite of myself.

I have done some things that I'm not proud of. God loves me anyway.

God never gets sick. He is never busy. He hears me. Jesus intercedes for me without me asking. He has plans for my life. Better ones than I have for myself.

Most importantly, God's love and approval doesn't cost me anything. It is free.

Lord, thank You for never leaving me in spite of who I'm not.

OCTOBER 11

[8] Jesus Christ is the same yesterday and today and forever.

Hebrews 13:8

Today, I will be loving and caring. Tomorrow, I may not want to say a word. Yesterday, I was fun and spontaneous. That's the nature of the human being. But God, Jesus Christ, the creator of everything, never changes – not even for one moment.

Jesus Christ is the being whose actions I imitate in an effort to become more like Him. He is worth imitating. He is perfect.

Yesterday, He forgave me. Today, He forgives me. Tomorrow, He will forgive me. But we are not able to do that. We may forgive but on our terms in our time. Not God.

Overnight, we change about any little thing. Today, your favorite color is red. Tomorrow, it is blue. We are not consistent in our behavior or our preferences or sometimes our decisions.

Our loyalties move as well. Consider your friendships. We don't love unconditionally. If your friend upsets you, you may select a new friend rather than working on the relationship. It's the fickleness within us.

I'm glad that God doesn't treat me this way. When I am wrong, He exposes my wrongs only to me. He allows me time to ask for forgiveness. He forgives immediately. He never mentions it again. This is only one example of how He is always the same.

This also means that the rules are still the same. They are not wavering and not negotiable. His laws are to be obeyed. He is to be respected.

He is a loving God. He will love us no matter what. You are the most important person to Him that He created. Always.

Jesus, if I could be like You, then I would not waver.

On This Journey

OCTOBER 12

¹⁷Obey your leaders and submit to their authority. They keep watch over you as men who must give an account. Obey them so that their work will be a joy, not a burden, for that would be of no advantage to you.

Hebrews 13:17

Leaders include parents, siblings, pastor, church leaders, law enforcement, government officials, teachers, school personnel and other similar authorities. Obedience is hardest when you don't agree with what you're asked, but it doesn't matter because they have authority over you and are in the right if you don't obey. My only rule is not to do anything illegal your leaders ask you to do. This scripture assumes that the leaders are obedient to God.

One reason we don't worry about what they ask of us is because they answer to God as the supreme leader and authority for their every action. They are leaders to protect us. Consider your parents. You were given as a gift to your parents. As parents, they are charged with the mission of raising you, using godly counsel and wisdom. God protects His children. While no one can answer why some people are blessed with children and others are not, we can say that children are important to Christ and your upbringing is critical to Him.

"Obey them so that their work will be a joy, not a burden, for that would be of no advantage to you."

Teachers are paid the least among all professions where less education is required. They also have the toughest jobs: they teach us and they teach us to succeed. Most teachers make $44,000. But they could earn double or triple by doing something else. Why do teachers teach?

Human beings are hard to teach. We don't listen. We are disobedient. We are contrary. We are ungrateful for their sacrifice for the knowledge they share with us. Teachers are unselfish. They prepare for us – they have do their homework before they ask us to do ours. They prepare for us – they studied before they asked us to study. They give us their best and they get our leftovers. They come each day dedicated to feed us knowledge. We go to sleep in class. We talk in class. We don't turn in our homework, on time or at all. We don't read the text. We don't take notes. My mother said to me one day, "I got mine. You have to get yours." You sacrifice your own education when you are disobedient and when your disobedience renders your teacher unsatisfied with her position.

Obedience is an act of love of God. Obey – it's best for you.

Lord, remind me to be obedient to my leaders and allow those I lead to obey me.

OCTOBER 13

[18] Pray for us. We are sure that we have a clear conscience and desire to live honorable in every way.

Hebrews 13:18

This is my prayer. I pattern my lifestyle such that the Lord can be pleased. I make mistakes, sure I do. But the clear conscience cannot exist by doing purposefully opposite of what God has commanded. Now, there are decisions I make which God can't possibly be pleased with, however, He still forgives and loves me.

My decisions are carefully made in order not to error. I like to feel good about what I do.

As a Christian, we have to guard our lifestyles such that we are representative of Christ. Deciding at an early age to maintain your Christian lifestyle and virtues is a great decision. This is critical for your adult life. I started praying at an early age and I keep an active prayer life by praying with several partners as well as alone. Similar decisions will ensure a sound foundation which cannot be easily shaken by life's curves and obstacles.

Now, my desire to live honorably every day is primary. Life is all about order. I have to have a clear conscience in order to live honorably. You have to decide for yourself what honorable living means. For me, honorable living means avoiding lies, no sex until married, treating people as I want to be treated, praising and worshipping the Lord, attending church regularly, and participating in ministry at church. My lifestyle has to include these things.

Lastly, don't be afraid when you have trials to ask those around you to pray for you. They will uplift your needs and concerns to the Lord on your behalf, called intercessory prayer.

Let's review:

1) Desire a clear conscience
2) Make decisions about lifestyles
3) Desire an honorable lifestyle
4) Ask for prayer

Lord, each day I need to be renewed that I may live honorable in every way.

OCTOBER 14

^{2}Consider it pure joy, my brothers, whenever you face trials of many kinds, ^{3}because you know that the testing of your faith develops perseverance.

James 1:2-3

My first thought when I first read this scripture was that God was joking. How exactly was I supposed to be joyful about my trials? Then I read it over and over until it became real for me. Now, I get excited about my trials. I get excited about the tests and trials because of several reasons:

1) God loves me. He wouldn't give me anything I cannot live through. He promised to protect me and I believe Him. Elders say that what doesn't kill us will make us stronger. He is also investing in me.
2) My trials cause me to lean and depend on God more. I pray more during trials which overall increases my prayer life. He wants me to depend only on Him.
3) When my trials end, I have a new testimony of what God has done in my life. My tears turn into my testimony. My testimony then helps others weather their storms. Learning that my experiences are designed to help others and are not for me or about me was a big lesson.
4) At the end of that trial, I am stronger as a Christian. My faith is stronger. I know I can persevere more. God knows He can depend on me to remain faithful.

It's hard to persevere sometimes. There may be times you will want to give up but understand God gets the most glory. Your testimony is that much more powerful and impacting and touches more lives.

I get excited when God tests me. His tests translate into His love for me and His belief in me. The fact that God has faith in me is powerful.

Perseverance is necessary for life's journey. It is a valuable trait for surviving life's questionable moments, twists and turns and the unforeseen.

Thank You for my joy. Thank You for my trials. Thank You for testing me.

OCTOBER 15

[4]Perseverance must finish its work so that you may be mature and complete, not lacking anything.

James 1:4

Perseverance is groomed within each of us. Through trials, tests and tumultuous moments, perseverance is a result of surviving those tests. Perseverance fuels our determination to survive our situations and circumstances. Perseverance overcomes and withstands adversity. Perseverance also withstands suicide. Once I asked was suicide a sin and I received a lot of attention – more than I intended to of course. I asked because I had a fleeting thought of suicide once. I don't know why because I can't recall anything that was so difficult that I would consider my own death. The answer I got was startling. My mother responded that it was a cop out, meaning it was a cowardly solution for a temporary situation. She didn't answer yes or no but the answer is yes, suicide is a sin. Some may argue against that but I know that suicide is a sin.

1) Murder is a sin so murder of oneself is also.
2) Suicide means you have given up on all of God's ability and Biblical teachings.
3) Suicide means you don't believe that God can do exceedingly, abundantly more than we can imagine.
4) Through suicide and any attempts, you minimize Christ's death.
5) You have rejected Christ's help. He said He would answer when we called. Did you even call?

So, just those 5 points alone, I conclude yes, suicide is a sin.

Perseverance by design keeps suicide out of the option pool. You will develop an attitude of a conqueror as you mature through tests and trials. You determine that with Christ you overcome and accomplish anything. You discovered this ability through the successful end of your trials. Perseverance will mature you and complete you. In order for that maturity and completion to take place, you know that trouble will come your way. Troubles, trials, and tests ensure you are a Christian, rather than not, as most people believe. They ensure that God loves you and is pressing you to the next stage of your Christian development. You can persevere through your tests. Just believe.

Thank You for grooming me to persevere anything.

On This Journey

OCTOBER 16

⁵If any of you should lack wisdom, he should ask God, who gives generously to all without finding fault, and it will be given to him.

James 1:5

Be careful what you ask for. Wisdom develops through experience. So if you lack wisdom and you ask for wisdom, then you are sure to experience some events, circumstances and situations. On the other hand, if you lack wisdom and you ask God for wisdom then I feel that you have acted wisely. Wisdom exists when you acknowledge that you lack wisdom. Maturity exists because you know to ask God and you asked Him and you are willing to receive that wisdom however He chooses to present it to you.

He will give you wisdom but I feel that we earn that gift through our experiences.

In our youth, we need to be wise about our choices regarding sex, friends, school, future, parents, drugs, alcohol, and on and on. We need to make wise choices as these choices affect the rest of our lives. Wisdom increases the range of our foresight.

Let's spend a little time on consequences of our poor choices and how any amount of wisdom could change our future. Consider you fall into peer pressure and try drugs as a teen, or even in college. You try just a "little" of an illegal substance. Twenty years later, you want to be an elected official but you are painstakingly reminded of your experiment with drugs. Your future is at stake because of poor judgment as a young person. There are several people to whom this happened. At least one was elected but others were not. Society is quite judgmental of elected officials and hold public figures to quite a different standard.

You have unprotected sex just once because you both forgot the condoms. (Don't be confused. I don't condone sex outside of marriage. The example would also apply to the use of a condom and it broke during intercourse.) You have intercourse and discover you are pregnant or your partner is pregnant. Now what do we do, you ask. Each option has its own consequence. Be a young parent is one option. Give up the baby for adoption is another option. This comes with several consequences, one of which is there will be a child who will become an adult who one day may ask about you. Another option is to abort the pregnancy, which you may regret as an adult. Although abortion is wrong and may not be an option for Christians, we are in a worldly society where abortion will be presented as an option.

Bad grades and poor study habits affect your ability to get into the college of your choice, which will alter your future. Wisdom is important. Be aware how you become exposed to your additional wisdom. It also comes from your parents, teachers and church leadership. You need to take heed from their experiences as well. He said He'd give you the wisdom. He didn't say how it would come.

Lord, thank You for Your wisdom.

OCTOBER 17

⁶But when he asks, he must believe and not doubt, because he who doubts is like a wave of the sea, blown and tossed by the wind.

James 1:6

This scripture refers to the previous scripture when it advises on asking God for wisdom but this scripture can extend to anything you ask of God.

Just a thought: if you ask and don't believe you will receive, what incentive does God have to give you what you have asked? Another thought: If you don't believe, why did you ask? If I question whether I will get what I want from anyone, then I normally don't ask.

God has three answers to our requests: yes, no and wait. Yes is definitive and certain. He answers promptly and issues descriptive instructions on whatever conditions are attached, if any. Of course, this is the answer I like the best. It's not the one I heard the most.

No is also quite definitive. Again, He answers promptly. I have learned to avoid asking why, although I may want to know. Later in life, I found that I will eventually know why. I have also, as an adult, now thank God for His "no" answer. I have been abundantly blessed when He says no because He has other, better plans for me of which I can't see or have no knowledge. I have been blessed tremendously by Him telling me no on several occasions.

Wait is the response that concerns me. He doesn't answer immediately, nor in a definitive manner. In fact, the biggest concern is that I wonder what I am waiting on. I try not to be impatient but sometimes I do. Even when He says wait, I believe He will answer and do what only He can. Of course, when He does answer, what He delivers is more than worth the wait and more than what we can imagine.

Don't doubt. Sometimes it's hard but believing is trusting. It you don't believe God, then it's just like not trusting Him. We say we love Him but then our actions reveal disbelief and distrust, which don't match. The Lord deserves our belief and our trust without hesitation. There are enough reasons why in His word.

Thank You for keeping Your word and knowing that I believe.

OCTOBER 18

[12]Blessed is the man who perseveres under trial, because where he has stood the test, he will receive the crown of life that God has promised to those who love him.

James 1:12

Maintaining your composure during trials is synonymous to 'weathering the storm.' Perseverance results from overcoming trials and apply that experience to future situations. Perseverance builds character. It proves you have fortitude.

The crown of life is quite a gift. Your perseverance brings you blessings.

As a younger person, I persevered my parent's divorce. They divorced. There was the initial shock of the divorce. My mother left me with him and I developed a bitterness for her because of that. It was during summer when it started so you can imagine how I spent my summer and you know when you are in elementary school that's your first assignment when you return to school, "How I Spent My Summer." So needless to say the beginning of third grade was difficult. I spent time reading about how other children survived divorce. There were moments when my father discovered that he had messed up a great life by being stupid. He tried to make me feel responsible and guilty. I stood up to him and denied any responsibility in their divorce. It was his hope I could help him win her back. This behavior lasted until I was an adult.

My biological father is not a role model and of course I'm being kind. But the awesome news is that God blessed me with a stepfather who ignored the fact that I wasn't his biological daughter and I ignored that, too. So I got a new father. My mother got a real husband and some real joy. Perseverance and blessings prevailed. God's crown of life is special and everlasting. I gained a better relationship with my mother. I experienced a new father-daughter relationship. I know what my husband and our daughter's relationship should be. I saw their marriage as a model for my future marriage. I haven't seen or heard from my biological father since I was 18. I would've never thought that our relationship would be this way but it has and I'm better because of it. Not all divorces happen this way and I encourage you to keep a great relationship with your parents. You can live successfully through divorce and remember it is not your fault.

Christ, thank You for Your blessings and standing by me through these storms.

OCTOBER 19

¹³When tempted, no one should say, "God is tempting me." For God cannot be tempted by evil, nor does he tempt anyone.

James 1:13

God will test you but this test is of faithfulness and loyalty. Tempting usually relates to the sinful nature. Tempting also lures you away from God. God's tests lead you closer to God and involve Christ and the Holy Spirit.

Evil and the devil will not tempt God. The devil respects God and knows this is outside of his range of power.

Temptation comes at our most vulnerable points. This however, means that we can overcome this low point. Temptation is designed to lead us away from God, but if we remain focused, the ability to resist temptation and seek God's face will surface and we are then closer to God as a result of the temptation.

Temptation comes in many forms: cheating on tests or other assignments, stealing from stores or money from parents, taking the car without permission, coming home after curfew, sex before marriage or outside of marriage, alcohol consumption before legal age or over-consumption, drug use and abuse and any other sin.

The easy thing is to say don't fall into temptation. The hard behavior is calling on God to rescue and help you avoid temptation.

The best way to overcome any sort of temptation is to seek God's face at the moment you are aware of your vulnerability.

As an example, you haven't studied for your test and you won't be able to study. You're tempted to cheat. You know your neighbor studied. Your solution however is to ask God to bring to your remembrance all the knowledge to which you have been exposed and that you don't cheat during the exam. He grants your requests and your exam is graded on its merits. You then pray for help with your obstacles of studying in the future.

God tests not tempts, but helps us through both.

Lord, help me resist and not be led into temptation.

OCTOBER 20

[19]My dear brothers, take note of this: Everyone should be quick to listen, slow to speak and slow to become angry.

James 1:19

Knowing the whole story is valuable and a lesson I learned the hard way several times in my life. This scripture increased my compassion and patience for others. I want the bottom line first, then the details, not the long story then the results or outcome. But most people do not share in that manner, and I was seen as impatient when in fact I just like to get to the point. I soon realized that people don't respond well that way – not even me. I want to be listened to just like you do but I wasn't listening like I wanted to be listened to.

I had to learn to listen to everyone. Listen completely to everyone without anticipating (guess or assume) what they were going to say next. Listen and not think about my response. Listen until the other person is complete.

My husband and I memorized this scripture as a tool to increase communication in our marriage. I know that my daughter will benefit from me learning to listen. I don't want to have to say 'you don't listen to me,' so I don't want her to have to say that either.

It is as important to listen to your parents as it is important for them to listen to you. Speak so that they understand and let them know it is important for you to have their undivided attention when you speak. Your relationship depends on the efforts of both you and your parent(s). I hope this helps you – it did for me.

I told my mother these things and it worked wonderfully for our relationship.

Lord, thank You for teaching me to listen.

OCTOBER 21

[20]For man's anger does not bring about the righteous life that God desires.

James 1:20

Anger is one letter from danger. Danger follows anger, even in the dictionary. I ask myself is this worth getting angry? How do we get angry? Why do we get angry? Consider the circumstances under which you've gotten angry. Do you really remember the details? Are you still angry? Does it matter any more? Did your anger change the outcome of the situation? Did your anger alter the situation in anyway?

These questions are designed for us to consider the benefits of our anger. Are there any? Normally there are not any benefits to our anger.

We have all seen someone angry and the behavior which identifies that anger. You may have even asked yourself why are they angry and what has happened. Anger happens for many reasons but the important issue becomes: how to redirect the energy anger requires. I found my mother's wisdom true, which is that when you are angry you really aren't thinking clearly. If we aren't thinking clearly, then our decisions are bad. So in order to avoid these obstacles, between me and God, I ask some questions:

1) Before I get angry, I ask myself will this concern me later?
2) While I'm angry, can others see Jesus in my life at that moment?
3) Will my anger change the situation or the outcome?
4) Does my anger effect my health?
5) Is this really worth getting angry about?

Then, I made some decisions:

1) Ephesians 4:26: When I'm angry, I decide not to sin. I make it my business not to do anything I'll need to ask forgiveness for.
2) I make sure I don't hurt anyone else while I'm angry.
3) I decide to make responsible choices. If my anger will not change the situation or its outcome, I then decide whether I can walk away from the situation or not. If I can, then I do.
4) I address my anger with whom I'm angry and carefully explain why.
5) I will not allow my anger to endanger my health.
6) I ensure my anger doesn't interfere with my relationship with God and my pursuit of righteousness.

God, I desire a righteous life so please help me avoid anger.

On This Journey

OCTOBER 22

[22] Do not merely listen to the word, and so deceive yourselves. Do what it says.

James 1:22

Love is an action. In order for God to know we love Him, we have to show Him – through our actions. One of our duties is to obey His word. If we know His word and deny it, then we demonstrate our lack of love. We don't intend to act without love through our disobedience but when we do we hurt God. Our actions display lack of love and we cannot reverse those actions.

There are Christians who listen to God's word on a regular basis, maybe every Sunday and each Bible Study, but we never see them do what the word says. We unjustly start to scrutinize their behavior. Just as with Christ, if we continue to say we are Christians but don't do what He says, how do you think Christ feels about that? It makes it seem like we take Him and His word for granted.

How can we justify not doing what it says? We really can't but we create excuses for not doing what it says. Those excuses include and are not limited to: I didn't know, I forgot, I didn't understand it to say that (one of my favorites to hear people use), I really didn't think of it that way, among others. Christians lose portions of Christ's wealth He promised to us when we ignore God's word.

When we know the word, we are accountable for what it says. We are also accountable for sharing God's word. Lastly, we are accountable to hold other Christians accountable to God's word.

Lord, help me do what It says.

Daily Devotional for Young People

OCTOBER 23

²⁶If anyone considers himself religious and yet does not keep a tight rein on his tongue, he deceives himself and his religion is worthless.

James 1:26

Our religious practice is measured by our talk. Interesting? Sure it is; our talk, part of our behavior should support the religion we profess. Our religion should govern our speech. Our tongue should not make others question our religious practices or our religion, but sometimes we do.

Keep a rein, a tight rein, on our tongue – those are the instructions. What does that mean? Well, let's make a list:

Do's	**Don'ts**
praise God	gossip
encourage	foul language
truth	lies/deceit
promote love	criticism
positive	negative

Well, these are just a few but important all the same. Keeping a tight rein on our tongue is also an exercise of self-control, a characteristic of Christian behavior. Have you used a foul word? Some adults use them often. You look at those adults with a bit of confusion because you question their behavior, usually because we would have disciplined you if you did it. Foul language is one of the most obvious ways we don't keep a tight enough rein on our tongues. Foul language use decreases your maturity and will not impact long term popularity and casts a negative image. In our home, use of foul language constitutes a language violation. Most of the time, a limited vocabulary promotes frequent foul language use.

Criticism and gossip of others impacts your religion just as much as foul language. Why do we put others down? What exactly do we gain and why do we choose to highlight the negative about others? For various reasons we do this but it is not in accordance with God's word.

Perfection requires practice. Thinking before we speak starts the practice of keeping a tight rein on our tongues.

Christ, please help me keep a tight rein on my tongue.

On This Journey

OCTOBER 24

³If you show special attention to the man wearing fine clothes and say, "Here's a good seat for you," but say to the poor man, "You stand there," or "sit on the floor by my feet," ⁴have you not discriminated among yourselves and become judges with evil thoughts?

James 2:3-4

When we assigned ourselves as judges of others, we made one of the most critical errors ever. When we judge others, we make ourselves vulnerable to be judged using those standards by God, who ultimately has power over us and our actions and being. Just that thought should eliminate our desire to judge others. It doesn't, but it should. When we judge others, we make two mistakes: (1) we judged them and we have no authority, and (2) we judged them by different standards than God because in that judgment, we offer no forgiveness.

My mother often asks me how I would like to wear those shoes. She asks me this mostly when she either didn't approve of my behavior or she wanted me to think beyond my thought process. Either reason required me to develop a thought process and, ultimately, compassion for others.

When she challenged me, she forced me to consider others' circumstances as if they were my own. Her challenge eliminates the original urge to discriminate. The question we've come to ask as well is what if God treated us like we treated others. Would we like it? How would we handle that?

Considering those questions when we interact with others curtails poor behavior. There are things I have done and said to others, which I never want imposed on me – this is what governs my behavior. Remember the Golden Rule.

Lord, remind me not to judge or discriminate.

OCTOBER 25

¹⁷In the same way, faith by itself, if it is not accompanied by action, is dead.

James 2:17

Faith here is defined as our religious belief and practice. For us, our faith means believing in God, accepting Christ as our Savior and believing the Christ will return for us. These are the professions of our faith.

Our actions should support our profession of faith. This is not easy all the time but it is important we examine some common issues which often impede our faith.

1) Our body is a temple which we are to keep clean and pure because it is Christ's dwelling place. Thus, we have to protect our body from drugs and excessive alcohol. Also, we can't have sexual intercourse with anyone other than our spouse.
2) The Golden Rule revised: Do unto others as you would have Christ do unto you. If we continue to mistreat others, this is not obedience to God's word and those deeds will come back in that same measure.
3) Faith and religion are great but God expects us to attend church regularly, contribute our talents to the growth of the church, tithe, and share our faith with non-believers. If we lack in any of these areas, our faith is jeopardized causing observers to question our beliefs and question their pursuit of Christianity.

If Christians' behavior doesn't differ from non-believers and that of the world, then what purpose does faith serve? That's the question non-believers and new Christians ask themselves. When they ask, that's when we know our faith is dying. We do not want a dead faith so we need to modify our behavior. Remember, they see Jesus through us so how are we projecting Him?

Lord, I want my faith to live.

On This Journey

OCTOBER 26

[1]Not many of you should presume to be teachers, my brothers, because you know that we who teach will be judged more strictly.

James 3:1

Teachers are responsible for our knowledge. Teachers study to provide us with quality instruction so we are equipped to do battle with the enemy. Those persons are held to a higher level of accountability.

So with all this responsibility and accountability, why would Christ come forward to teach? Well, it's because it's a gift. To be able to teach the doctrines of God through the use of the Holy Spirit and His word is an awesome honor. This is a gift that definitely rewards if used properly and demands to be used. If given the gift of teaching, you won't be able to ignore the gift.

Consider how we treat our teachers. Do we treat them the best we can? Not always. But considering who they are and what they do, shouldn't we treat them better; meaning with dignity and respect and giving them our undivided attention in class, answering questions, participating in the discussions and doing all assignments. It is our responsibility to do those things because they submitted to their gift and are obedient to God. They deserve our attention and respect. When we don't do those things, we are in disobedience and God will judge us.

When in doubt, though, keep in mind one day, you too may teach. How would you respond to the student who talked while you were talking, and who was late and who never participated or who never did their homework? Now, you have just a glimpse of what you have to look forward to. Overall, most of us are respectful to our teachers, but for those of us who are not, we need to revise our behavior to an acceptable behavior and attitude. God judges us on our behavior so we need to leave out the other "stuff" we use to justify our poor behaviors.

If we are focused on learning, nothing else matters.

Thank You, God for the gift of teaching.

OCTOBER 27

⁵Likewise the tongue is a small part of the body, but it makes great boasts. Consider what a great forest is set on fire by a small spark.

James 3:5

If I am careless, my tongue will get me into trouble. The definition of trouble is my having more work than I want to do, more expectations to meet and the more I commit and the more I say. So I should learn to keep quiet but that doesn't always work. The important rule about tongues is to remember not to hurt people with its use.

Gossip and negative comments about others is a sin, a hurtful one at that. Usually, it's the misuse of the resource that costs us the most. Give great effort to uplifting others with your words rather than the reverse. Once the words leave your lips, you cannot get them back, no matter how hard you try. Once your words hurt someone else, we don't know how extensive that damage is. Our words impact others in so many ways. The more positive the better. As usual, the Golden Rule supports positive words based on the outcome possible if the words are not. In other words, how would you feel if those same things were said to you. I reflect on things I've said that I never want to hear again. I also guard myself against persons who gossip and speak negatively about others. I simply don't want to be associated with such persons. And as a rule, if they talk about others, nothing keeps them from talking about you.

My goal in life is to use my tongue to enhance the lives of others. The positive impact of the spoken word reaches beyond your wildest imagination. Try it. Walk up to someone and give them positive words of encouragement. Notice their reaction and behavior. It will be different. Use your tongue wisely – it could make the difference between life and death. Which do you want to effect?

Imagine your words influencing others to reach their full potential. That's time well spent and words well used. It's the least we can do if we won't use our tongue and ears in proportion (two ears and one tongue) – listen twice as much as we talk.

Let the words of my mouth be few and pure, Lord.

OCTOBER 28

⁹With the tongue we praise our Lord and Father, and with it we curse men, who have been made in God's likeness.

James 3:9

Does this imply that we are cursing God? In a manner of speaking, yes. You have criticized God's work. How can we criticize God and His work? What right do we have? We don't. We shouldn't curse God either. Let's investigate the wisdom of this act.

First of all, let's talk about why that's not wise. God's plan and wisdom you have cursed. He created us for a purpose and us cursing others demeans them and their purpose. Secondly, He made us, too. When we are being cursed, how do we feel? Not good, huh? Of course, not. However, this feeling doesn't deter our bad behavior. We continue to curse others. God's likeness translates into us being similar to His behavior, His patience, His love, His wisdom, and countless other attributes which distinguishes Him as God. While we will never be exactly like God, we were created with the pattern of God, except now we have our sinful nature, which He despises.

Because of this likeness, we should strive to uphold the attributes of God, to be like God; to do what Jesus would do. That is certainly not to curse others, but to uplift others. Our tongue is to uplift God and bring praise and honor to Him. Our tongue was designed to bring others to Christ, not to curse them. Our tongue can deter others from becoming Christian when it curses, this defeats our purpose as ambassadors for God. As an ambassador we have responsibilities to God. Not to curse is among the list.

Father, bridle my tongue, when I choose to curse others.

OCTOBER 29

¹⁶For where you have envy and selfish ambition, there you find disorder and every evil practice.
James 3:16

Envy is more severe than jealousy in that envy usually involves evil activity. Envy is the desire to have what others have and invokes a vengeful spirit to pursue that person or their possessions. It is sinful to lust over others' materials or blessings. When we do this, our behavior translates into disbelief of God's abilities and distrust of God's plans for your life. Envy tells God that what He has provided for you and His plans for you don't meet your standards and expectations. How insulting is that to God? How can our standards be higher than God's?

Envy houses disorder. Once we reach disorder, it is difficult to return to order. Orderly living consists of prayer, fasting, study, fellowshipping with other believers, and hearing God's voice directing your path. Not only is disorder the opposite of order, it is the definition of sin and sinful living. Disorder is not a recipient of forgiveness and does not seek wisdom nor Godly counsel. Disorder is content without God's mercy and often does not choose to seek order or anything which relates to order. Disorder breeds and thrives on its own behavior. Consider that someone lacking God's abundant gifts inclusive of joy does not encourage others to seek God's love and joy. Rather they encourage others to dismiss your joy and inner peace. Persons of disorder gossip, degrade, dismantle, manipulate and corner the market on negativity.

Overcoming disorder is not easy but anything worth having is worth working for. In other words, order is achievable. Asking God to impose order on our lives is step one. Submitting to His will is step two. Knowing His will is step three. Seems opposite but it's not. When we submit to God's will, we are ready to obey Him, then we can study and know God's word. If we did it in the reverse, we might assume submitting is optional.

Seek God's order for your life.

Lord, remove any envy or selfishness. I don't want them in my spirit.

On This Journey

OCTOBER 30

[17]But the wisdom that comes from heaven is first of all pure; then peace-loving, considerate, submissive, full of mercy and good fruit, impartial and sincere.

James 3:17

Wisdom is a gift from God and when used properly glorifies God. God wants us to be wise but only if it's used to build the kingdom. The scripture implies that wisdom could come from elsewhere, however, I think that knowledge used for scandal or evil could never be confused as wisdom.

Wisdom moves you to these traits and gently, rather than forcefully, or with manipulation. If we want wisdom, we desire those attributes as well. So when we accept wisdom, we accept purity, peace-loving, consideration, submissiveness, mercy, good fruits, impartiality and sincerity.

Wisdom demands an inward change for positive outward behavior. Further, responsibility accompanies wisdom. I also consider the attributes of wisdom to be a reward as well. If you've ever heard the phrase to whom much is given, much is required, then you realize how applicable it is to wisdom. If God gives you wisdom then He expects you to act wisely—at all times, not when it's convenient. Our use of wisdom is not optional. Our Father holds us accountable for the wisdom and knowledge we possess.

Wisdom is a blessing. Wisdom engages us in a trust relationship with God. God offers us wisdom because He can trust us to do the right thing: act wisely and in truth with peace-loving and all of the attributes synonymous with wisdom.

Thank You for Your wisdom—it's purity, peace and sincerity.

Daily Devotional for Young People

OCTOBER 31

¹⁸Peacemakers who sow in peace raise a harvest of righteousness.

James 3:18

Peacemakers are usually accused of being passive because they are not confrontational and they oppose confrontation. They avoid arguments and other disagreements because of the potential they can reach. At the same time, they will spend hours to reach a peaceful agreement, no matter what it takes. Peacemakers seek God's favor and submit to His will through their peaceful efforts.

How do we become peacemakers? Find the positive in all situations. Help others reach agreements when they have confrontations or misunderstanding. Be a listener. Share with others the positive in their situation. Peacemakers don't gossip and diffuse all arguments. She encourages people to mend their differences and points out the "bright" side, the positive of the circumstances. Believing that God's forgiveness is truly important, the peacemaker encourages the forgiveness of one another. Knowing that God forgives us without any conditions or strings attached, peacemakers forgive and encourages forgiveness.

Righteousness doesn't cost anything for some but for others, righteousness costs them their souls because they can't be righteous. They cannot submit to righteousness. So peacemakers are already under the umbrella of righteousness because of what they do in Jesus' name.

Righteousness is not hard to achieve but obedience and peacemakers meet the criteria for achieving and maintaining righteousness. They also influence righteousness in others.

Help me to help peace exist, God.

NOVEMBER 1

²You want something but don't get it. You kill and covet, but you cannot have what you want. You quarrel and fight. You don't have, because you do not ask God.

James 4:2

My mother and I made an agreement to follow God's word and hold each other accountable for our behavior. Rule #1 is "you have not because you have asked not." This is not new. She imposed it on me when I was a child. She didn't let me slide not even on one occasion. She never let me borrow anything of hers without asking. I thought that was terrible. When I realized its origins, God, I then held her accountable and asked her to do the same.

I received the desires of my heart because I asked God for them. It was as simple as that. God gives the desires that we have in our hearts. Once we have the desires that we have in our heart, it's up to us to act on them and translate them into actual results. This is when we ask God to deliver the desires of our heart to us. He is waiting on your request in order to fulfill the desire.

If He influences the development of the desire then waits on us to ask for it, why is that? Initially it made no sense to me either but I remember another childhood lesson. When I ask my mother for something, she is more inclined to give me what I ask for because she feels that I'll take better care of what I have asked for rather than for something I didn't ask. Same concept applies with God but further, asking God is recognizing that He is in charge and the giver of all things and desires. He must be assured that we are totally dependent on Him. Asking Him assures Him that we recognize His power as Lord in our lives. When He answers our prayers, He reminds us of His love.

I remind myself then I don't have what I want: "did I ask for it?"

Lastly, I have implemented the same rule in my family and often remind my husband of our agreement. And sometimes he has to remind me.

Father, thank You for hearing and answering my requests.

NOVEMBER 2

[3]When you ask, you do not receive, because you ask with wrong motives, that you may spend what you get on your pleasures.

James 4:3

God gives to people whose motives are pure and whose rights are relinquished. That was the title to a sermon Pastor West preached in January, 1998. I have never forgotten the self-assessment I engaged in following that stewardship series.

Why do I want this and are my motives pure and will this bring glory to God are questions I have to ask myself and answer before I approach God with certain desires. I am growing and maturing as a Christian when I don't have lengthy conversations about motives because my life is focused on Him so well that my desires revolve around Him so there's no question about motives.

Should God give you the desires without an examination of motives? Certainly not. If He cannot trust me to remain committed to Him, then should He give me what I've asked for? Certainly not. Will He give us everything we ask for? Certainly not. Should promises be made to God to encourage God to fulfill our desires? Certainly not. Does God have the right to withhold granting our desires based on our maturity and our ability to use them to glorify Him? Certainly. God is the judge of what we deserve and He certainly has the right to give us just what we deserve. Mostly, He chooses to give us what we don't deserve and He judges that, too.

When I got my first car, I promised God I would never miss church. I didn't uphold my promise to God because I missed church. I had great intentions but I didn't fulfill my promise. Most importantly, when I made the promise, the Lord knew my heart and He knew what I would do even though I didn't. He even knew that I would forget to keep my promise. He gave me the car anyway and He forgave me for making the promise and not keeping it. He is a wise God.

Lord, purify my motives and keep me focused on You.

NOVEMBER 3

¹⁷Anyone, then, who knows the good he ought to do and doesn't do it, sins.

James 4:17

If you were supposed to feed the homeless with the school or church and you didn't go and your reasons weren't sufficient, you are clearly in the wrong. This is only an example, but the truth exists that you were going to be a blessing to others but missed your opportunity to be used by God. Missing such an opportunity is a sin.

Knowing what's right and doing what's right is not optional. You commit a sin each time you know the right thing to do and don't do it.

Why do we neglect to do the right thing?

- peer pressure (not cool to do the right thing)
- don't want to do it (specific act; not conceptual)
- our sinful nature prevails and prevents us from doing the right thing

Doing the right thing has become a slogan for the anti-drug campaign, a company's motto, and general theme for various functions, including proms and graduations. But better than a saying tattooed on a souvenir glass or t-shirt, knowing the good we ought to do and doing it becomes a lifestyle we mature into as Christians. This is to be treated as a cliché. We as Christians are charged to do the right thing.

Why do we do the right thing?

- because of our respect for God and His word
- because we want do the right thing no matter the situation
- because our maturity overpowers our sinful nature into submission
- because we are accountable for the right thing; no excuses accepted
- because we want to avoid sin at all cost

Jesus, thank You for being my conscious and my redeemer and my guide.

NOVEMBER 4

[11] As you know, we consider blessed those who have persevered. You have heard of Job's perseverance and have seen what the Lord finally brought about. The Lord is full of compassion and mercy.

James 5:11

Society teaches and supports the 'dog-eat-dog world' and 'the every man for himself' and the 'survival of the fittest' mentalities. All of this is void when we speak of God, His kingdom and His blessings. Society teaches us 'by any means necessary.' Another philosophy which doesn't exist in Heaven or with God.

The Lord blesses us to survive the art of daily living. Further, God blesses us to persevere the issues and the situations life presents. This is not often easy. It is not easy to live through these situations and it is not easy to receive His mercy and compassion. But God's love for us is so deep and strong and real, He offers His mercy and compassion unconditionally, repeatedly and without prejudice.

For the rest of our lives we will be presented with challenges. How we handle those challenges will be the measure of our Christianity, our dependence of God. I remember when my parent's divorced. There were days when I thought I would never make it but the Lord proved me wrong. I made it through each day just as He designed. In the process of the divorce, I learned more about life and God's will for my life than ever. My experiences benefit others whose parents have or will divorce. I can share with others how the Lord will bring you through this test and trial.

Whatever your circumstance, situation or storm, God will show you mercy and compassion. He will see you through and support you every step of the way. You will gain strength through your perseverance.

Lord, thank You for Your compassion and mercy which enables us to persevere.

NOVEMBER 5

⁶Who through faith are shielded by God's power until the coming of the salvation that is ready to be revealed in the last time.

1 Peter 1:5

As you grow as a Christian, your faith will be tested, stretched, challenged and questioned (mostly by you). Assuming that you know how important faith is simply based on the number of times the word faith appears in the Bible, faith is continually renewed. Faith is intangible, similar to energy. Faith is your spiritual energy. Faith is how you withstand various trials and situations and circumstances. Faith reminds you that God promised never to leave us nor forsake us – no matter how bad we think we've messed up. Our faith protects us from His wrath and provides us with His strength. Our faith prevents us from attacks designed to dismantle our courage. This same faith keeps us encouraged to achieve our goals and the desires of our heart. This same faith keeps us focused on Jesus as our Savior, realizing that His plan will prevail through all situations. This faith reveals secrets even to ourselves. It is amazing what our faith reveals to us. We don't really know what we can survive until we experience it, live through it and share that testimony with others.

Faith is the evidence of things hoped for and not yet seen.

> Father's love, fearless
> Active, adoration
> Innovative, ingenious, inquisitive
> Thought-provoking
> Humble

Faith is a life-style, not a destination. Faith is a success but not an achievement. Faith is the source of journeys, not the moral of the story. Faith is your life preserver not your convenience stop.

Lord, help me remain faithful.

NOVEMBER 6

⁶In this you greatly rejoice, though now for a little while you may have to suffer grief in all kinds of trials.

1 Peter 1:6

What doesn't kill you, will strengthen you. Your trials aren't for you; your trials are designed to develop your testimony. Your testimony is for others to hear and be uplifted. After your trials, you are an example for others of what God can and will do in our lives. God made us so He knows what trials to present such that He gets our attention, He gets the glory and we recognize Him for His power.

God knows what He can trust us with. He knows us better than our parents know us. My mother knew how to get my attention when she disciplined me. She took my phone when I needed discipline. She knew that television didn't bother me. Extra chores didn't mean anything, but without the phone, I was miserable. My mother didn't give in because of my hints and requests. She was determined that I would learn from my disobedience. She knew that the phone was the key.

God will try us and test us and stretch us so that He can grow us up, so that we can rejoice from the outcome. Grief comes in many assortments inclusive of deaths, illness, divorce, heartbreak, trouble in school, finances, and other circumstances which test your faith and stretch your ability to believe.

When the trials pass, you are able to rejoice and praise Him for you perseverance through the trials. You and I understand how trials happen and why. We know trials are for our growth but it doesn't make trials easier – that's not how it's designed.

Rejoice that you can share with someone what it means to lose a loved one or how to survive a divorce or what it means to persevere through the lowest points of your life. Rejoice that God chose you to have those trials. He trusts us when we He selects us for these trials.

So even when the worst happens that you could ever imagine, remember God has not left you nor forsaken you. Trust Him. Cling to Him. Love and obey Him. Rejoice and praise Him. Share Him.

Lord, I know that I grow through my trials.

On This Journey

NOVEMBER 7

⁷These have come so that your faith – of greater worth than gold, which perishes even though refined by fire – may be proved genuine and may result in praise, glory and honor when Jesus Christ is revealed.

1 Peter 1:7

Our faith impacts every aspect of our lives, greater than what we are aware. If you have little or no faith when God is in the lead then you certainly have no faith in anyone or anything else. You may ask why I would say that; well, I'm glad you asked. Because of my faith in Jesus, I place my burdens at His feet and leave them there. I pray in faith that He will answer and He does answer. He answers because He promised He would and He answers because I'm faithful. Faith is accompanied by trust. I have to trust God to keep His word. Faith and trust are mutual. When I am faithful, He delivers His promises, then He is praised.

But it's not that easy. Having faith is not always easy. It's safer for your emotions to doubt God's power, reject your faith and distrust. But what if God felt that way about me. What if God said, "I have no faith that she regrets her sins, downfalls, and mistakes so I'll just stop blessing her. I'll stop keeping her out of harms way. I'll stop hearing her prayers. I won't meet her needs nor the desires of her heart." He doesn't though. He believes in me even though He knows me and what I'm going to do before I do it. He forgives me even though He knows my thoughts – all of them. He still offers me His love and compassion in spite of my "ugly ways" and I don't always exemplify the highest Christian standards as I should.

So why is it hard to have faith in the God who created us? Why is it difficult to offer all of your trust to the God who loves us without one condition or reservation? Why do we hesitate to totally surrender to the Owner and Creator and the all-knowing God who has yet to make a bad decision?

I have faith in Him because He loved me first and in spite of all I've done and who I am and am not. I trust Him because it's not wise to distrust Him or trust anything or anyone else including myself. He is a jealous but wise God and since He created the universe, made Eve from man, flooded the continent but saved the species, impregnated a virgin and a barren woman, let Jesus be born into sin but live 33 years without sin, died and resurrected Him, and promised to return for me, I can trust Him and have faith in Him if He doesn't do anything else for me for the rest of my life.

Thank You for honoring my faith and remind me to always give You the glory. I can at least start toward what You deserve.

NOVEMBER 8

⁸Though you have not seen him, you love him; and even though you do not see him now, you believe in Him and are filled with an inexpressible and glorious joy, ⁹for you are receiving the goal of your faith, the salvation of your souls.

1 Peter 1:8-9

The goal of our faith is the salvation of our souls. He saves our souls. Our souls needed saving from all of our stuff and ourselves:

1) greed
2) jealousy
3) hatred
4) gossip
5) no faith
6) no trust
7) theft
8) sex
9) drugs
10) alcohol
11) idol worshipping
12) inconsistent worship
13) impure heart
14) disobedience
15) law breaking

Just to name a few – these separate us from God. But what we know is that He loves us unconditionally without judgment but He's fully authorized to judge each of us because He made us.

When I first learned of God, I was amazed. Totally. At first, I questioned in detail His love for me. I wanted to know how much He loved me. Then I wanted to know why He loved me, of all sinners, why me. Then I wanted to know if there was anything I could do to have more of His love. That was some question.

He loved me when I didn't love myself because I couldn't love myself because I didn't know how. He loved me most when He should've scorned me, when He should've disowned me, when He should've ignored my pleas and my cries. He held me tightest when I not only didn't love myself but when I hated myself. The scripture is correct. I haven't seen Him and I love Him because I look at me and I know what He's seen me through and I love Him. I believe in Him because He's saved me from some impossible situations. I am proof there is a God just by waking up everyday because I don't deserve to be here. Inspite of what I do deserve, He still loves me and comforts me and fills me with His joy and His love, mercy and grace.

I love Him because He loved me first. I love Him because I don't deserve Him but He continues to bless me and love me. He saved my soul because He wanted me to be saved.

I love Him and believe in Him because He won't give me what I truly deserve.

Lord, I love You because You loved me first.

On This Journey

NOVEMBER 9

^{13}Therefore, prepare your minds for action: be self-controlled, set your hope fully on the grace to be given you when Jesus Christ is revealed.

1 Peter 1:13

Life is full of lessons and time spent on preparation. 'Prepare your minds for action.' At every stage of life, there is preparation for the next stage. In pre-kindergarten, we prepared for kindergarten. Kindergarten prepared us for first grade. Fifth grade prepared us for sixth grade and middle school. Eighth grade prepared us for high school. High school prepares us for college. College prepares us for our life and careers.

Well just as school prepares us for "life" as society would have us imagine it, our parents help prepare us for school. The most important preparation we can do is to study and meditate on God's word. Reading the Bible prepares us for life's loves and battles. Reading His word brings us closer to Him and prepares us for greater intimacy with Him.

Knowing His word prepares us to share Him with others – one of the most important parts of your Christianity. This is part of the action He expects us to engage. When we have the opportunity to share our faith, we need to be prepared to act immediately. Intuition doesn't come to an unprepared mind. In order to make intuitive decisions or instinctive decisions, you need to have that knowledge stored already. How do you prepare for action? Well, the solution is simple. It's not easy, but it's simple.

1) Read the Bible daily. Put it on your daily agenda. Pray before you read for understanding of what you read and application of what you read. By reading we will find answers to most of our questions and some of our prayers.
2) Prayer is the tool where we talk and we listen. Pray without ceasing.
3) Study the notes from church sermons. That's right – take notes from the church sermons. Go back and read those notes. Reread the scriptures. Make notes of any new questions or revelations so that you can discover the new truths you've learned.
4) Memorize scriptures as you read them. Select a few to start, then as you master a set, add a few and continue forever to memorize scriptures.
5) Give God His tenth. His tenth of your time. Two hours and twenty-four minutes is 10% of a day (24 hours). This is the hardest component.

All of these leads to preparation. Action is inevitable by nature of our Christianity. We need to be ready.

Thank You for preparing my mind for action.

NOVEMBER 10

¹⁴As obedient children, do not conform to the evil desires you had when you lived in ignorance.

1 Peter 1:14

Obedience is an action which translates into love for God. He knows we love Him by our ability to obey. When we sin and disobey we demonstrate our lack of love for God. Obedience is a choice. We can decide to obey or disobey. When we stay out beyond curfew, we made a choice.

In order to remain obedient and continue to choose to be obedient, I need help. I constantly need Christ to help me remain obedient. I decided to be in full obedience to God and rededicated my body to God by not having sex without being married. I stopped engaging in pre-marital sex. The decision was influenced by God. He directed my steps. After I made the decision, because of God's direction, I needed Him more than ever. I was tempted more than ever. To avoid that temptation, I called on God to help sustain me in my commitment to Him. Because of Him I was able to keep my commitment and avoid temptation and not conform to the past desires.

I had to know when I was vulnerable to such temptations so I could seek God's help to avoid the situations. This is a difficult commitment where there was very little support from the public. My friends wished me well but they didn't understand my reasons for such a commitment. I had to reevaluate my circle of friends for support of my commitment. I needed to talk to others with a similar commitment so that they could tell me that this would be hard. I also needed someone to tell me that when I said no to sex that I would not be disappointed in the results.

I discovered that several people weren't interested in me but rather interested in sex – I don't know if I was a factor or not. In other words, they would've had sex with anyone who would say yes. Once I got pass the initial shock, I realized that sex was not designed to be casual but a soul-sharing commitment with the person God designed for you. I was so happy with myself when I realized that God had something in store for me and the important point was that I ready to receive His gift.

Lord, help me remain obedient. Keep me away from evil.

On This Journey

NOVEMBER 11

¹⁵But just as he who called you is holy, so be holy in all you do, ¹⁶for it is written: "Be holy, because I am holy."

1 Peter 1:15-16

Easier said than done? In some instances, being holy is easier said than done, however, how much effort do we put into being holy? What does it mean for us to be holy? It is somewhere between what we do and what Jesus did.

Holy doesn't mean we quote scripture in every other sentence. It does mean knowing the scriptures, and being able to apply the scriptures to our daily living.

Holy doesn't mean turning water into wine or walking on water, but it does mean that we are able to tell others about Jesus' miracles and that we believe in His miracles. While we don't see the same types of miracles, we need to realize He still performs miracles. Just because He's not physically present, He is still present and performs miracles regularly.

Holy doesn't mean we don't have fun or friends. It does mean that we maintain self-control. Jesus was at a wedding party when He performed the first miracle, turning water to wine. The Bible doesn't say that Jesus wasn't doing anything which cast a poor light on Him or our faith. Jesus had friends, the disciples, and they held each other accountable for their actions. Jesus was able to recognize those who didn't love and weren't His friends; Judas is our example for this. Even when He spoke of His betrayal, He didn't change His attitude nor His demeanor. He remained the same. We have to measure what kind of fun we have and what company we keep. Holy does mean keeping God first and reminding yourself would you do the same thing if Jesus were here.

Holy doesn't mean that you stop living. I still listen to music but music which uplifts Jesus and doesn't influence me to sin. I still have fun when I travel with my family, when I visit museums and go to movies. I have fun and am fulfilled when I teach youth Christian values. Holy means that Jesus is first and our behavior honors our commitment to Christ.

Jesus, help me to be holy.

NOVEMBER 12

¹⁸For you know that it was not with perishable things such as silver or gold that you were redeemed from the empty way of life handed down to you from your forefathers, ¹⁹but with the precious blood of Christ, a lamb without blemish or defect.

1 Peter 1:18-19

We were saved from death because of our sins by Christ through His death, but He had never sinned. Christ died for something that He never did. Does it seem fair? Could we have been Christ?

No, it doesn't seem fair. We never would consider giving our lives to save strangers from dying – or would we? So many people do daily – police officers, fire fighters, the armed forces, Federal Bureau of Investigation (FBI), Central Intelligence Agency (CIA), the National Guard, and others who have died in the line of duty for people they don't know. Their loved ones miss them and love them and had no prior notice of their death(s). Their families don't find that fair either. So how do you think that Mary, Jesus' human mother, felt when He was crucified? How do you think your mother would feel if it were you which had to die to save others?

I imagine it was hard for Mary to be joyous about such a powerful act of God but I am certain that God had prepared her as He had for earlier events, (i.e. her pregnancy). Mary also had the wisdom to know that she had to be redeemed so she had to understand the sacrifice she was about to make.

Are you "Mary" material? I define "Mary" material as a person God trusted to carry the life of Jesus, or something with the precious status, then He trusted her with the upbringing and care then He performed the ultimate – He sacrificed His only Son to save our lives. He trusted her to spread the news that Jesus had been resurrected. She did all that God asked her with neither doubt nor hesitation.

Am I that Christian? We all have to conduct a self-examination to discover the answer. If the answer is yes, then great. But if the answer is no, then we need to ask Him to help us get there. He died for us, so we need to be that Christian He can trust with everything He has for us.

Lord, remind me that I was saved at a great price.

NOVEMBER 13

²⁵But the word of the Lord stands forever.

I Peter 1:25

The beginning of time is marked by God's words, "Let there be light." If I say let there be light, I had better have my hand on the light switch.

Just consider that God imagined us before He created us and the universe. A portion of His creation is the word. His word is how everyone knows how the world was created.

Since He started time, and continues to define time, He of course determines forever. This is not why His word lasts forever though.

His word lasts forever because His word is lasting and never-changing. His word is the same from the first day His word was created and it is timeless. His word applies to all situations and all seasons. Although we may not want to admit this, it does. Keep in mind, the Bible is the instruction book. When your parents cannot program the VCR or cannot make the transition from VCR to DVD, we refer them to the instruction manual. Most times we fix it for them but my mother wants me to show her rather than do it for her. It's not the same as the instruction book but I showed her and explained the steps and refer to the manual often. Then there are things I cannot do like make the PIP work, that's picture-in-picture. I then refer to the book.

The same holds true for the Bible. It's life's instruction book by the Creator of life. We can refer to the Book. We can refer others to the Book. Also, we can share the contents of the Book. By whichever method is appropriate, the Book remains the same and available for us. God wants us to know His word. The Bible is God-breathed, which means that God used those co-authors based on their ability to be used. God selected each person based on their obedience to Him. He picked persons He trusts. He knew the impact of His word – particularly the longevity and the power of His word. Could He have picked us?

When you need answers, pick up the instruction book, the Bible. It is everlasting and it will give you the answers.

Thank You for Your everlasting word.

NOVEMBER 14

[20]But how is it to your credit if you receive a beating for doing wrong and endure it? But if you suffer for doing good and you endure it, this is commendable before God.

1 Peter 2:20

When we suffer, we often feel we are being punished. I know I do. By suffering, it may not be as severe as Job did. Job lost his home, land, livestock, children, friends and his wife wanted him to curse God. Job truly suffered but never cursed God nor doubted God's love and power. Job's attitude and disposition glorified God. He set the example for all Christians of how to suffer. Job showed us how to suffer gracefully.

As a part of suffering, there is also suffering for doing good. I wonder how we can suffer for doing good but we can and will. One instance is the women who were on a mission trip in a foreign country during a time when the United States was entering war with a foreign country. Those women were captured and held captive by those people. They were later released unharmed and God was glorified because of the unfortunate ordeal. They endured it.

Another instance is the reporter who was on assignment in the same war. He was killed but God smiled on him. He endured it. It doesn't seem that He endured it because he was killed. He endured that situation though. He stayed to report the story and events as they happened. He could've come home as soon as he knew there was danger and all its possibilities. He survived and God was uplifted and honored. When he finally died, he was honored because most of us would've come home at the first sign of trouble. He suffered more than what we will know but what we do know is that God received credit for such a powerful act. Because of all he endured, there is a book published of all his writings.

Lord, I'll suffer for You and Your will.

On This Journey

NOVEMBER 15

²⁴To this you were called, because Christ suffered for you, leaving you an example, that you should follow in his steps.

1 Peter 2:21

To what are we called? Suffering? Service? Suffering while serving? What is our purpose? How are we to fulfill our life's purpose and calling? By His example, suffering ranks amongst firsts for our calling. What kind of suffering though? Christ fasted for 40 days and nights. Are we expected to fast that long? No, but we are expected to fast for a period of time. Fasting and praying eliminates the space created by sin between you and God.

Most of us know nothing about a sheet made into clothing with a tie to keep it closed and some sandals as our entire wardrobe. However, while we may not consider that suffering then, now is a different story. Some consider anything not name brand clothing as suffering. In His word, it states we should not worry about what we will wear. Our argument always relates to our peers and their opinion. We grow up to realize that designer clothes don't contribute to our education nor character. The other fact about designer clothing is its short lived lifespan.

You have never heard of Chic, Jordache or Gloria Vanderbilt – the designers of the late 70's and early 80's. Now it's Hilfiger and Polo. While Polo has lasted longer than most, consider the reaching ramifications that in an effort to be "hip" and "in," you can be broke. What good are $80 pants and a $40 shirt with $120 shoes when you can't afford a $12 movie with $8 popcorn and a $20 meal at the local hamburger place. Or you wear your $240 outfit but you put $5 in the gas tank until Friday. This is not the suffering He had in mind.

Suffering is synonymous to sacrifice. What are we willing to give up for the good of others is what we need to examine within ourselves. This is what we are called to do.

Christ, reveal my calling to me.

NOVEMBER 16

[23] When they hurled their insults at him, he did not retaliate; when he suffered he made no threats. Instead, he entrusted himself to him who judges justly.

1 Peter 2:23

'Sticks and stones may break my bones, but your words will never hurt me.' Do you remember learning that phrase as a child? This was designed to increase our self-esteem and to remind ourselves that they were only words and should not damage us. While that chant presented a valiant effort, we all know that certain insults and comments have wielded us hurt and unable to recover. We have that in common with Jesus, insults do hurt and some deeper than others.

His example is remarkable based on what we may want to do. When we humans are hurt, we try to figure out a way to recover from our hurt. We fight, curse, threaten to fight and argue and we say hurtful things back. God handles that though; we are just simply impatient for Him to do His will. We are to endure the insults. I know it's hard to hear and understand but we are not supposed to retaliate. As Christians, we are to ignore the hurtful words and trust God's judgment and not take any actions on our own.

Easier said than done, huh? I know it is because it's hard for me. I remember in elementary school when the other kids insulted me because I was "fat." I fought this girl because she always talked about me. What I realized as I grew older was that the insults resulted from jealousy. "Fat" children are healthy, happy and loved. "Fat" is in quotes because I define it as being slightly larger than others your age. I reviewed my school pictures and discovered that I was not "fat." However, during my investigation I found that I was the smartest in my class and I was pretty and my mother was active in my education. Later, I also found out those insults were based on jealousy because of the attention I got from the teacher and other administrators.

Jealousy influences people in the worse ways. Jealousy and envy will prompt the rudest comments and brings out the worst in people. Just imagine that Christ was resurrecting the dead, turning water to wine, walking on water and healing the sick. Who wouldn't be jealous and have ugly things to say?

When people insult me, especially now, I simply remember that their comments are based on their own shortfalls and don't have any relevance to me. And most importantly, I know I will be insulted because they insulted Christ first and I am a child of God so I'm not exempt.

Lord, teach me to ignore their ignorant comments and insults.

NOVEMBER 17

^{24}He himself bore our sins in his body on the tree, so that we might die to sins and live for righteousness; by his wounds you have been healed.

1 Peter 2:24

For 33 years Jesus lived on this earth and didn't commit any sins. Not even one. We can't spend 33 minutes without a sin. When I reflect on that fact, I simply cringe. I remind myself to be meek and humble and pray to be shielded from sin.

Let's talk about us dying for the sins of others. Would you? Would you die for someone who lied, stole, murdered, committed idolatry and adultery, coveted their neighbors, dishonored their parents and on and on? Probably not, because our judgment yields them unfit to trade our life for theirs. But Jesus did it for us – all of us, no matter what we did, no matter how big or small the sin. He saved us from it. He did it because His Father said to die for us. It hurt Him as it would hurt us if God would ask us to make such a huge sacrifice. Your life in exchange for others to be forgiven and to live. For us, impossible. Christ did it.

Christ was wounded so that my sins are forgiven and my soul saved and my wounds healed. So if He died so that our sins are forgiven and we are supposed to live for righteousness, why do we continue to sin? Can He just stop our desire and ability to sin? At one point, we were without sin but Eve couldn't live without that apple and as a result, we grow up and get to know the world. Sin starts when we know there is wrong and make a choice to do wrong. Only God can make allowances for our future sins and forgive us before we sin. Only God can sacrifice His only Son, resurrect Him and reward Him. All for us.

Christ, thank You for saving me.

NOVEMBER 18

⁸Finally, all of you live in harmony with one another; be sympathetic, love as brothers, be compassionate and humble.

1 Peter 3:8

Finding harmony with others is a learning experience. Living in harmony provides peace for you. Getting along with others is a gift as well as being charming draws people to you. While that's a blessing it can also be a curse, so be careful. Living in harmony is important.

Being sympathetic is a gift. Very similar to compassion, sympathy for another's troubles is Christ-like. Sympathy is listening to another's issues and problems and understanding the other person's "stuff." Our sympathy for others is an extension of God's love. It's how we want others to treat us.

Compassion is helping to make the situation more comfortable. Compassion means extending yourself to accommodate the needs of another. Extending myself for another means I have truly put God first by putting the needs of another in front of my own. I want others to be compassionate to me because I want my needs and issues to mean something to others. I also want others to be understanding and help my burdens to be lighter.

'Love as brothers' assumes that siblings love each other in a manner which fosters growth. But I will encourage you to love as you want to be loved. Love is hard enough to find so we have to be love in all we do and are. Remember, we are defined as Christ's ambassadors which means we represent Christ so our love needs to also be representative.

Humble is defined as modest and is the opposite of arrogant. Again, being Christ-like revolves around love, compassion and humbleness. It's hard to be humble sometimes, especially when we are blessed. But this is when it's most important to be humble. When God blesses us, He trusts to be mature, which includes being humble. He frowns when we are proud and arrogant. This scripture is one of a few of God's simple commands. They may appear difficult but if we compare His demands on us to our requests of Him, it is extremely simple.

Lord, help me follow Your commands.

NOVEMBER 19

⁹Do not repay evil with evil or insult with insult, but with blessings because to this you were called so that you may inherit a blessing.

1 Peter 3:9

"Kill them with kindness" is an old cliché designed to encourage us to win hardened hearts over with a kindness, which represents God. It is hard to treat your enemy kindly especially when your enemy has no intention of stopping their evil ways. God has a plan for those who do evil to Christians. That plan doesn't include our help. Yes, it's hard to smile and speak to the person who waits until you turn the corner to talk about your outfit. Or the person who pretends to be your friend but gossips about, or repeats your secrets to others. Or the person who picks a fight in order to become more popular.

As a child, I experienced fat jokes, wardrobe remarks and even was provoked to fight. (Yes, I should've walked away.) I had two fights with the same person in the second grade. After those two confrontations, she didn't bother me anymore. It doesn't always work out that way, but for me it did. My other incident was when my neighbor hit me in the back with her white patent leather shoe after the first grade promotion exercises. What makes children so angry and evil? I was six at that time. While I don't have an accurate or specific answer, my educated speculation is that they lacked love. When you are loved and experience love on a regular basis, you are less likely to be evil and mean to others. As a child, we are gifts and a signal that God will allow life to continue. But most children are cruel because of what they experience in their homes.

I have found that the best way to combat evil is with kindness and love. When you seek the root of the evil you typically find issues which don't relate to you at all.

The shoe in the back related to jealousy. I had just won the spelling bee and graduated second in the class. So she took out her anger on me, but I treated her kindly; at least I tried to be kind. I was glad I didn't repay her with a shoe in her back because later I realized why. Besides, she was hurt inside for longer and deeper than I was from the shoe.

Thank You for allowing me to ignore the evil and insults directed at me.

Daily Devotional for Young People

NOVEMBER 20

[14]But even if you should suffer for what is right, you are blessed. "Do not fear what they fear; do not be frightened."

1 Peter 3:14

Let's count our blessings:

1) We are blessed when we know that God's will is taking place in our lives, regardless of what is happening around us.
2) We are blessed to know God and His word. There are people who don't know God at all. There are those who know of God but choose not to walk with Him.
3) We are blessed to suffer because out of suffering comes growth.
4) We are blessed to have quality examples of suffering and the marvelous outcomes that God provides.
5) We are blessed when we can speak the truth to each other.
6) We are blessed not to be frightened or afraid. God did not give us the spirit of fear, therefore we need not be afraid. 'But the word says, "Fear the Lord our God."' Yes, but this means respect Him with the ultimate respect and revere Him because He is God. 'Do not fear what they fear' starts with the truth. Most people fear the truth because it's opposite of what we've become.
7) We are blessed to love a forgiving God.
8) We are blessed to be loved by God. Consider that God has choices about what can happen. He decides whether it will rain or shine. He decides what time the sun will rise and set. He decides if, when and how we will suffer. We are blessed because He wants us to prosper.
9) We are blessed because God is all knowing. I was running late one day to an event. As I was on my way, I passed an accident where people were hurt. My thoughts ranged from I pray God's favor over their lives to thanking God for His timing. Had I not been late, would I have been part of that accident?
10) We are blessed because He teaches us things. He shows us His power. And it is awesome.

Lord, thank You for the gift of distinction about what to fear.

On This Journey

NOVEMBER 21

[17]It is better, if it is God's will, to suffer for doing good than for doing evil.

1 Peter 3:17

Even when I want to do evil, I reconcile that it's wrong and I do right. This is often not an easy choice because of worldly pressure.

If your friends steal, then you may be inclined to steal. By reviewing the facts, my first question is if we have friends who steal, why are they our friends? Well Christ hung out with some questionable characters but Christ was never confused as a questionable character. He shared the truth with them about God; the distinguishing factor between them. How do we affect our friends you ask? Well, first things first – approach them in truth. Tell them stealing is wrong. Refuse to associate with them if they continue. Ask them why they do it knowing it's wrong. You will find some interesting things during your investigation, which may include they couldn't have it because they can't afford it or they really didn't know differently or because they want others to accept them as popular. Now that you know, it's up to you to say that you will share the truth with them. You continue to share the truth with them until it changes. You be sure though you are not mistaken for a thief.

As a Christian, you will be challenged to do right. You will be presented with numerous opportunities to do wrong. God will help you to do the right thing. This is often labeled the moral high ground. While that may be true, it is the right thing to do.

Avoiding evil is a decision based on wisdom. Wisdom, maturity and forethought contribute to avoiding evil. I think God honors our desire to avoid evil and provide an escape when evil presents itself. We then need to recognize the exit and take it.

Evil continues to present itself in various ways. It is our duty to avoid it and call on God for help at that time. So as to have an escape from it.

Lord, I want to do Your will. Help me avoid evil.

Daily Devotional for Young People

NOVEMBER 22

⁸Above all, love each other deeply because love covers over a multitude of sins.

1 Peter 4:8

The more we love someone, the easier it is to forgive him or her. Our love for one another makes our ability to sin and desire to sin less likely. When my child does something, I have a different reaction when another person's child does it. That's because I have a deep love for my child, deeper than for someone else's child. The same applies for your parents. Further, the love between siblings is easy to explain but strange to understand. They treat each other so badly, but if someone else mistreats one of the siblings, the other one runs to their aid. Isn't that how it is at your home? That's the depth of the love we're talking about.

God's love is the definition of deep love. His love for us covers all of our sins. We are to love such that it covers over a multitude of sins. Does this mean we forget the sins of others because of our deep love? Yes, it does. Does this mean that any sin is forgiven? Yes, it does. Does this mean that all sins are forgotten? Yes, it does.

We've all done some things that God ought to hold over our heads for the rest of our lives but He doesn't. That's deep love. There are some events that God should never forget but He forgets. That's deep love.

How do we reach that depth of love? Prayer. That's my first suggestion to reach deep love because He can heal the hurt which results from sin allowing deep love to develop.

Secondly, forgive yourself so you can forgive others. Forgiveness is difficult when we are out of practice. It is also difficult when the love is shallow. Love is the answer to 90% of life's issues.

Lord, remind me to love deeply.

On This Journey

NOVEMBER 23

¹⁰Each one should use whatever gift he has received to serve others, faithfully administering God's grace in its various forms.

1 Peter 4:10

How can we serve others with our gifts is not typically the first thing on the to do list. But serving others is the basis of Christianity and the example Jesus provided.

So how can we serve others with our gifts? We'll examine what you are gifted with and what you do well. Then use that to help others. When you serve others, you fulfill their needs and you are their gift and blessing from God. Our gifts are designed to benefit others – not for ourselves. How can we serve others? Based on your gifts, you simply start there. Perhaps your gift is prayer. You may be called to pray for your peers and their needs. Your prayers are not optional for your peers. Perhaps you gift is organization. You may be asked to go to the home of an elderly person to sort their bills and help them organize their homes. Again, this is not optional.

If we recall the parable in Matthew about the talents, the man who was given one talent didn't do anything with the talent and returned it unused because of fear of failure. The other two men doubled their talents. They were rewarded for their use of their gifts. Remember, your life depends on others using their gifts for your benefit, so you then influence the life of others when you use your gifts to benefit them.

This scripture directly states that our gifts are ambassadors for administering God's grace. You deliver God's grace through your use of your gifts. So why would you want to block someone else's grace by being stubborn or disobedient?

I don't know where this story came from but it's useful for this occasion. There is a community of people and they only have long-handled spoons with which to eat. They tried incessantly to feed themselves and could never eat. They lost weight and were close to starvation. One day, one of the members used the spoon to feed another member of the community, then that member feed the original member. The rest of the community caught on until they all fed each other. They then lived and survived as a true community because they served each other for the growth of each other.

Lord, remind me to use Your gifts according to Your will and purpose.

NOVEMBER 24

¹²Dear friends, do not be surprised at the painful trial you are suffering, as though something strange were happening to you.

I Peter 4:12

When I read this scripture, it always applies. As Christians, we will be tried and tried and tried, but we apparently forget that we will be tried. Our trials are painful and when we suffer them, they are not designed to be neglected. What that means is that our trials are designed to:

1) Bring us closer to God through prayer, study of His word and more intimate understanding of Christ's human experiences.
2) Show others how trials are survived
3) Remind us of God's love for us.

That last one is hard to understand I'm sure. But if God didn't love us, trials wouldn't exist. Job is one such example.

Trials are not a surprise; they are a given. Jesus endured many trials. I have learned to expect a trial or two. But what I do in response to a trial is what makes the difference. In preparation for the trials that will come, pray. Pray for preparation for the trials. Pray for perseverance. Pray for your testimony. Pray for obedience during your trials.

Just a question: why wouldn't trials happen to us? They happened to Jesus. Nothing strange is happening. We should expect it – the Word clearly states that we will be tried.

Our trials strengthen our faith and draw us closer to God. Trials increase our trust in God. Trials create our testimony.

Lord, when my trials come, help me to be prepared.

NOVEMBER 25

[13]But rejoice that you participate in the sufferings of Christ, so that you may be overjoyed when his glory is revealed.

I Peter 4:13

As I think of the overjoy to which this scripture refers, I am overwhelmed. Putting the scripture in plain English, it says that we are to be glad we suffer like Christ and then we can really be happy when we can say that God is glorified.

As we examine the difficulty in rejoicing in suffering, we need to realize that we are able to be excited because of God's selection. We are chosen because He trusts us to be faithful and obedient to His calling. Often we miss our mark and move away from the suffering before the lesson is done.

When you are someplace and unhappy, ask God what is His purpose. It may be that you are there to learn something. It could be that you are to teach something and someone else benefits. Or it could be that we need certain experiences. We will need to be patient during this time. We need to focus on the outcome rather than the situation or circumstances.

His glory is our testimony that we learned or benefited or that we sacrificed for another after this suffering. His glory is revealed when we can thank Him for His view of certain situations.

God just wants us to learn more and be a better blessing to those we come in contact with. People cross our path for a reason and God is at the root of the reason. We are to share with everyone in our reach the goodness of Christ. This is His true glory. We can share this because He is truly good to us.

His glory is powerful through our daily lives. The more dominant He is in our lives, the more powerful He is. Our trials bring Him glory.

Lord, I suffer so that You may be glorified.

Daily Devotional for Young People

NOVEMBER 26

¹⁹So then, those who suffer according to God's will should commit themselves to their faithful Creator and continue to do good.

1 Peter 4:19

In my insufficient words: don't give up and keep our eye on the mark.

Don't give up. Don't stop pressing toward the mark. What's the mark? Pleasing God. The great thing about pleasing God is that He doesn't change therefore the mark doesn't move. This fact makes it easy to commit to Him and remain faithful.

Let's focus on "continue to do good." What does 'good' mean? I've compiled a list but it is non-comprehensive:

- Obedience to God, parents and others in authority, inclusive of teachers.
- Avoid gossip; avoid putting down your peers and classmates.
- Offer your help to elderly and younger persons.
- Save your money (a word to the wise most everything goes on sale and video games get old.)
- Listening is a component of obedience; tell your parents where you'll be and with whom you'll be.
- Tell the truth; honesty and integrity speaks volumes of your character.
- Give your time to your church. You could answer the phones, make phone calls or stuff envelopes.
- Clean your room, do your homework and go to bed without being asked. Your room would be easier if we manage it each day, then make sure we do the heavier cleaning on the same day each week. I recommend a night during the week so that you won't have to commit any of your weekend. Your rest is your responsibility. It impacts your attitude and your learning ability. You are more fun if you are rested. They shouldn't have to tell you to go to bed. You should agree on a time they feel is reasonable and be obedient. Doing your homework impacts your future, not that of your parents. It may seem cruel but they have their education. It is a fact that your education is directly related to your future.
- Avoid sex, drugs, alcohol and negative peer pressure to cut school and steal and other ungodly things.

That's a short list but a great starting point for the areas that are most critical to your spiritual growth.

Help me, Father, to continue to do good.

On This Journey

NOVEMBER 27

⁵Young men, in the same way be submissive to those who are older. All of you, clothe yourselves with humility toward one another because, "God opposed the proud but gives grace to the humble."

1 Peter 5:5

Humble, meek and gracious are synonymous. Humble is the opposite of arrogant and haughty. Humility is acting without pretense. It all means down to earth.

But why don't we act that way toward everyone? To some people we act all knowing. To others we act better than them. To still others, we act totally respectful. What makes the difference between them and how you treat them? One difference is age. We respect those we consider older or elderly.

Another difference is money. The money assumption is derived from material items, such as clothes, car, house and other material indicators. If we perceive a person has less, then we look down on them. We don't treat them the same. If we perceive that they have more than us, we tend to treat them with respect and give them our full attention.

A third difference is cultural differences. We treat people differently if we don't know about their culture. I define culture as unique foods, unique eating habits, unfamiliar dress practices, different religion or anything different from what we have grown to define as 'normal.' Anything outside those parameters we consider to be different. Unfortunately, we judge those persons because of their differences rather than attempting to understand their differences. I decided long ago that if I didn't want to be judged, then I shouldn't judge. Likewise, I have differences, as do we all and I want people to understand me and be compassionate to my differences, especially if I have needs because of my differences.

Lastly, I wish to be the recipient of God's grace. I pray that God teaches me to omit the differences of others, as well as my pride.

Lord, remind me to act with humility and act humbly.

NOVEMBER 28

⁶Humble yourselves, therefore, under God's mighty hand, that he may lift you up in due time.

1 Peter 5:6

For this scripture we will focus on God's due time. God's timing is awesome but we question His judgment of the occurrence of events. "He may not come when we want Him, but He'll be there right on time. He's an on-time God. Yes, He is" is a portion of a popular Christian song. This verse reminds us that God's will occurs in God's time, not in our time. This is hard to embrace when we want God to do great things in our lives but on our timing. Again, we want God to do the great things He has planned for us but in our "in a hurry" timing. We want to rush His blessing.

These last three sentences should sound really strange to you, but they don't. We really want that. The answer is no. A resounding no. We will not rush His blessings nor His plans for us.

In God's timing is when great things happen. Then and only then. When we get that understanding, life will be much better for us. Life will change immediately when we accept that as fact. The hardest thing I have had to do as a Christian is remember that my testimony comes from trials and if I had my way, I would never have any trials but would God get the glory as He should? Not likely.

In due time is when God is ready to move us to the next stage. In due time is when we have learned the lesson God has in store. In due time is over after we submit to God and give Him the glory. In due time is when we are mature enough to receive what He has for us. In due time is when we can appreciate God's greatness and vision. In due time is when we can accept God as Lord and we move out of His way.

In due time is time when we accept His love unconditionally. In due time changes when I thank You for Your timing.

Remind me of Your timing, Lord. Remind me not rush You.

On This Journey

NOVEMBER 29

⁷Cast all your anxiety on him because he cares for you.

1 Peter 5:7

What worries you? What keeps us awake at night? What distracts us from focusing on matters at hand? Anxiety. Worry. These two answers seem simple enough, but are a tall order to overcome.

Anxiety as defined by the Random House dictionary is distress or uneasiness caused by danger or misfortune. Your anxiety probably falls into one or more of these categories: grades, school, college, parents, money, and friends. Of course to all of those topics presents simple but hard to achieve answers:

Issue	Solution
grades	study
school	maintain good attendance
college	study, apply early and follow instructions
parents	obey and respect
money	God will supply your needs
friends	don't spend lots of time on this; it is rare to have the same friends as you grow up older and closer to Christ

The real solution is give the anxiety to God. All of it. Right now. Pray to God confessing that there are some issues and then telling Him what they are and lastly, depending on Him for the solution. It sounds easy. And it is.

Pitfalls to avoid: don't take it back. Often we say that we have given our anxiety over to the Lord but we keep trying to fix it ourselves. You're thinking how is that. Well, if you continue to worry about it then you didn't completely give it to Him. Also, if your behavior doesn't change, then it cannot be fixed because we haven't repented (turned away and stopped sinning). How can He handle it if we continue to interfere? He could but He won't. And He shouldn't. He told us to cast all our anxiety on Him because He cares for us.

All means all and it means all of the time; each anxiety – not the big one or the small ones. All. Finally, if you keep giving attention to the anxiety, does that say to God that you don't believe He can handle it or that you don't believe He cares?

Thank You for wanting my anxiety. Thank You for caring for me.

NOVEMBER 30

[10]And the God of all grace, who called you to his eternal glory in Christ, after you have suffered a little while, will himself restore you and make you strong, firm and steadfast.

1 Peter 5:10

Job's story is such a powerful one but a clear example of this scripture and more so evidence of God's actual work. It's proof of what God will actually do.

When we read scripture we need to believe the contents. We need to diligently research the evidence or proof of that actually happening. The word of God is all encompassing. Our worldly nature encourages us to question His word, pick which parts we believe and spend minimal time with His word.

Questioning God's word is not a practice I've adopted. This is the same as questioning God. Now when I say question, I mean actively challenging His word and the appropriateness. This is not to be confused with asking for clarification on a scripture and once you get an answer consistent with God's word, you accept that answer and move on. Rather, questioning should not involve dissecting God's word in order to find fault, flaw or contradicting information. Just a word to the wise, we are usually likely to engage in this behavior when we are attempting to justify a wrongdoing.

The Bible is a living, breathing document. We have to take all the parts together. It is whole, not a bunch of parts. Further, we can't pick out the scripture that suits us or supports us today, but we don't "like" the other pieces. If you like John 3:16 'For God so loved the world that He gave His only begotten Son that whosoever believes in Him should not perish but have everlasting life,' then you also need to like John 14:15 'If you love me, you will obey what I command.' All scripture works together for a total and sufficient representation of God's word. It's like wanting to keep the heart but discard the liver. You really need all parts to live.

Lastly, we owe God 2 hours and 24 minutes daily with Him, total, focused attention. We actually spend the minimum time available, which some days means no time at all. Intimacy happens after we have spent time with that which we are intimate. We cannot expect to become stronger and more faithful and steadfast unless we study and pray daily. God has something new and different and exciting for us each day. We have to make ourselves available to receive His grace.

Thank You for Your grace.

DECEMBER 1

³His divine power has given us everything we need for life and godliness through our knowledge of him who called us by his own glory and goodness.

2 Peter 1:3

So all I need to live a life of godliness is knowledge of Him and I already have everything I need for my life. Wow, are you sure?

Need versus want dictates the better part of our lives. It is a definite distinction between need and want. We often blur the lines but clearly there are differences between what we need to survive and what we want to make life more fun and convenient.

God spoils us because we have imagination and thoughts and creativity. If we can think of it, then we can have it. Most often this is true, but it doesn't mean you have to have it.

Need	**Want**
food	specific items/specific brands
clothes/shoes	name brands (Polo, Nike, Gap, etc.)
shelter	fancy neighborhood, largest house on block
transportation	foreign, popular, expensive name brand

What we want is not out of reach and nothing is wrong with that, however, basics need not be neglected. Be able to decide when you must have your 'wants.' As a young person, we will not have everything we want because our parents provide for us. They cannot afford everything we want and everything they want, too. Remember to ask yourself when you demand the newest and latest in video game technology, if they will have to sacrifice anything for you to have that gadget. What could they do for themselves rather than buy you this gadget that has no real value, other than entertainment. Your parents want to give you everything you want but know that that is not good for you so they won't. God won't either, so don't be surprised when you ask and the answer is no. Realize that nothing really changed – your needs continue to be met.

Thank You for supplying all of my needs and some of my wants.

Daily Devotional for Young People

DECEMBER 2

⁴Through these he has given us his very great and precious promises, so that through them you may participate in the divine nature and escape the corruption in the world caused by evil desires.

2 Peter 1:4

'He has given us his very great and precious promises.'

He promises to be faithful. Deuteronomy 7:9
He remembers His promises and covenants. Psalm 105:8
He keeps His promises. Numbers 23:19
He promises everlasting life. John 6:47
He promises eternal life. I John 2:25
He promises to return for us. 1 Thessalonians 4:16
He promises that the old life will go away. Revelation 21:4
He promises a place for us with Him after His return. John 14:2-3
He promises to save us. Ephesians 2:8
He promises the fruit of the Spirit. Galatians 5:22-23
He promises life without fear. Proverbs 1:33
He promises relief from suffering. Isaiah 14:3
He promises to help us. Isaiah 41:13
He promises to keep our foot from being snared. Proverbs 3:25-26
He promises to purify us. I John 1:9
He promises mercy. Job 11:6, Exodus 33:19
He promises compassion. Lamentations 3:31-33
He promises love. John 3:16
He promises grace. II Chronicles 30:9
He promises forgiveness. Luke 6:35-38, Matthew 6:14
He promises to keep us from falling. Psalms 37:24
He promises us strength. Psalms 73:26
He promises protection for us. Psalms 32:7
He promises us refuge. Psalms 46:10, Nahum 1:7
He promises us joy and laughter. Job 8:21
He promises us light from darkness. Micah 7:8-9
He promises peace. John 16:33
He promises deliverance. Psalms 34:19
He promises to be our rock. Psalms 18:2
He promises to provide for our needs. Joel 2:26
He promises direction, counsel and instruction. Proverbs 3:6, Psalms 32:8
He promises to remove our transgressions. Psalms 103:12
He promises newness. II Corinthians 5:17
He promises to never leave or forsake us. Joshua 1:5

Thank You for keeping Your promises. Help me better keep Your commandments and my promises.

On This Journey

DECEMBER 3

⁵For this very reason, make every effort to add to your faith goodness and to goodness, knowledge; ⁶and to knowledge, self-control; and to self-control, perseverance; and to perseverance, godliness; ⁷and to godliness, brotherly kindness; and to brotherly kindness, love.

2 Peter 1:5-7

Faith is the price of admission. It is required. Not optional. Faith is believing in God and His word and works. Faith is knowing and sharing the good news about God and His blessings. Faith is hard. Faith is also commitment to God and His will.

Goodness exists within each of us. We may have to dig for it or fight for it. We have good within us. We need to share our goodness with others. Likewise, we need to accept the goodness of others. Our goodness represents God and His work within us.

Knowledge is acquired several ways, but the most important is we study for ourselves. Study is what we like least but is the best method for learning and retention. Knowledge stimulates maturity and growth. Knowledge also makes us accountable as Christians.

Self-control accompanies knowledge, maturity and goodness. It is a result of submission to God and His will. Self-control is the evidence of God's work and the result of prayer. Self-control is required for the journey.

Perseverance is staying in the race. Not giving up. Knowing that our finest hour will come after our most bleak moment. Perseverance cannot exist without faith. To persevere means to withstand pain and endure struggle. We have to be durable. We have to act like the person God made. He did not specialize in quitters.

Speaking of God, godliness and perseverance operate together as a unit, not independent but rather interdependent. Godliness means acting within the will of God and all the time.

Brotherly kindness is treating others the way God treats us. It's realizing that we need other people to live comfortably in this world. It's having compassion for others. Brotherly kindness embraces the soul of another and assures them that God is in control and has the last say.

Love combines all of these and propels us into the bosom of God. Love needs nurturing. Love cleanses us from sin. Love captures the essence of who we are and absorbs all that we lack and presents a perfect work named Christian or God's child.

Lord, thank You for faith, goodness, knowledge, self-control, perseverance, godliness, brotherly kindness and love. I want to be in Your will.

DECEMBER 4

⁸For if you possess these qualities in increasing quantities in increasing measure, they will keep you from being ineffective and unproductive in your knowledge of our Lord Jesus Christ.

2 Peter 1:8

In other words, we are to pursue faith, goodness, knowledge, self-control, perseverance, godliness, brotherly kindness and love so that we are better Christians and our knowledge of our Lord Jesus Christ. We are also expected to be effective and productive in our knowledge of our Lord.

How do we increase the quantities of those qualities is one such question we will answer in the next few paragraphs.

We agree that these qualities are wonderful attributes to possess. We can expect God's favor even if we possess these qualities in even the smallest proportions. We also agree that increased quantities of these qualities will also yield God's favor.

I would start with increasing our study time. This will increase our knowledge. The more I know about God influences my increase in love, brotherly kindness, and faith. The more I experience in my life with Christ, the more godly I want to be and become. Godliness requires God's help. He will help you become more godly – more like Him. We have to desire goodness to regularly achieve goodness. There will be times when you will not be good. There may even be times when you want to be good but don't. The fact we need to remember about goodness is that there will be obstacles designed to prevent us from being good. Goodness is more than behavior, it also encompasses your spirit and heart. So is your spirit and heart good?

Lastly, perseverance increases the better we know God and can testify of His goodness. As Christians, we know a change will come because we know God will not allow us to suffer forever. We also know that our experiences and sufferings produce our strength and increase our testimony and faith.

Our effectiveness and productivity also depends on remembering the lessons we've learned and knowledge we've acquired, and the trials we've endured. Finally, we are most effective and productive when we realize our testimonies are to benefit others and remember to remain focused on Him.

Lord, help me be effective and productive as I serve You.

DECEMBER 5

⁹But if anyone does not have them, he is nearsighted and blind, and has forgotten that he has been cleansed from his past sins.

2 Peter 1:9

To be nearsighted and blind in the sight of God is suicidal, a spiritual death. We may not possess the same quantities of faith, goodness, knowledge, self-control, perseverance, godliness, brotherly kindness and love but we should all possess all of the qualities. This is a reasonable expectation.

To be nearsighted and blind also indicates we also need to focus on gaining these qualities. By focusing on these qualities we acknowledge that God is Lord and that He has cleansed us from our sins. It is important we acknowledge that He is Lord. It is also important we honor Him as Lord. We honor Him by remembering that He has cleansed us from our sins and cast them on the sea of forgetfulness. He also sacrificed a lot for us to enjoy this. Often I thank Him because He is a man of His word and He didn't change His mind. He could've easily decided that after Eve and Adam sinned He would wipe the slate clean and restart but He didn't. Because that change certainly would've impacted our lives today.

Why wouldn't you want to possess those qualities? I do not know what I would do without faith or goodness or without knowledge or self-control or without perseverance or godliness or without brotherly kindness? But without love, surely I would die. I'm sure of it. Love is all encompassing. Love started with God. God defines love over and over and over again. So surely, I couldn't live without it. I wouldn't even want to try to live without love. Living without love means without ALL love. ALL cannot start without God's love. No way – no how. There's no life without God's miraculous love.

We want to possess these qualities in as large of quantities as we can. Our possession of these qualities upholds the standards that God has for us. Fostering these qualities shows God our commitment to Him. It shows God that we want to be neither nearsighted nor blind.

Lord, allow me not to be nearsighted nor blind.

DECEMBER 6

Daily Devotional for Young People

[10] Therefore, my brothers, be all the more eager to make your calling and election sure. For if you do these things you will never fall, "and you will receive a rich welcome into the eternal kingdom of our Lord and Savior Jesus Christ."

2 Peter 1:10-11

As humans, we often need the definite direction that if we do _____, then the results are _____. Not every situation will have this outcome. Most things are not that easy or simple.

The calling and election the scripture refers is our calling to serve God and our election that Christ is Lord of our lives. God calls us to Him. If we listen for His voice, He directs us, calls us to Him and reassures us of His love. How can we be sure of His voice and how can we be sure that He has called us are two questions we'll answer.

His voice is authoritative. His voice declares the just and righteous response. His voice is distinctive and distinguished. It is bold and charismatic. It is not you or your voice. It does not always support your desires. That's when you really know you've heard His voice and that He is calling you. He does not support or encourage or condone your inappropriate desires, so that's a firm indication that it's God voice. We are promised a "rich welcome into the eternal kingdom of our Lord," if we are "eager to make your calling and election sure." In order for that reward, we must answer His voice.

Yet another cliché: 'your attitude determines your altitude.' Our eagerness makes the difference. Our eagerness speaks volumes about the intensity of our commitment. Eager is synonymous with zeal, so we can conclude that the more zeal we exhibit, the better response we will receive.

I like this promise because my attitude and behavior directly impact my future. I like this promise because of its huge in magnitude and content.

Thank You for preparing a place for me.

On This Journey

DECEMBER 7

¹⁶We did not follow cleverly invented stories when we told you about the power and coming of our Lord Jesus Christ, but we were eyewitnesses if his majesty.

2 Peter 1:16

While experience is the best teacher, we do need others' experiences with certain instances. We will not experience everything personally and certainly not the experience of the disciples.

The disciples' firsthand experience is the only recount from which we will benefit. Neither will our experience be the same. Does that mean that one experience is better than the others? No it doesn't. While each experience has its benefits, it most certainly has its disadvantages, too.

Disciples Benefits
- Firsthand knowledge of Jesus in the flesh
- Witness the miracles as they happen
- Get answers to their questions immediately
- Question Jesus about God's word and will
- Present for monumental events in our Christianity
- Personal teaching and leadership
- Able to finish His work

Disciples Disadvantages
- Greater accountability
- Witnessed His death
- Left with questions (i.e. did we learn enough? can we do what is expected?)

Our Benefits
- Our suffering has been answered and provisions made for survival
- We know the consequences of our actions
- We know the reward of God's love and plans
- We benefit from their experiences
- We have the knowledge and history of their experiences
- We have the Holy Spirit available

Our Disadvantages
- Our trust is low
- Our faith is lukewarm
- We think we can question God and His power and challenge His plan and His will
- We are not prepared for His return

It is unfortunate that people challenge the story of the disciples. But it still happens today. People will challenge our testimony and beliefs and our commitment to God. Even though we don't have the same experience, we do have the benefit of the Holy Spirit and its intercession on our behalf. Likewise, we are able to see the differences and know that those differences are by God's design. He knows us and therefore knows who could handle the responsibility of being a disciple then and now.

Lord, thank You for Your plan and Your vision.

DECEMBER 8

[17]For he received honor and glory from God the Father when the voice came to him from the Majestic Glory, saying, "This is my Son, whom I love; with him I am well pleased."

2 Peter 1:17

I want to hear Him say those words to me, too. Christ had died for sins and the prophecy of His coming was then fact. God expressed His gratitude to Jesus for doing what He was asked – being obedient and with a meek and gracious spirit. Christ submitted totally to His Father. He followed His instructions to the letter. I'm sure His gratitude made all the difference.

Having said all of this, I wonder if we did all of the things our parents asked us, then I wonder if they would express their gratitude. Further, if we did all that God asks, would He then express His gratitude? Last question: does He express His gratitude in other ways other than direct conversation?

Our parents would probably show us more gratitude if we were more obedient than not. My mother once told me that the more obedient I was, the easier it was for her to grant my requests. I put some thought into that. I realized that my obedience expressed my gratitude. It also expressed my respect. She didn't have to provide anything for me except food, clothing and shelter, but she did. Did I always deserve her generosity? No. We can grow to a level as a child where we are consistently obedient. Also, we will understand that we may not receive everything for which we ask. Our parents work hard to provide for us. We need to be mindful of that with our actions. Maybe then they would show us more gratitude.

Our Holy Father honors us in the same fashion. Our obedience expresses our true love (John 14:21) for Him. Our disobedience and sin sends the opposite emotion. He wants to bless us but often our behavior delays the process.

Finally, if I was waiting on Him to say the exact words then that may not happen instead He answers my prayers, blesses me with things for which I haven't asked. So if we do our part, then God will do His and interestingly enough, He never needs a reminder.

Thank You for offering me Your gratitude.

DECEMBER 9

⁹If this is so, then the Lord knows how to rescue godly men from trials and to hold the unrighteous for the day of judgment, while continuing their punishment.

2 Peter 2:4-10

Hope is factual. There is hope in this scripture. Since we know that the Lord knows how to rescue godly men from trials, maybe when our trials come, He would rescue us from our trials. This possibility of being rescued brings hope, which should help us to endure trials better. This thought process doesn't always work, but this hope should motivate us to endure with a better attitude.

This hope also reminds us that God is aware of our trials. I think sometimes that we feel God doesn't have any idea that we are experiencing this trial, when in fact, He knows everything. Because He knows of the trial, this reminds us that He would not allow us to experience more than we can bear.

We experience trials to accomplish several things. The first of which is a more dependent posture towards God. God needs to know that we are totally dependent on Him. God needs reassurance that He is our only God. God is a jealous God and does not intend to be second in our lives – not to anyone or anything. Our trials force us to turn towards Him and find our comfort within Him and His word. Our trials also remind us where our source of strength is.

Secondly, we grow stronger from our trials. They increase our strength and our faith.

Lastly, our trials remind of us of Christianity and our true mission: to serve God. Christianity brings certain responsibilities and rewards. Trials are part of our new life.

This scripture presents the hope which God provides for us in order to encourage us to keep focused on Him. This hope saves us from everything that will try to undermine God and His plans.

Lord, thank You for providing us with hope.

On This Journey

DECEMBER 10

¹³They will be paid back with harm for the harm they have done. Their idea of pleasure is to carouse in broad daylight. They are blots and blemishes, reveling in their pleasures while they feast with you.

2 Peter 2:13

No place for laughter nor rejoice. 'But they deserve it,' you think. When others do harm to one of us, does it ever occur to you that they need attention? They may also need our empathy and our prayers. They also need our witness and our forgiveness. People's motives for doing harm range from jealousy to immaturity.

You may be saying 'why are they jealous?' The answers range from grades to overall attitude about life. No, it doesn't make any sense but it's true. The most popular person at school could be popular for the wrong reasons. This status won't last and this façade and image proves difficult to maintain because it's not really you. I consider jealousy a compliment because in order for jealousy to occur, there has been observation, contemplation and decision. Although jealousy is unhealthy, it does involve a lot of energy. Energy which could be used to glorify the Father. When people are jealous of you, they have the potential to harm you.

People also harm people they don't want to respect but deep down they really do respect them. You may have other qualities which potentially causes others to scrutinize you and cause them to harm you because of their respect and their desire to be like you. You may ask why do people harm others when they could simply strive to achieve what they want. The answer is not simple enough to investigate all of the options but it is important to note that their own thoughts block them from achieving what they desire. They don't believe in God; they don't believe that God can do immeasurably more than what we can imagine; they don't believe in themselves; and they have become consumed with themselves and have turned away from God.

I don't like to be harmed and I don't like the thought I can't stop the potential for being harmed. My concern is that those who harmed Jesus were saved, too, even though they harmed their Savior. They showed no remorse when they discovered who He really was. My encouragement comes in the fact that my trials won't last always and He will protect me from harm.

Thank You, Father for taking care of me and protecting me from those who harm me.

DECEMBER 11

¹⁴With eyes full of adultery, they never stop sinning, they seduce the unstable; they are experts in greed – an accursed brood!

2 Peter 2:14

Let's not be greedy. It's hard not to be greedy but try to avoid greed at all costs. Greed is a concentration on the accumulation of material things past the basic requirements. There is nothing wrong with having things and nice things, even exactly what you want. God wants to know how we will respond to these things.

Why do we need to accumulate significantly more than we need? It's the race for who can accumulate the most. There is no real reason for this accumulation. We are all guilty in some way of this greed. Just think of your blessings. Most kids have more toys than they actively play with. Most teens have more videos and video games and music discs than they actively listen to. Most humans have more clothes and shoes than we need.

Further, we have more stuff than we really need. We can achieve our goals without greed. The average family has two more television sets in their homes than 15 years ago. We buy more because we can afford more. Also, there is more to buy. There is more technology producing more goods for us to consume. We fall into the trap of wanting what others have. Also, we fall into the trap of thinking we need to have the latest technology. We want to be knowledgeable about the latest technology. In order to do that, we need to own them or so we think.

Avoiding greed is simple. Hard but simple. Not having to have everything we see is a start. Secondly, we need to recognize when to stop acquiring material things. Lastly, we need to share and learn to give some things up and away. Others need "stuff" too. We need to give them some of our "stuff." We need to give it without reservation or hesitation.

When God knows He can trust us to let some things go then He knows that He can trust us with more. Besides, being greedy requires too much energy. Who has time for that?

Lord, help me to avoid greed.

DECEMBER 12

^{19}They promised them freedom, while they themselves are slaves of depravity – for a man is a slave to whatever has mastered him.

2 Peter 2:19

"What has mastered me?" That's what I asked myself when I read this scripture. It would make sense that something has mastered us. It may not be permanent but there's a point when something will master us.

Short list of possibilities:

1) clothes – being obsessed with what to wear and how we look.
2) video games – always playing and making sure we master them
3) electronics/DVD's – who has the latest one first, who has the most
4) whatever else distracts us from spending time with God

Freedom has several definitions. Slavery means service: to serve something or someone. Also, to be at the mercy of that person or thing. Not being able to live without that person or thing.

This example probably applies to many of you but it's true so I'll share it with you. Each year for Christmas we travel to Tyler, Texas to spend our holiday with our extended family. My nephew cannot leave home without two things: his basketball and his video game system. Does that make him a slave to those items or is that simply his entertainment for the week? We stay four days. Does he really need those items for a 4-day stay? I can't answer that but what I do propose is that he could probably do without them but he chooses not to.

The question we need to ask ourselves can we live without or why do we choose to not live without them. We also need to ask ourselves what would happen if we lose these items or they break and are not repairable.

Lastly, why are they so important to us or why do we like them so much.

Once we answer those questions then we can better determine what we serve and to whom or what we are a slave.

Lord, let me not be slave to anything or anyone.

DECEMBER 13

⁹The Lord is not slow in keeping his promise, as some understand slowness. He is patient with you, not wanting anyone to perish, but everyone to come to repentance.

2 Peter 3:9

We are truly selective in determining when we want God to hurry up. We want Him to hurry to bless us and give us our desires. But we are not in a hurry for Him to punish us as we deserve. So why do we say that He is slow? If we wait on Him to bless us and punish us in His timing, we will be ready to receive all that He has – punishment and reward.

We know the main reason we don't have something or haven't reached a specific stage is because we are not ready for everything we want or deserve. In His infinite wisdom, He exerts His patience for us so that we may be ready to receive what He has for us.

He doesn't want anyone to perish so He offers us time to repent for our sins and shortcomings. He allows us time to ask for forgiveness for each and every sin individually and specifically. He already knows what we've done, so He needs us to confess those sins, even the tiniest indiscretion. When we don't confess our sins, we deceive ourselves. Further, our actions demonstrate that God is a lie. When we don't confess our sins, we act as if they weren't sins or that we didn't do them. When we don't confess, we are in disagreement with God. God doesn't lie nor is He wrong, so we are to confess our sins. Quickly. If you were God, would you want someone to imply that you were a liar? As God, I would be angry.

How do we become more patient and avoid accusing God of being slow? Well, patience is acquired but easy once we've mastered some areas of our lives. One such area is faith. Faith that God is in control and His plans for us are in progress and we will experience those results. The second area is hope. We need to know that waiting on the Lord has always proven beneficial. Sarah (Isaac's mother), Elizabeth (John's mother), Mary and Magdelene (Lazarus' sisters), and Naomi (Boaz's wife). Each of them has a testimony about the wonderful results of waiting on the Lord our God.

Sometimes His slowness is a great thing. God is known for His excellent timing.

Lord, thank You for Your slowness and keeping Your promises, promises I don't deserve.

On This Journey

DECEMBER 14

[11]Since everything will be destroyed in this way, what kind of people ought you be? You ought to live holy and godly lives.

2 Peter 3:11

What does it take to live a holy and godly life? Unfortunately, this is an area you will examine more than once during your life. I always need to have check points to ensure I am in line with His will.

The following is not a comprehensive list, but it covers the highlights and the most controversial issues we are faced with as Christians.

1) Put God first. We owe God time. He deserves our attention. Besides how will we hear His voice if we are not still. (Exodus 20:3-17).
2) Tithe. Give 10% of everything we have, including our time (Malachi 3:10, Leviticus 27:30).
3) Follow His commandments. (Exodus 20:3-17).
4) Only have sex with your spouse.
5) Exhibit the fruits of the spirit (Galatians 5:22-23).
6) Forgive others of their trespasses as we expect God to forgive us. (Matthew 6:9-13).
7) Put on the whole armor of God. (Ephesians 6:10-20).
8) Be obedient as an exhibit of our love for Him (John 14:21).
9) Be still and know that He is God (Psalms 46:10).
10) Know and act with that knowledge that God truly loves us (John 3:16).

So those are just a few tools to assist us with holy and godly living. The rest is pure determination and perseverance. We are charged to fight the good fight of faith. This is not easy and has no immediate gratification. This fight requires patience and spirit. It requires love. The good fight is not popular and typically lacks frills. But the fight is worth each day and each step. The reward of the fight is the holy and godly life we all strive to achieve.

Lord, help me live a holy and godly life.

DECEMBER 15

¹⁴So then dear friends, since you are looking forward to this, make every effort to be found spotless, blameless and at peace with him.

2 Peter 3:14

There are some times when we don't try hard or at all. So when the scripture reads 'make every effort,' this means that we have to give all that we have. We have to give 110%. We have to focus and remain committed to excellence. All of this requires concentration, avoiding distractions at all costs and all of our attention on Christ.

Difficult? For the normal ones of us – yes. It is hard to keep our total attention on Christ. We have to try harder to combat the difficulties which are presented to us.

Spotless and blameless refers directly to a sin-free lifestyle. We can speculate on how to live totally sin-free. We can make every effort to avoid sin as often as possible.

Peace is achievable. Achieved via submission to God. Peace is worth all the costs. Further, peace is not temporary nor is it surface. Peace comes from the within then contributes to the outside. Peace offers us a comfort which exceeds all logical understanding. His peace overcomes all situations. His peace transcends all understanding.

Peace with Him also means our total submission to Him. We have to be a vessel ready to receive all that He has. Job is always a great example of how God's peace will transform you. In summary, Job suffered deep loses: his family, his material possessions and his desire to live. Eventually, he was restored to a greater place with God. All of his family and material possessions and his will to live was restored. Job exhibited a trust in God that was based on his love and faith in God and his peace with God. Job already had the promise that during his darkest hour God was with him (Psalms 23).

There were times when it didn't feel like a blessing to be Job but it was always a blessing to be Job. He had to suffer so that we could benefit from his testimony and witness another of God's miracles. Job truly lived spotless, blameless and at peace with Him.

Thank You for Your peace, which transcends all understanding.

On This Journey

DECEMBER 16

⁸If we claim to be without sin, we deceive ourselves and the truth is not in us.

1 John 1:8

Denial delays healing and forgiveness. If we deny ourselves the healing and forgiveness He has in store for us, we only hurt ourselves.

We must confess our sins, first to ourselves through acknowledgment of our sins. Yes, it's hard to admit that we sin. How can we openly admit our sins so as not to commit additional sins?

First, we were born into sin. God's word clearly states that fact. Accepting this fact should relieve us of any guilt typically associated with sin. All have sinned and fallen short of His glory. (Romans 3:23)

Second, sin is not personal. It is inherent and it is not new. Sin is old. You didn't create sin and even with our best intentions, we will sin. Sin continues until we die. Jesus is the only person who never sinned while on this earth.

We are usually the last to admit our personal sin. God already knows and has already forgiven us and waits for us to ask for it. I learned to ask for God to help me forgive myself. When we don't forgive ourselves for our sins, we find ourselves in denial. Our spiritual growth and subsequent maturity depend on our confession of sin. Once we confess our sins, change can occur in our lives.

In 1998, I ask God to help me turn away from my sin and seek a new life, specifically about pre-marital sex. God knew I was serious about my request, so He helped me to commit to abstinence until I married. Because of my confession and commitment, I attended a conference called "True Love Waits," which is a national Christian Initiative to promote and influence teen abstinence. With 3 other adults and 21 young people, we committed with a ring to remain abstinent until marriage. Before any of that could happen, I had to admit to my sins. I wanted to stop sinning but I needed help and only God could help. I can't and won't imagine where I would be without admitting my sins then requesting His help.

Father, help me admit my sins. Thank You for forgiving me of my sins.

DECEMBER 17

⁹If we confess our sins, he is faithful and just and will forgive us our sins and purify us from all unrighteousness.

1 John 1:9

God promised us the desires of our heart. "And we know that in all things God works for the good of those who love him, who have been called according to his purpose (Romans 8:28). The events occurred as follows:

1) I prayed for a husband. He didn't come when I expected him to come.
2) I admitted my sins. I was having sex without a husband.
3) I corrected my behavior. I stopped having sex.
4) I started a purification process where my study became more serious and focused. I read books on being a wife. I studied scriptures about marriage. I prayed that God prepare me to be a wife, a great one.
5) I admitted that my self-esteem was attached to how men felt about me, but their opinion was based on sex. When I stopped engaging in sex, they no longer showed the same interest.
6) God renewed my self-image and self-esteem based on His word and His love.
7) He sent me my husband, who was prepared for me, and for whom I was prepared.

God answered my prayers. He gave me the desires of my heart and I was prepared to receive His blessing. God readied me for the role as a wife – which is different from anything in life and requires preparation.

He granted me my heart's desire and did it quickly. He didn't wait. He answered several prayers at once and several others shortly thereafter.

My sins didn't stop but I admit them quickly and commit to correct them quickly as well. I never have to question God's intentions. He grants me what I'm ready for and He wants me to have the desires of my heart. I have to do my part. He will not bless me if I am dishonest about my wrongs. My confession allows God to bless me, forgive me, and purify me from all unrighteousness. He'll answer my prayers and give me my dreams.

Thank You for being faithful.

On This Journey

DECEMBER 18

¹⁰If we claim we have not sinned, we make him out to be a liar and his word has no place in our lives.

1 John 1:10

Denying our sins negates our commitment to God. Why claim Christianity if we are not willing to confess our sins? When the Bible refers to judgment, it relates to those who won't confess their sins, and are disobedient to God.

Why would we want our behavior to demonstrate God as a liar? He is not a liar. We need to change our behavior so that this is not the case. Confession is hard but the only way to avoid confession is to avoid the sin. While this is not always possible, it is possible to confess all sins to Him.

Most of the times, the reason we don't confess our sins is that we have a problem admitting our wrongdoing. However, that fact doesn't seem to prevent us from doing wrong. So if we could face ourselves, then we can face God? Is that logic sound? Not exactly. If I can't face God, I haven't faced myself. It's not likely I'm able to face myself. The most important lesson here is that we learn to admit we're wrong and then to confess our wrongs to God.

I'm sure we don't intentionally imply that God is a liar, either. So what is the root of the problem? My problem is forgiveness. Most people share that issue. We don't forgive ourselves. We let our issues linger on and on, sometimes for years before we rediscover what they are and address them in order to forgive ourselves.

Love prompts and provides forgiveness. It is His love which provides His forgiveness. So I'm saying that we don't love each other enough to forgive ourselves. It's true. If it weren't true then we would forgive ourselves more easily and we would have less to forgive ourselves for.

Practice forgiving. God only forgives when we can forgive.

Lord, I don't want You to be a liar. I have sinned.

DECEMBER 19

⁵But if anyone obeys his word, God's love is truly made complete in him.

1 John 2:5

I have yet to realize my mother's reward she promised if I obeyed because I never obeyed long enough. Are we consistent when we obey God? Not always. We benefit regardless. But imagine what He might do if we obeyed versus what He does even if we don't obey.

Why is it so difficult to obey His word? His expectations are clearly outlined. He leaves nothing to our imagination or interpretation. Most of what He expects is not hard or unreasonable. There are things which seem more appealing but put us out of God's will. This is one such reason obedience is difficult. A second reason is we are not disciplined enough to consistently obey. One way to overcome this difficulty may be to consider His discipline when we lack discipline. The outcome of His discipline is not always our favorite thing.

Don't we owe Him our obedience? It takes so much of us to obey Him, or so we think. We owe Him our obedience because of all He continues to do for us.

His unconditional love answers all woes, worries, loss, needs, wants and fears. Why isn't this enough to ensure we obey Him?

God's love is boundless and it's magnitude is indescribable. So for His love to be made complete in us by our obedience is extraordinary. How do we achieve the obedience consistently?

1) Decide to be obedient to God. When we decide to do something we are certain to achieve our pursuits. When you put your mind to it, you can achieve all of your pursuits.
2) Know what we need to do to be obedient. Reading His word and praying to Him will increase our knowledge of Him.
3) Pray and ask God to help you obey. He is the one who can see you overcome your obstacles and achieve obedience.

Lord, I want to obey You. All the time.

On This Journey

DECEMBER 20

⁹Anyone who claims to be in the light but hates his brother is still in the darkness. ¹⁰Whoever loves his brother lives in the light, and there is nothing in him to make him stumble. ¹¹But whoever hates his brother is in the darkness and walks around in the darkness; he does not know where he is going, because the darkness has blinded him.

1 John 2:9-11

Hate is so powerful. Hate stops your blessings – not the other person. Hate hurts you – not the other person. Hate requires too much energy. When we hate, we have to remember what we hate and why we hate. Then you have to remember who you hate so that you don't mistakenly interact with that person. Hate requires that you turn off your love meter. Hate requires you stop being Christ-like. Hate interrupts your relationship with God. Hate interrupts your loving relationship with God.

Why do we hate others? Several reasons: (1) they may have hurt you; (2) they may have offended you; or (3) we may be envious.

Although we get hurt, we need to offer them the benefit of the doubt and tell them you were hurt. You may find out that they had no idea you were hurt. Further, they may acknowledge that they had no intention to hurt you. You then will renew your relationship.

Being offended is subjective. Why are you offended? Have you taken the time to fully understand what the other person is communicating. Most of the time when we are offended, we also have other things going on.

But let's talk about love. Love fixes most everything. Love only exists in light. Growth can only happen in light. God does not like darkness. You cannot see in darkness. You can't receive God's love in darkness.

Why would you want to hate someone when it interrupts your relationship with God?

Lord, help me not to hate.

Daily Devotional for Young People

DECEMBER 21

¹⁵Do not love the world or anything in the world. If anyone loves the world, the love of the Father is not in him. ¹⁶For everything in the world – the cravings of a sinful man, the lust of his eyes and the boastings of what he has and does – comes not from the Father but from the world. ¹⁷The world and its desires pass away, but the man who does the will of God lives forever.

1 John 2:15-17

If you take a minute to count all of the times you use the word love in an average day, you may note that you said you loved the food you ate for lunch, the backpack you carry, the clothes you wear, the television show you watched or the movie you watched. So if you are honest, we will admit we use the word for most things but inappropriately because they are things - not what love was designed to be.

What is the correct use of the word love? First, of all love is defined as an emotion which is where your passion is staked. So, the correct use of the word focuses on what our passion is. With that being said, if you focus on material things, then you are of the world. As we focus on the world, we lose sight of God and what our focus really should be.

The correct use of the word is to love the Father. The way to really love Him is through our actions.
Here is a short list:

- avoid sins; learn to walk away
- take an aggressive stand about your commitment to God
- pray
- study
- obey His commandments
- the Golden Rule Revised: "Treat others as God treats you."

Every once in awhile, God sends us to people because He needs a physical presence. Can He trust us to do what He sends us to do? If He sent us to hug someone, did we do it? Did we hug that person the way God desired? If not, then we failed to do what God needed us to do.

There is a song which always moves me that I want to share. "Teach me how to love and adore You. With my whole heart I will bless You precious Lord. There's no burden You can't see me through. There is no worry. Always on time. When I'm alone, You raise my spirit with Your touch. You make my day bright Lord."

That's overflowing with love – unconditional and abundant – only the way God delivers love.

Lord, let me love You the way You are supposed to be loved.

On This Journey

DECEMBER 22

³Everyone who has this hope in him purifies himself, just as he is pure.

1 John 3:3

Purity. How is our purity measured? How can we remain pure? What does purity cost? Who is the authority on purity and who defined the word? Why is it so hard to maintain? Is my purity lost forever if I make one unpure decision?

Six questions we ask ourselves when no one is around but Jesus. Let's get some answers. The purity authority is Jesus Christ. He was tempted in all ways known to man and never sinned. He lived 33 years without one sin. I have often asked about sex and was Jesus tempted with sex and I never confronted the issue because the other temptations were very clear. He clearly set the boundaries and a method by which to maintain a pure life.

Our purity is measured by sin but there is no purity meter. God is black and white and in the question of purity, yes or no. God is fair but there is no somewhat pure, almost pure nor too far gone to be pure ever again.

We remain pure because of our decisions and choices. We decided to or not to have sex, smoke, drink alcohol, curse, skip school, disrespect our parents and disrespect God and whatever else we do when we dishonor Him and His word. In these cases, the answer is a simple no. Purity is a decision for a lifestyle – one ordained by God, thus protected by God. God helps us maintain our purity if we ask.

Purity among us is hard to find so maintenance is hard. Satan shows up in many formats, often when we least expect it, and through avenues we never thought possible. Satan's arguments are so compelling. "If you loved me then you would prove it." (Sex) Your response needs to be "if you love me then prove it and don't ask." One of my youth ministers said that to us. I added that "the last time someone proved His love for me, He stretched out His arms and died. Are you willing?" Normally, that fixes it if they last that long. Don't be misled, some females will push the envelope too. Same responses apply. When I renewed myself to God through sexual abstinence, my life turned in a new direction. He forgave me. He poured more love out for me. He lifted me up and carried me some days. No, your purity is not lost forever. He is faithful and forgiving.

Satan does not want us to be pure. He will do whatever is necessary to prevent our purity. But he does not overrule God. We can remain pure.

Help me remain pure, Lord.

DECEMBER 23

⁶No one who lives in him keeps on sinning. No one who continues to sin has either seen him or known him.

1 John 3:6

The difference here is between someone who sins and never repents and the Christian who sins, repents and turns away from sin.

Yes, Christians can't live without sin but we can decide to turn away from sins. Our repentance speaks volumes of our commitment to Christ and recognizes that He is Lord and the amount of sacrifice it takes to save us and allow us eternal life even though we commit new sins every day.

Persons who sin without remorse don't have any knowledge of Christ. They possibly don't even know there is a Christ. I find it hard to really believe but I know it's possible the greatest number of people without a relationship with Christ don't believe in Him and His miraculous works. Non-believers spend time attempting to prove that God is make-believe or fantasy. They depend on scientific evidence that God does not exist. However, to date they haven't been able to disprove there is no God. One day you may find yourself asking is our God real? And of course, the answer is yes. Then you may ask how do we know and how are we sure. The answer is simple: "He lives. He lives. My Savior lives today. He walks with me. And talks with me along life's narrow way. You ask me how I know He lives. He lives within my heart."

God invented rocket science. God created it all. He is real. It is astounding the amount of time others spend on disproving Him and how little we spend with Him and obeying Him.

Be prepared to teach others about Him. Be prepared to defend Him and all of His work. Pay close attention to Him and His word: It is true and real and will come to pass.

Father, help me to be honest about my sins when I confess them to You.

On This Journey

DECEMBER 24

⁹No one who is born of God will continue to sin, because God's seed remains in him; he cannot go on sinning, because he has been born of God.

1 John 3:9

Our sins disappoint and hurt God. I imagine God crying and pouting when I am wrong and have sinned. That image halts all wrong actions that cross my mind. Just a note here: as we grow older, life adds layers of complications, so although we know to say no, it's not any easier.

The other thought is that I was created in His image and others are looking to me for guidance, leadership and an example, I cannot keep sinning. Satan would love to flaw the image God has created through me, so I have to do everything I can to ensure it doesn't happen.

These thoughts coupled with the fact that I don't want to have to explain to God why I sinned and why I didn't ask for His help or recognize His escape. He knows each of our weaknesses and I believe He works diligently to strengthen those weaknesses. He depends on our prayers and communication to help us through our weaknesses and trials.

I want God to be happy with me so I try hard to make sure that I do things that are pleasing in His sight. I want Him to smile when He thinks of me. I want Him to cheer when I take the escape He has provided for me when sin arises. I want God to be proud of me and my behavior. My mother reminds me of my behavior and now she can be proud of my choices. At one point, she would complain about my behavior. Then one day, I told her that I always act better when I'm away from home than I do at home. I added that my goal was never to embarrass her. Eventually, she recognized that was true. The last day I heard her comment about my teenage behavior, we reminded her that our (my sister and I) behavior was not as bad as she portrayed nor remembered. This reminder came only after she remembered that the woman she was talking to had a child who had been addicted to drugs. After that we counted our blessings for each other because neither was as terrible as we remembered or seemed.

I will remain in You at all times and in all seasons.

DECEMBER 25

¹⁷If anyone has material possessions and sees his brother in need but has no pity on him, how can the love of God be in him?

1 John 3:17

God's unconditional love offers us unending compassion. He shows us that compassion in order for us to be compassionate to others. It is hard for us to offer ourselves to others. Why is that? Why do we have problems helping others in their time of need?

'Maybe they won't accept my help.' 'The last time I tried to help she said no.' Our direction is to help others, so we have to offer no matter what we anticipate the answer to be. This is the time the answer may be yes and they really need you to ask.

'I don't know if I can help.' If you ask, God will do the rest. God equips us for every perfect work. He will give you exactly what you need to help them.

'I can't help myself. Certainly I can't help another.' This may be your help, too. You helping the other person may serve as your help and solution. You have what they need and they have what you need. Both of you will win instantly from your obedience.

'Why does God test me in this?' God wants to trust us. He really does. He wants to know we respond when others suffer. Do we act superior to them as they suffer? Do we treat them as lesser beings? Neither of these are acceptable. This is not how He treats us.

The parable of the woman comes to mind. Someone told her Jesus was coming. She prepared all day. While she prepared for Jesus, a person knocked on her door hungry. She told him she could not feed him because she was waiting for Jesus. A second person needed clothing. She told him that she was waiting on Jesus and couldn't help them. A third person needed shelter. She was frustrated by then because they kept interrupting her as she prepared for Jesus. She refused because Jesus was coming to stay with her. Finally, Jesus showed up and she was excited. She said I waited on You all day. He responded to her saying I came by but you sent me away. I returned needing clothing. You refused. I needed shelter. Again you refused. The woman was stunned. The message is when we help others we have served Him.

Lord, let me answer and recognize You.

DECEMBER 26

[20]Whenever our hearts condemn us. For God is greater than our hearts, and he knows everything.

1 John 3:20

We should examine this scripture with the previous passage in mind. Verse nineteen reads: "This then is how we set our hearts at rest in his presence." There are means for us not to condemn ourselves. One such way is God's hand and presence.

God is greater than my heart. He is greater than my fears. He is greater than my issues. God is greater than my faults. God is greater than my tears. He is greater than my stuff. He is greater that my thoughts. He is greater than my thoughts. He is greater than me.

God designed us to be smart and wise and He is greater than those too. God's knowledge is remarkable – He knows everything! ALL! About everything. He is the expert on everything. With all that said, why do we challenge Him? We question Him about His decisions and His timing. We question His plans for us and His judgment over us. We sometimes think we know more than God and that our decisions are the best ones. We also don't think we need to be judged.

Most of this behavior results from the fact that God trusts us but we take that trust too far. The mistake is that we don't have the foresight nor all the facts.

Is there a time that you remember when your decision was 'overruled' by God and the outcome was better because God took control. I can think of several examples, but the one thing that I recall from each of those situations is that God didn't ignore me even though I wanted something outside God's will.

God has kept me away from financial ruin because a venture capital program rejected my plan. He kept me from building the wrong house in a flooding neighborhood with a dishonest builder. He kept me from the wrong career – a career where hundreds of people are losing hundreds of thousands of dollars. He kept me from marrying the wrong man, which would've led to a lifetime of unhappiness.

There is no way to know the full consequences of our actions but one thing is certain – He knows everything and He uses this knowledge for our good, even when we interfere.

Lord, this is just one more exhibit of Your abundant love.

DECEMBER 27

>[21]Dear friends, if our hearts do not condemn us, we have confidence before God [22]and receive from him anything we ask, because we obey his commands and do what pleases him.
>
> *1 John 3:21-22*

I have the most confidence before God when I have studied His word, prayed as I should, being obedient and doing what pleases Him.

Do I always manage to do this? No. Do I do it sometimes? Yes. When I don't do all of those things, I wonder what God thinks of me and I get discouraged, but then He lifts my spirit, forgiving me of my transgressions and encouraging me to restored confidence. When I follow Him and accept His forgiveness, I am confident again because then I have pleased Him. When I stop my own condemnation, He is pleased and restores my confidence.

The difference is do I readily accept His gift of confidence. Confidence is relative to self-esteem. Self-esteem stems from our opinions of ourselves usually relating to others. Here is where we make the mistake. Who we are is defined by God, our Creator, rather than by others, who He also created. We want to be like others, just the good stuff though. We want their looks, clothes and the stuff. We don't always realize that they have had to endure some "stuff" to acquire some of that. We don't always consider how the items were acquired.

Although easier said than done, don't let others assist you with building negative self-esteem. Guard your soul against insults and negativity and counterproductive behavior and activities.

Confidence is relative to our ability to operate within God's parameters and guidelines. When I go outside those guidelines, I feel guilty and that's when my confidence lacks. So, I stop the guilt trip, I forgive myself because God had already forgiven me and regain my confident, zealous self. Then God is pleased.

I have also noticed the more confident I am, the greater able I am to share Him with others. So He always wants us confident so we can share Him with others.

Thank You for my confidence.

DECEMBER 28

⁴You, dear children, are from God and have overcome them, because the one who is in you is greater than the one who is in the world.

1 John 4:4

"Them" is referred to here as anything or anyone who stands against you. Because of God and the Christ who resides in you, you have overcome them. The 'fight' is already won. The 'fight' was fixed from the beginning. God has fought all of our battles for us, so we have no need to fear or fight or worry.

Don't misunderstand me. Sometimes it's difficult to remember that the 'fight' is fixed. But as soon as you remember, you need to change your demeanor and your actions. I start looking for my opportunity to grow, the lesson I'm supposed to experience, someone I need to share my faith with, and I look for the addition to my testimony because this was only a test. Also, I modify my behavior to exemplify God and then you know that 'they' now know whose you are.

When you experience adversity, remember to smile in the presence of 'them.' "They" will not know how to respond. "They" will wonder why you are smiling and "they" may even ask you. Your opportunity to witness and share your faith has come. The moment you were waiting on. The moment of truth. The moment you anticipate and hope for as a Christian. The moment you can stand and say, "Greater is He that is in me than he that is in world." "They" will respond, "Who is He?" "He" is Jesus. Our Savior. The One who fights my battles including the one you "waged against me." Everything, if anything else, that needs to be said will be guided by Jesus.

When you are done, thank God for His victory and for using you to accomplish His goals and being a part of His plans. Praise Him for the victory you witnessed. Then go and be forever mindful of how "they" can appear and remember that He has already done all that needs to be done.

I love you, Lord for You are greater than me, "them" and the world.

DECEMBER 29

¹⁹We love because he first loved us.

1 John 4:19

There is no greater love than the love of God and Jesus Christ. They are the definition of love. They created love. They act in love. They breathe life into love. Love lives because of them.

"For God so loved the world, that He gave His one and only Son, that whoever believes in Him shall not perish but have eternal life." John 3:16

"For god did not send His Son into the world to condemn the world, but to save the world through Him." John 3:17

"And hope does not disappoint us, because God has poured out His love, into our hearts by the Holy Spirit, whom he has given us." Romans 5:5

"But God demonstrates His own love for us in this: While we were still sinners Christ died for us." Romans 5:8

"In my Father's house are many rooms; if it were not so, I would have told you. I am going there to prepare a place for you." John 14:2

"Before I formed you in the womb I knew you, before you were born I set you apart; I appointed you as a prophet to the nations." Jeremiah 1:5

"It was just before the Passover Feast. Jesus knew that the time had come for him to leave this world and go to the Father. Having loved his own who were in the world, he now showed them the full extent of his love. 5After that, he poured water into a basin and began to wash the disciples feet, drying them with the towel that was wrapped around him." John 13:1, 5

Those are just a few scriptures which describe His love for us. Love is an action which God demonstrates daily. We repay Him as sinners and disobey Him at will. Yet, He still loves us daily, more than we will ever know or can conceive. He deserves our love in all the ways possible just to make a small comparison to what He does for us.

Thank You for loving me, God.

On This Journey

DECEMBER 30

[20]If anyone says, "I love God," yet hates his brother, he is a liar. For anyone who does not love his brother, whom he has seen, cannot love God, whom he has not seen.

1 John 4:20

Jesus appeared to people in various ways. He showed up to the disciples in various ways as well. He performed many miracles whether His identity was known or not. Often the audience only responded after He made His identity known and certain miracles and events took place.

As for the disciples, He showed up performing miracles: they witnessed His baptism, He walked on water and He showed up on the roadside. There were occasions when they were overwhelmed by His presence and the methods by which He appeared. I said all that to say God determines how we will really treat Him by how we treat humans, loved ones and strangers. We don't know how Jesus will appear, so we need to treat them all with the spirit of Christ – as Christ treated the people He met – rather than like strangers.

We love God because of who He is and what He does and what we want. We love others because we are Christians and we know what our love may mean to others. Some people are love-starved and it is our responsibility to love them. People who are love-starved are a gift from Christ because He measures our hearts based on our response to them.

He's said that if you [love] the least of these, then you have loved me.

Loving others means loving God. Being obedient means loving God. Hating anyone is completely opposite of loving God, especially since God created us all. So in order to hate someone is to hate God's creation. That's bold and unreasonable. Don't forget He created you too.

Lord, let my love for them be clear because I want my love for you to be clear.

DECEMBER 31

²⁴To him who is able to keep you from falling and to present you before his glorious presence without fault and with great joy –

Jude 24

This is the verse that is an answer to prayer: keep me from falling. Keep me from falling into the traps set for me by the enemy.

Strength and renewal comes from this verse. It is also about reverence to Him.

He indeed is able to do ALL things, inclusive of keeping us pure and from falling.

The most compelling portion of this scripture is that He can present me faultless before His throne. Faultless. I am not faultless – not by a long shot. But He can make me faultless despite all of my wrongs. Faultless! Without stain of blemish of spot – ME. This is what He does for us. This is nothing short of amazing and so important for our future.

Why, you may ask, would He do this? Because He loves us. It is as simple as that – LOVE conquers all. He wants us to be faultless. His forgiveness is monumental and this is a further exhibit of that.

When I first heard this scripture, I heard it like this: "Unto Him who is able to keep us from falling and to present us faultless before His throne." Now the translation is not exact, not to mention as I was researching the scripture I couldn't find the exact translation. That may mean I didn't look far enough or my then teacher/pastor tailored it to impact his message at that time. The important point is that it didn't lose its meaning. While there's no crime in that, it provides the example that we need to study His word for ourselves so we are not surprised when it does read differently.

The scripture is truly powerful once we consider the impact it has. Just consider that He can have anything and do anything because He created everything. He forgives us, wipes our slates clean to the point of faultlessness, then He tops it all off with great joy. Joy the world can't give us and they can't take it away.

While I don't deserve anything but death for my sins, I truly thank You for Your overwhelming forgiveness.

On This Journey

WITH YOUR WHOLE HEART, WALK WITH GOD

No one respects an indecisive person. Why should God be different? He shouldn't. He expects us to live for Him decisively. He demands we leave our worldly possessions behind and pick up our cross and follow Him—fully and completely.

What does "with your whole heart, walk with God" mean? To me, it means I don't sin and expect to do repeatedly the same sin. It also means avoid Peter's mistake of denying God. Whole means all, all the parts making up one. Whole heart means all that you have inside.

During my praise and worship, which can happen anytime, I sometimes cry. I cry because He blessed me to accomplish some things or He's given me something, or mostly because I am holding something back—an unconfessed sin, or a burden I'm still carrying. This means I have withheld from God a portion, a fraction if you will, of myself. Withholding negates the wholeness He requires.

With your whole heart, walk with God means (this is the short list):

- obedience to parents and other authorities
- purity (sexually, drugs, and alcohol and other impurities available)
- anything or anyone who separates you from God through study, praise and worship

One of my favorite songs says 'with my whole heart I will bless You, Precious Lord.' Exchange bless for praise, worship or walk and it applies the same.

God tells us to come to Him as we are. This has nothing to do with our outerwear but our inner self. We try to convince ourselves that we can present ourselves to God better than we are, but only He can do that. He can clean us up from all unrighteousness and impurities and everything. He will fix and repair all that is broken or dysfunctional. He just asks us to come to Him.

Secondly, He wants all of us—not some of us. We have to commit our whole self to Him. Give yourself to God totally, and fully. NOW. With your whole heart is the only way to experience success.

The total surrender to God is an intimate encounter. And well worth it. There is no risk involved. Your whole heart. Your heart will become stronger and more whole.

He deserves your whole heart. Walk with Him by giving Him your whole self—starting with your heart.

RESOURCES

FOR

THE JOURNEY

THE NAMES OF GOD

Elohim	The Creator
El Elyon	The God Most High
El Roi	God Who Sees
El Shaddai	The All-Sufficient One
Adonai	Lord, Master
Yahweh	Lord, Jehovah
Jehovah-jireh	The Lord Will Provide
Jehovah-rapha	The Lord That Healeth
Jehovah-nissi	The Lord My Banner
Jehovah-mekoddishkem	The Lord Who Sanctifies You
Jehovah-shalom	The Lord Is Peace
Jehovah-sabaoth	The Lord of Hosts
Jehovah-raah	The Lord My Shepherd
Jehovah-tsidkenu	The Lord Our Righteousness
Jehovah-shammah	The Lord is There
El Olam	The Everlasting God

THE PRAYER OF SALVATION

Salvation is defined by Random House as the act of saving or protecting from harm or loss. God provides salvation for us, His children, free of charge. In order to receive His salvation, we only have to accept Jesus as our Lord and Savior. Salvation is a gift, which we have nothing to earn and can do nothing to achieve. God planned salvation before He created each of us. The scriptures listed will show you God's plan and provision for your salvation. Then follows a prayer of salvation, which confesses your sin to God and will assist you in accepting God's gift of salvation.

Romans 3:10-12, 23	We are all sinners.
Romans 6:23	The penalty for sin.
Romans 5:8-9	The payment God made for sin.
Romans 10:9-10, 13	Confess Jesus as Lord.

Dear God: I know You love me. I realize I am a sinner. I have not lived as You have wanted me to live. I believe Your Son, Jesus, died for me on the cross and was raised from the dead to provide forgiveness and eternal life. Please save me as I turn from my sins, place my faith in Jesus and receive Him as Lord and Savior. I will no longer live according to my selfish desires and plans but will follow Your desires and plans for my life. Thank You for saving me and giving me eternal life. I pray this prayer in Jesus' name, Amen.

What do I about my family and friends who are not saved?
Your prayer for God to become Lord of their lives is critical. You have to pray for them diligently. You don't have to pushy. The Lord will handle the rest. You share with them what you know through your study and prayer and the Lord will do the rest. Invite them to your church. Don't be afraid to ask them about what they know and don't be afraid to share God with anyone, believers or not. Eventually, God will bring them to Him. Pray then watch Him work.

On This Journey
ADDITIONAL SOURCES FOR THE JOURNEY

Disciple Youth Bible
True Love Waits Bible
Worth the Wait by Tim Stafford
Choosing God's Best by Dr. Don Raunikar
The Five Love Languages of Teenagers by Dr. Gary Chapman
The 7 Habits of Highly Effective Teens Sean Covey
Love Letters to God From a Teenage Girl by Onedia Gage
The Notebook for the Christian Teen by Onedia Gage

INDEX

Genesis 1:3	23
Exodus 20:4-6	24
Exodus 20:7	25
Exodus 20:8-11	26
Exodus 20:12	27
Exodus 20:13	28
Exodus 20:14	29
Exodus 20:15	30
Exodus 20:16	31
Exodus 20:17	32
Numbers 6:24-26	33
Nehemiah 6:16	34
Nehemiah 9:6	35
Nehemiah 9:13	36
Psalms 3:4	37
Psalms 8:1	38
Psalms 46:1	39
Psalms 46:10	40
Psalms 54:2	41
Psalms 55:5	42
Psalms 55:16	43
Psalms 56:3	44
Psalms 62:1	45
Psalms 62:2	46
Psalms 63:1	47
Psalms 63:8	48
Psalms 81:7	49
Psalms 81:10	50
Psalms 103:3	51
Psalms 103:10	52
Psalms 103:12	53
Psalms 117:2	54
Psalms 121:1	55
Proverbs 1:10	56
Proverbs 3:5-6	57
Proverbs 5:12-13	58
Proverbs 10:4	59
Proverbs 10:12	60
Proverbs 10:14	61
Proverbs 11:13	62
Proverbs 11:14	63
Proverbs 11:16	64
Proverbs 12:1	65
Proverbs 13:10	66
Proverbs 14:30	67
Proverbs 16:7	68
Proverbs 17:3	69
Proverbs 17:9	70
Proverbs 18:8	71
Proverbs 19:11	72
Proverbs 20:27	73
Proverbs 21:30	74
Proverbs 22:1	75
Proverbs 22:15	76
Proverbs 24:17	77
Proverbs 25:15	78
Proverbs 25:16	79
Proverbs 25:21-22	80
Proverbs 27:17	81
Proverbs 31:8	82
Ecclesiastes 11:1	85
Ecclesiastes 11:10	86
Isaiah 55:8	87
Jeremiah 1:5	88
Jeremiah 17:9	89
Jeremiah 17:10	90
Jeremiah 18:5-10	91
Jeremiah 18:11	92
Matthew 5:39	93
Matthew 5:44	94
Matthew 6:6	95
Matthew 6:13	96
Matthew 6:14	97
Matthew 6:25	98
Matthew 6:33	99
Matthew 6:34	100
Matthew 7:1	101
Matthew 7:7	102
Matthew 7:12	103
Matthew 8:26	104
Matthew 9:20-22	105
Matthew 10:39	106
Matthew 11:28	107
Matthew 14:27	108

On This Journey

Reference	Page	Reference	Page
Matthew 14:28-29	109	John 6:38	155
Matthew 14:30	110	John 8:31-32	156
Matthew 14:31	111	John 11:35	157
Matthew 18:15-17	112	John 13:14-17	158
Matthew 18:19-20	113	John 14:15	159
Matthew 22:37	114, 129	John 15:18-19	160
Matthew 22:39	115	John 16:7	161
Matthew 25:31-46	116	John 16:33	162
Matthew 26:39	117	John 17:1-5	163
Matthew 26:42	118	Romans 1:17	164
Matthew 27:29	119	Romans 1:21	165
Mark 3:29	120	Romans 2:11	166
Mark 8:36	121	Romans 3:23	167
Mark 9:40	122	Romans 4:7	168
Mark 9:41	123	Romans 4:8	169
Mark 10:9	124	Romans 4:21	170
Mark 10:43-44	125	Romans 5:5	171
Mark 11:24	126	Romans 5:8	172
Mark 11:25	127	Romans 6:23	173
Mark 12:17	128	Romans 7:17	174
Mark 12:30	129	Romans 7:18	175
Mark 14:30-31	130	Romans 7:19	176
Luke 11:1-4	131	Romans 7:20	177
Luke 11:9-10	132	Romans 8:1	178
Luke 14:28	133	Romans 8:5	179
Luke 14:33	134	Romans 8:8	180
Luke 15:4	135	Romans 8:10	181
Luke 15:8-9	136	Romans 8:26	182
Luke 16:15	137	Romans 8:28	183
Luke 22:40	138	Romans 8:31	184
Luke 22:62	139	Romans 10:9	185
Luke 23:34	140	Romans 12:2	186
Luke 23:46	141	Romans 12:9	187
Luke 24:6	142	Romans 12:14	188
Luke 24:32	143	Romans 12:15	189
Luke 24:36	144	Romans 13:1	190
Luke 24:38-39	145	Romans 14:13	191
Luke 24:45	146	1 Corinthians 2:5	192
John 1:26-27	148	1 Corinthians 2:9	193
John 2:1-11	149	1 Corinthians 2:10	194
John 3:16	150	1 Corinthians 3:16-17	195
John 4:34	151	1 Corinthians 4:5	196
John 6:35	152	1 Corinthians 4:7	197
John 6:36	153	1 Corinthians 4:10	198
John 6:37	154	1 Corinthians 4:12	199

Reference	Page
1 Corinthians 6:13	200
1 Corinthians 6:16-20	201
1 Corinthians 7:25	202
1 Corinthians 7:34	203
1 Corinthians 10:13	204
1 Corinthians 10:23	205
1 Corinthians 10:24	206
1 Corinthians 10:32	207
1 Corinthians 11:26	208
1 Corinthians 12:12	210
1 Corinthians 12:22-25	211
1 Corinthians 12:26	212
1 Corinthians 13	213
1 Corinthians 14:33	214
1 Corinthians 15:33	215
2 Corinthians 1:3-4	216
2 Corinthians 4:16	217
2 Corinthians 4:18	218
2 Corinthians 6:14	219
2 Corinthians 9:6	220
2 Corinthians 10:3	221
2 Corinthians 12:9	222
Galatians 5:19-21	223
Galatians 5:22-23	224
Galatians 6:10	225
Ephesians 2:4-5	226
Ephesians 2:8-9	227
Ephesians 3:20	228
Ephesians 4:23	229
Ephesians 4:24	230
Ephesians 4:26-27	231
Ephesians 4:29	232
Ephesians 4:30	234
Ephesians 4:31	235
Ephesians 4:32	236
Ephesians 5:10	236
Ephesians 5:18	237
Ephesians 5:30	238
Ephesians 6:1	239
Ephesians 6:2-3	240
Ephesians 6:4	241
Ephesians 6:11	242
Ephesians 6:13	243
Ephesians 6:14-17	244
Ephesians 6:18	245
Ephesians 6:19	246
Ephesians 6:24	247
Philippians 1:27	248
Philippians 1:28	249
Philippians 2:9-11	250
Philippians 2:14	251
Philippians 4:6	252
Philippians 4:7	253
Philippians 4:8	254
Philippians 4:11	255
Philippians 4:13	256
Philippians 4:14	257
Colossians 1:16	258
Colossians 3:2	259
Colossians 3:5	260
Colossians 3:10	261
Colossians 3:12	262
Colossians 3:13	263
Colossians 3:14	264
Colossians 3:15	265
Colossians 3:16	266
Colossians 3:17	267
Colossians 3:20	268
Colossians 3:21	269
Colossians 3:23	270
Colossians 3:24b	271
Colossians 4:2	272
Colossians 4:5	273
1 Thessalonians 4:11	274
1 Thessalonians 4:12	275
1 Thessalonians 4:16	276
1 Thessalonians 4:17	277
1 Thessalonians 5:12-13	278
1 Thessalonians 5:14	279
1 Thessalonians 5:15	280
1 Thessalonians 5:16	281
1 Thessalonians 5:17	282
1 Thessalonians 5:18	283
1 Thessalonians 5:19	284
1 Thessalonians 5:20	285
1 Thessalonians 5:21	286
1 Thessalonians 5:22	287
1 Thessalonians 5:23-24	288
2 Thessalonians 1:6, 7a	289

2 Thessalonians 3:10	290	James 4:17	336
2 Thessalonians 3:13	291	James 5:11	337
1 Timothy 6:12	292	1 Peter 1:5	338
2 Timothy 1:7	293	1 Peter 1:6	339
2 Timothy 2:22	294	1 Peter 1:7	340
2 Timothy 3:2-5	295	1 Peter 1:8-9	341
2 Timothy 3:16-17	296	1 Peter 1:13	342
Titus 1:6	297	1 Peter 1:14	343
Titus 1:8	298	1 Peter 1:15-16	344
Philemon 1:6	299	1 Peter 1:18-19	345
Philemon 1:7	300	1 Peter 1:25	346
Hebrews 1:13	301	1 Peter 2:20	347
Hebrews 7:25	302	1 Peter 2:21	348
Hebrews 10:22	303	1 Peter 2:23	349
Hebrews 10:24	304	1 Peter 2:24	350
Hebrews 10:26-27	306	1 Peter 3:8	351
Hebrews 11:1	307	1 Peter 3:9	352
Hebrews 12:1	308	1 Peter 3:14	353
Hebrews 12:10	309	1 Peter 4:8	354
Hebrews 12:14	310	1 Peter 4:10	355
Hebrews 13:1	311	1 Peter 4:12	356
Hebrews 13:5	312	1 Peter 4:13	357
Hebrews 13:8	313	1 Peter 4:19	358
Hebrews 13:17	314	1 Peter 5:5	359
Hebrews 13:18	315	1 Peter 5:6	360
James 1:2-3	316	1 Peter 5:7	361
James 1:4	317	1 Peter 5:10	362
James 1:5	318	2 Peter 1:3	364
James 1:6	319	2 Peter 1:4	365
James 1:12	320	2 Peter 1:5-7	366
James 1:13	321	2 Peter 1:8	367
James 1:19	322	2 Peter 1:9	368
James 1:20	323	2 Peter 1:10-11	369
James 1:22	324	2 Peter 1:16	370
James 1:26	325	2 Peter 1:17	371
James 2:3-4	326	2 Peter 2:4-10	372
James 2:17	327	2 Peter 2:13	373
James 3:1	328	2 Peter 2:14	374
James 3:5	329	2 Peter 2:19	375
James 3:9	330	2 Peter 3:9	376
James 3:16	331	2 Peter 3:11	378
James 3:17	332	2 Peter 3:14	379
James 3:18	333	1 John 1:8	380
James 4:2	334	1 John 1:9	381
James 4:3	335	1 John 1:10	382

1 John 2:5	383	1 John 3:20	390
1 John 2:9-11	384	1 John 3:21-22	391
1 John 2:15-17	385	1 John 4:4	392
1 John 3:3	386	1 John 4:19	393
1 John 3:6	387	1 John 4:20	394
1 John 3:9	388	Jude 24	395
1 John 3:17	389		

ACKNOWLEDGEMENTS

God, thank You for Your plans for me. Thank You for **On This Journey** and choosing me to complete Your project. **OTJ** has brought me to the next level. I just want to please You. Thank You for continuing to anoint me and to invest in me and my gifts, which keep surprising me. Thank You for loving and forgiving me.

Hillary, and Nehemiah, thank you for enduring my late nights, your ideas, the sounding board, the love and the support. Thank you for loving me, especially when I do nothing without a pen and a clipboard.

To my inner circle: keep me in your prayers. As one of you asked: "how do you match 2001-2002?" I responded you ask God. You know I have asked God for much, so for me much is expected.

On This Journey

Daily Devotional for Young People

ABOUT THE TEACHER

Minister Onedia N. Gage believes in the study of God's word. She wants youth to have the help she wanted and needed as a former youth so that you can grow with God. She hopes that you will seek God for a closer relationship so that you can have a closer relationship with your family and friends.

Her life philosophy is three – fold:
A) "What have you done today to invest in your future?"
B) Reading is essential to your positive contribution to our community; and,
C) "If not me, who? If not now, when?" She feels her time is best spent when youth benefit from her experiences.

Minister Onedia invites you to share her study at her retreats for couples. Minister Onedia would like to pray for and with you. Please contact her via email onediagage@onediagage.com
Via twitter @onediangage, on facebook.com/onedia-gage-ministries and phone 512-715-GAGE (4243).

Minister Onedia Gage

On This Journey

Preacher ♦ Prayer Warrior ♦ Teacher

To invite Rev. Gage to preach, coach, teach, and pray, Please contact us at
@onediangage (twitter) ♦ onediagage@onediagage.com ♦
facebook.com/onediagage
youtube.com/onediagage ♦ blogtalkradio.com/onediagage ♦
www.onediagage.com

On This Journey

Publishing

Do you have a book you want to write, but do not know what to do?

Do you have a book you need to publish but do not know how to start?

Would publishing move your career forward?

Let us help

onediagage@purpleink.net ♦ www.purpleink.net

713.705.5530

281.540.7143